DFI = direct foreign investment (of US in foreig. count

FDI = foreign direct investm. in C

str. 198 = URA

W9-COS-414

THE DYNAMICS OF TRADE
AND EMPLOYMENT

THE DYNAMICS OF TRADE AND EMPLOYMENT

Edited by
LAURA D'ANDREA TYSON
WILLIAM T. DICKENS
JOHN ZYSMAN

BALLINGER PUBLISHING COMPANY
Cambridge, Massachusetts
A Subsidiary of Harper & Row, Publishers, Inc.

Soc
HD
5710.75
U6
D96
1988

ROBERT MANNING
STROZIER LIBRARY.

SEP 8 1988

Tallahassee, Florida

Copyright © 1988 by Ballinger Publishing Company. All rights reserved. No part of this publication may be reproduced, stored in a retrieval system, or transmitted in any form or by any means, electronic, mechanical, photocopy, recording or otherwise, without the prior written consent of the publisher.

International Standard Book Number: 0-88730-158-4

Library of Congress Catalog Card Number: 87-37416

Printed in the United States of America

Library of Congress Cataloging-in-Publication Data

The Dynamics of trade and employment/edited by Laura D'Andrea Tyson. William Dickens. John Zysman.
    p.   cm.

    Includes index.
    1. Foreign trade and employment—United States—Case studies. 2. Clothing trade—United States—Case studies. 3. Automobile industry and trade—United States—Case studies. 4. Semiconductor industry—United States—Case studies. 5. Telecommunication equipment industry—United States—Case studies.
I. Tyson, Laura D'Andrea, 1947–   . II. Dickens, William.
III. Zysman, John.
HD5710.75.U6D96   1988   331.12—dc 19   87-37416
ISBN 0-88730-158-4

CONTENTS

LIST OF FIGURES

LIST OF TABLES

ACKNOWLEDGMENTS

This book grew out of initial research sponsored by the Office of Technology Assessment. Further research was supported by grants from the Carnegie Corporation of New York and the Carnegie Forum on Education and the Economy.

1 TRADE AND EMPLOYMENT An Overview of the Issues and Evidence

Laura D'Andrea Tyson and John Zysman

Between 1979 and 1985 the United States lost almost 1.7 million full-time equivalent jobs in manufacturing—a decline of about 8.5 percent. During the same period, the U.S. trade deficit in manufactured goods climbed sharply, rising to $101 billion by the end of 1985. What was the relationship between the drop in U.S. manufacturing jobs and the declining fortunes of U.S. producers in world trade? This is the subject of the research presented in this book.

To many observers, the links between the worsening trade position in manufactured goods and the loss of manufacturing jobs in the United States are self-evident. Soaring imports and stagnant exports represent a decline in demand for U.S. manufactured goods and for the workers who are employed to produce them. The image of American workers losing their jobs as their factories scale back operations or close down altogether in response to a flood of foreign-made substitutes has become deeply ingrained in the American consciousness. This image has fueled growing sentiment in favor of protectionist measures to solve the crisis of America's trade imbalance.

What makes the most recent period different from past periods is not that American employment opportunities are affected by the ability of American producers to compete internationally nor that the industries that are adversely affected by foreign competition have lobbied for

1

protectionist measures in the name of the American worker. There is a long history of import pressure and dwindling employment levels in such labor-intensive industries as apparel, textiles, footwear, and television receivers.[1] In all of these industries, policies have been adopted to stem the flow of imports—not always with noticeable success.

What distinguishes the latest period is the fact that the trade threat to American production and employment levels has spread throughout the manufacturing sector, encompassing not just labor-intensive industries but also capital- and technology-intensive industries, where U.S. producers were only recently thought to have a significant competitive edge. Moreover, the threat in many industries has come not from low-cost, unskilled workers in the Third World but from high-wage, skilled, often better educated workers in the developed countries, especially Germany and Japan. Finally, the sheer number of American manufacturing jobs that are tied to the trade fortunes of American producers makes the most recent period distinctive.

Although there is widespread agreement that the erosion in the U.S. competitive position in international markets has been partly responsible for the recent decline in manufacturing employment, we do not understand the relationship well. There have been few careful analyses of the links between the two developments. A large number of existing studies are summarized and criticized in chapter 2. For a variety of reasons, these studies use methodologies that often yield misleading conclusions. The standard approaches all tend to focus on how trade affects the demand for U.S. output and how that, in turn, affects the demand for U.S. workers. These approaches make the limiting and highly unrealistic assumption that the price, wage, technology, and location decisions of U.S. producers are unaffected by foreign competitive pressure. In an increasingly open U.S. economy, such an assumption overlooks the most important channels through which trade ultimately affects the type and number of jobs available to American workers.

To understand these channels better, this book relies heavily on case studies of the employment effects of trade in four industries—apparel, automobiles, semiconductors, and telecommunications equipment. These four industries differ in terms of growth rates, wage levels, profitability, labor intensity, technological change, market structure, and other economic indicators. Taken together, they provide a broad, representative picture of how trade has affected employment throughout the manufacturing sector. The case study approach, while lacking the methodological rigor of some of the standard approaches to the problem, yields important insights into how the responses of firms to foreign opportunities or threats have affected and will continue to affect employment trends in individual industries. The analysis also yields some insight into how existing methodologies must be modified to improve our understanding of the links between trade and employment in an increasingly open economy.

The results of our efforts force us to reconsider the causes of the deterioration in the U.S. trade position. Among the most widely cited factors are the dramatic rise of the dollar between 1980 and 1985, rising relative wages in the United States, protectionism and targeting of exports abroad, slow growth in foreign markets for U.S. products, and a long-term erosion in relative productivity and technological performance in the United States. In many popular discussions, the appreciation of the dollar is believed to be the most important factor. Recent studies by Branson and Love (1986) and Eichengreen (1987) indicate that the appreciation had a significant negative effect on U.S. employment levels throughout manufacturing, including the apparel and auto industries.

Yet a clear and quite different message emerges from the case studies, especially those for autos, semiconductors, and telecommunications equipment. The message is that while the dollar's rise aggravated the trade difficulties experienced by U.S. producers in the short run, more fundamental factors, especially a relative decline in U.S. productivity and technology performance compared to that of Japan, were at play over the long run. As a result of these factors, the dollar would have had to depreciate rather than appreciate between 1980 and 1985 to prevent growing import penetration and downward pressure on U.S. employment levels in these industries.[2]

The purpose of this introductory chapter is fourfold. The first section describes recent trends in U.S. trade performance in manufactured goods and manufacturing employment and unemployment in the United States. The second section analyzes the various factors that influence the size of the employment consequences of a change in trade. A basic theme is that the effects of trade on employment and unemployment are difficult to assess because so many interrelated factors come into play. To demonstrate that trade has reduced the demand for U.S. workers in a particular industry does not necessarily imply that employment in that industry has actually declined as a result of trade. To demonstrate that employment in an industry has actually declined as a result of trade does not necessarily demonstrate that the unemployment rate in the economy has increased as a result. Without case studies of the type contained in this book, one can say only that trade pressures on job opportunities in an industry have increased or decreased. Whether these pressures actually result in changes in employment depend on a host of other factors, including how prices, wages, and technology change in response to changes in international competition. The third section of this chapter summarizes some of the major results that are contained in the remaining chapters of the book. Finally, the chapter ends with a brief discussion of the policy options that are implicit in these results.

THE EVIDENCE

Over the past fifteen years, the role of international trade in the U.S. economy has increased dramatically. In 1960 imports and exports of goods and services amounted to 10 percent of GNP. By 1984 this figure had more than doubled to 22 percent. The growing openness of the economy has been particularly pronounced in manufacturing. As the data in Table 1–1 indicate, the trade content of the typical manufacturing industry—as measured by the ratio of imports and exports to total industry shipments—has increased significantly over the past two decades, although there is great variation across industries in the extent of openness.

The growing openness of U.S. manufacturing to international competition was not accompanied by a discernible trend in the U.S. trade position in manufactured goods until 1982. Between 1973 and 1981 the U.S. trade balance in manufacturing moved erratically but was positive in most years. Nonetheless, even in this period there were already signs of an eroding competitive position for U.S. producers. Despite a sharp decline in the dollar's value in 1977–78, the United States was unable to generate substantial and growing surpluses in manufactured goods to offset its substantial and growing deficit in energy products. In contrast, both Germany and Japan enjoyed large surpluses in manufactured goods that covered their energy import needs. In addition, the U.S. share of world exports of manufactured goods remained sharply below the level realized in the late 1960s, despite some recovery after the dollar's depreciation (Cohen and Zysman 1987).

There was a dramatic deterioration in the U.S. trade position in manufactured products after 1980. In 1980 the United States ran a trade surplus of about $22 billion in manufactured products. By 1986 it ran a

Table 1-1. Changes Over Time in the Level and Variation in the Importance of Trade in Manufacturing.[a]

Year	$M/(M+S)$ [b]	X/S [c]	$(X-M)/S$ [d]
1960			
Mean	2.29%	4.27%	1.57%
Standard deviation	4.57	5.89	9.75
1970			
Mean	4.60	5.64	0.22
Standard deviation	6.08	7.08	11.30
1980			
Mean	7.50	10.35	0.78
Standard deviation	8.48	11.41	18.43
1984			
Mean	10.02	8.60	−5.96
Standard deviation	10.40	10.17	47.00
Change, 1960–1984			
Mean	9.18	3.45	−12.55
Standard deviation	10.60	7.68	59.18
Change, 1970–1980			
Mean	3.21	4.04	−.72
Standard deviation	4.64	6.07	13.40
Change, 1980–1984			
Mean	3.11	−1.67	−8.39
Standard deviation	4.60	4.43	4.50

[a]The means are average trade ratios weighted by industry employment for the 430 four-digit SIC manufacturing industries with valid trade data.

[b]Imports/(imports + shipments by domestic producers).

[c]Exports/shipments by domestic producers.

[d](Exports − imports)/shipments by domestic producers.

Source: Katz (1986).

trade deficit of nearly $129 billion in such products.[3] By the end of 1986, U.S. imports of nonpetroleum products exceeded U.S. exports of nonagricultural products by 75 percent (Krugman and Baldwin 1987). The deterioration in the U.S. trade position in manufacturing was the result of both stagnant exports and soaring imports. Throughout the manufacturing sector—from technology-intensive, high-wage industries like computers and telecommunications equipment to labor-intensive, low-wage industries like apparel—the U.S. trade position eroded sharply. By 1986 the United States was running a deficit in almost all manufacturing sectors, even many high-technology sectors in which it had traditionally run a surplus.

At the same time its trade position in manufacturing was deteriorating, the United States was losing a record number of manufacturing jobs. Between 1979 and 1985, two years of roughly comparable levels of overall economic activity, it lost about 1.7 million full-time equivalent jobs in manufacturing. The 1979–1985 period has the highest average annual job loss in the manufacturing sector when compared to all other cyclical peak-to-peak intervals during the postwar period. It also has the highest average annual decline in the share of manufacturing employment in total employment. Although the share of manufacturing employment in total employment has steadily decreased throughout the postwar period, the pace of the decline quickened noticeably during this period. By 1985 only 20.1 percent of full-time equivalent employment was in manufacturing, compared to 23.7 percent in 1979 and 25.8 percent in 1973.[4]

There is an unanswered question, of course: How much of the decline in manufacturing jobs during the 1979–1985 period and earlier was the result of trade pressures and how much was the result of other factors, such as the 1981–1982 recession, a shift in domestic demand away from manufactured goods and toward services, or an improvement in manufacturing productivity that reduced the demand for labor even as manufacturing output continued to rise? To some observers, the fact that manufacturing's share in total gross output remained roughly constant during the most recent period and declined only slightly between 1973 and 1979 suggests that productivity improvements rather than trade flows are responsible for declining employment opportunities in manufacturing. As the case studies indicate, however, competitive pressures abroad motivate changes in the technology of production or the offshoring of parts of the production process that result in apparent labor-saving productivity improvements.

To put it differently, changes in the technology or organization of production that reduce domestic employment opportunities while maintaining levels of domestic value-added may themselves be caused by, rather than independent of, trade flows. The case studies reveal that corporate strategies to remain competitive in international markets may be successful in that they sustain domestic production, but this is achieved at the expense of domestic employment. Seen positively, competitive pressure from lower cost foreign producers may necessitate changes in production processes that result in higher productivity growth. Seen negatively, such changes may lower employment opportunities in domestic manufacturing. Whether the loss of manufacturing jobs in fact reduces national welfare, however, is not at all certain. It all depends on what happens to the displaced workers—on how quickly they find employment elsewhere in the economy and at what wage and productivity levels.

The dwindling share of manufacturing employment in the U.S. economy suggests to some observers that fewer and fewer U.S. jobs are exposed to international competition (Abowd and Freeman 1986). Since almost three-quarters of U.S. exports and imports are manufactured products and only about one-fifth of U.S. workers are now employed in manufacturing, it appears that most workers have jobs that are not directly threatened by growing import competition or dwindling export markets. This conclusion is misleading, however, because at least one-quarter of GNP consists of services that are tightly linked to manufactured goods production.[5] The demand for these services, which include most of the high-wage, business-service jobs held by professionals, comes from the domestic manufacturing sector. Therefore to the extent that the demand for domestic manufacturing is reduced by trade, the demand for such services and for the workers who provide them will also be reduced.

The sharp drop in the number of manufacturing jobs during the past eight years has caused concern for two other reasons. First, on average, manufacturing jobs pay wages that are significantly higher than those paid in services. In 1985, for example, the average hourly manufacturing wage was $9.52, while the average hourly wage in services, excluding retail trade, was only $7.95.[6] In retail trade the average hourly wage was only $5.97. Given these figures, it is not surprising to find that between 1979 and 1985, the average weekly wage of jobs lost— mainly in manufacturing—was $444, while the average weekly wage of jobs gained—mainly in services—was $272 (Council on Competitiveness 1987).[7] Between 1978 and 1985 more than one-third of net additional year-round, full-time equivalent employment was paid an annual wage below the poverty line for a family of four (Bluestone and Harrison 1987).

In addition to its deleterious effects on wages, the decline in manufacturing employment in recent years is thought by many to be an important reason why the unemployment rate has remained stubbornly high despite a sustained economic recovery. After correcting for cyclical conditions, it is clear that there has been a secular increase in the unemployment rate. With the exception of the economic boom of the 1960s and early 1970s, each business cycle has had higher peak, trough, and average unemployment rates than the one preceding it (Summers 1986). Although there is much debate about why the average unemployment rate has increased, there is evidence to suggest that at least since 1980 a substantial part of the increase has been the result of greater structural change in the demand for labor, caused in part by the effects of the trade imbalance on manufacturing employment opportunities. This argument will be evaluated in greater detail below. It is clear, however, that such an argument motivates much of the popular discussion linking trade deficits to the unemployment rate.

Looking back at the past several years, two features stand out: First, the U.S. economy has experienced unprecedented trade deficits in manufacturing products. Second, despite the longest economic recovery in the postwar period, the United States has lost a large number of relatively high-wage jobs and the unemployment rate has remained high by the standards of past recovery periods. It is not surprising that these two features are often linked together in popular discussion. To many, the evidence seems overwhelming that trade is deindustrializing the American workforce by destroying high-wage jobs in industry and driving the labor force into lower paying jobs elsewhere. But is this conclusion, however compelling, correct? To answer this question, it is necessary to examine the many factors that link trade and employment and unemployment levels.

THE EFFECTS OF TRADE ON EMPLOYMENT AND UNEMPLOYMENT

The Changing Dynamics of the American Economy

An increase in imports or a decrease in exports means a decrease in demand for U.S. output. Whether this decrease shows up in a decrease in U.S. production levels, and whether that in turn shows up in a decrease in U.S. employment levels, depends on several things, one of which is domestic demand. Despite the growing openness of the U.S. economy, domestic demand is still a much larger contribution to total demand for

U.S. output than are imports or exports, at least at the macro level. When domestic demand increases, U.S. output levels can rise, even if imports rise and exports fall at the same time. Indeed, this is exactly what happened during the 1982–1986 period, when manufacturing output in the nation grew by 30.4 percent.[8] Even at the industry level, changes in domestic demand have been a more important determinant of changes in output than changes in foreign trade, at least until recently. For example, Lawrence (1984) finds that changes in trade were more important than changes in domestic demand in determining changes in domestic value-added in only five out of fifty-two input-output industry categories—footwear, iron and steel, engines and turbines, special machinery, and aircraft and parts—between 1970 and 1980.[9]

In a more recent study, the Office of Technology Assessment (OTA) uses a similar input-output methodology to examine how the output of different industries changed between 1972 and 1984. Significantly, the OTA study reveals that trade changes began to play a much more important role after 1980. As a result of greater openness, the dynamics of the American economy have changed.

The OTA study contains results that are relevant to the findings that are presented later in this book. The study finds, for example, that a worsening trade balance almost eliminated what would have been a large gain in the auto industry's share in total domestic value-added stemming from strong domestic demand after 1980.[10] A growing trade deficit also played a major role in the decline in the value-added shares of low-wage, labor-intensive industries, including apparel. Finally, in high-technology industries, including office and computing equipment, and radio, television and telecommunications equipment, the study finds that the negative influence of the deteriorating trade position after 1980 dampened the increase in value-added shares that would have occurred as a result of impressive gains in domestic demand. In electronic components, an industry category that encompasses semiconductors, the OTA study finds that the decline in value-added share between 1972 and 1984 was nearly entirely the result of the growing trade deficits between 1980 and 1984 that reversed the overall positive trade effects that had occurred between 1972 and 1977.

Isolating and comparing the effects of changes in trade with those of changes in domestic demand on domestic output levels is even more difficult than input-output studies suggest because such changes are not independent of one another. For example, a high rate of growth of domestic demand in the economy may cause a growing trade imbalance as goods that might have been exported are instead sold at home and as foreign goods are imported to meet the growing demand of domestic consumers. The question of the dependence of the trade balance on domestic demand conditions is particularly important for examining the period from 1980 to 1986.

Most economists believe that macroeconomic imbalance in the U.S. economy was a major factor behind the deterioration in the U.S. trade position during this period. Domestically generated saving was insufficient to cover mounting federal government deficits and rising private investment rates as the economy moved out of recession in 1982. The saving gap pushed real interest rates to historically high levels, encouraging an inflow of foreign capital to dollar-denominated assets. This inflow pushed up the dollar's value, which had deleterious effects on the price-competitiveness of U.S. producers.

According to this interpretation, the mounting trade imbalance was not the ultimate culprit behind the loss in demand for U.S. manufacturing jobs after 1982—macroeconomic imbalance in the U.S. economy was. If foreign capital had not been attracted by U.S. interest rates, the dollar would not have appreciated, the trade balance would not have climbed so dramatically, and many U.S. manufacturing industries would have fared better in world markets. Without foreign capital inflow, however, if U.S. saving and government deficit levels had remained unchanged, U.S. interest rates would have been much higher and the U.S. investment rate would have been much lower, with negative effects on employment and production levels in many manufacturing industries and construction.

Seen from this perspective, it was inevitable that the combination of low saving rates and the huge financing needs of the federal deficit would "crowd out" demand from some sectors of the U.S. economy (Frankel 1987). If foreign capital flows had been smaller, interest rates would have been higher and interest-sensitive sectors would have been squeezed more tightly. As it was, heavily trade-dependent sectors, whose export and import performances were most sensitive to the appreciation of the dollar, bore a disproportionate share of the burden. According to the Branson and Love results, autos and apparel were among the most affected manufacturing industries.

This macroanalysis is misleading, however, because it assumes that all of the deterioration in the trade imbalance after 1982 was the result of macroeconomic imbalance. Other forces were working as well, including slow growth in traditional U.S. markets in Latin America, overt or implicit trade barriers to U.S. products in foreign markets, notably the Japanese market, and a long-term erosion in U.S. competitiveness. These forces, as well as such special industry conditions as the deregulation of the domestic telecommunications market, affected what actually happened to the trade balance in individual industries.

Trade, Output, and Employment

So far the discussion has focused on how a change in exports or imports affects the demand for U.S. output. It might seem that a change in demand would directly affect U.S. output and employment levels. However, the relations are not direct and the long-term consequences are not obvious. As an illustration, suppose there is a decrease in the demand for a particular type of U.S. product caused by an increase in imports. What actually happens to employment in the U.S. firms that produce this product—that is, how many workers are actually displaced—depends on the resulting changes in product price, wages, employer expectations, and production technology. Let us consider each of these in turn.

Product Price.   If price falls in response to foreign competition, the demand for the product will rise (the extent of the increase depends on how sensitive demand is to a fall in price—the price elasticity of demand). As long as domestic producers share in the resulting increase in demand to some degree, the domestic output and employment effects of the increase in imports will be smaller than they would have been if the price of domestic output had remained constant. This point is well-illustrated in the chapter on semiconductors. A drop in semiconductor prices caused by growing imports from U.S.-owned offshore plants in the 1970s actually increased the total demand for semiconductors in the United States, with positive net effects on the employment levels of nonassembly jobs and with moderating effects on the number of assembly jobs lost as a result of imports.

Wages.   The number of jobs lost to import competition depends on what happens to wages. If wages fall or fail to rise quickly in response to import competition, producers will be willing to keep on a larger number of workers. Import competition confronts the workers in an affected industry with a tradeoff between jobs and wages. The case studies indicate that wages have responded differently in different industries where imports have posed a substantial threat to domestic employment. In apparel, as in many other low-skill, labor-intensive industries that have been subject to strong import competition for many years, relative wages have declined. The average hourly wage paid to production workers in apparel declined from 68 percent of the average hourly wage in manufacturing in 1972 to only about 60 percent in 1984 (Katz 1986). The decline in relative wages has probably moderated the pace of employment decline in apparel.

In autos, as in steel, wages actually increased relative to the manufacturing average between 1972 and 1984, despite growing import competition in the 1970s. Most of the relative wage increase in autos occurred before the major thrust of import competition that began in 1978. The auto case study emphasizes that the failure of U.S. producers to exercise greater price moderation and the failure of the United Auto Workers (UAW) to exercise greater wage moderation after the imposition of voluntary export restraints in 1980 reduced the number of jobs that might have been preserved. Even more significant for the future, the persistence of very high relative wages in autos has hastened offshoring, subcontracting to foreign producers and suppliers, and labor-saving automation, all of which will further reduce domestic employment opportunities over the longer run.

Employer Expectations.   If employers expect that a demand reduction that is caused by imports is a temporary phenomenon, then they may decide to maintain employment that is close to current levels. If employers have substantial investments in the training of workers, and if workers with the necessary skills would prove difficult or costly to find at a later date should demand increase again, then they will be reluctant to lay these workers off. The result may be that existing labor is hoarded and employers accept a short-run decline in their profitability in order to maintain employment despite a decline in output demand.

Whether employers expect an increase in imports to have a temporary or permanent effect on demand depends on how large and how sustained the increase is. Between 1976 and 1978, when imports of small cars from Japan dramatically increased (partly in response to higher energy prices), U.S. producers might reasonably have expected the import surge to be temporary. By 1980, after five years of rapid increase in the Japanese share of the total number of autos sold in the United States, domestic producers undoubtedly thought that the import threat to both production and employment was a permanent one. Such a change in expectations would certainly influence employer willingness to retain labor, even highly trained, skilled labor, in the hope of improving demand in the future. In the apparel industry, where substantial import pressure has been a long-term problem and where many of the jobs threatened by import competition are low-skill jobs that require little investment in training, it is reasonable to assume that employers view a reduction in output demand that is caused by rising imports as permanent; they make their layoff and employment decisions accordingly.

Production Technology. The link between product and labor demand depends on the technology that links labor input to output levels. Technology in this context must be understood in broad terms. In its narrowest definition, technology refers to production techniques, most of which allow for some substitution between labor and other productive inputs, especially capital. However, the input-output models that are standardly used to assess the effects of trade on employment do not allow for such substitution. At the very least, the actual employment effects of a change in output demand depend on the substitution possibilities between labor and other inputs that are allowed by the production techniques currently in place.

In fact, the range of technological choices that are available to producers is broader since technological innovations that change production techniques, and hence the range of possible substitution, may also be an important response to foreign competitive pressures. Moreover, domestic producers may introduce new production arrangements, such as subcontracting, offshoring, or joint ventures, that change the links between domestic production and employment and that fall outside the usual definition of technological change.

A theme that is shared by all of the case studies in this book is that technological change (in the broad sense defined here) has been a major response of domestic producers to both domestic and foreign competition. The greater the role of such a response, of course, the less relevant or appropriate are traditional methodologies to understanding the issues at hand. Domestic semiconductor producers responded to growing import penetration from Japan in the late 1970s by accelerating the trend toward offshore assembly and testing. Domestic producers of apparel responded by developing and expanding subcontracting arrangements in low-cost Third World sites and by expanding automation of production at home. Domestic auto producers also responded by increasing their reliance on offshoring, joint ventures, and automation.

In each of these cases, such changes in the techniques of production, motivated by more intense foreign competition, may turn out to be more fundamental determinants of domestic employment levels than are the changes in product demand that are caused by a changing trade balance. Unfortunately, none of the existing methods for assessing the effects of trade on employment allow one to distinguish the effects of trade on the techniques of production. Most studies treat technological change as an independent cause of changes in the demand for labor and in employment. As a result, such studies probably seriously underestimate the effects of trade on U.S. employment levels in affected industries over the long run.

Clearly, the importance of each of the four factors discussed here varies over time. The shorter the time frame of analysis, the more reasonable it is to assume that prices, wages, and production technologies are fixed and that domestic employers view reductions in demand that are caused by a deteriorating trade position as temporary. The price and wage factors are likely to make the employment effects of an increase in foreign demand greater in the short run than in the long run, while the technology and expectations factors are likely to have the opposite effect.

All of the accounting and input-output studies summarized in chapter 2 measure employment effects under the assumption that prices, wages, and production technologies (in even the narrowest sense) are fixed or that variations within them are not the result of producer responses to foreign competition. These studies also implicitly assume that any increase in import penetration is a permanent phenomenon and that employers adjust their labor needs accordingly. Given these assumptions, such models are best suited for estimates of the short-run employment effects of foreign trade, and these effects must be interpreted as potential rather than actual since labor hoarding may drive a wedge between the two.

The model-based studies that are discussed in chapter 2 go some way toward relaxing the rigid assumptions of the accounting and input-output studies. For example, the model developed by Grossman (1984) allows for price and wage changes as well as employment changes, distinguishes between immediate and lagged responses to an increase in imports over an eighteen-month period, and allows for capital-labor substitution within the confines of a given production technology. The case studies indicate, however, that wage adjustments, broad technological changes, and other strategic responses to foreign competition are so different across industries and firms that even complicated model-based studies cannot capture their effects.

At best, what model-based studies and, to a more limited extent, input-output and accounting studies can do is identify and rank industries by the potential number of job opportunities that have been or are likely to be created or destroyed by trade over relatively short periods. This in turn yields an assessment of the potential effects of trade on the long-term composition of employment and on the long-term mix of skills and occupations and the long-term locational choices that such a composition requires. Of course, before policy measures are fashioned in response to these effects, it is important to emphasize their potential nature. For example, even if existing models were improved to give a more accurate picture of the potential employment gains or losses from trade, we would still know very little about actual job effects. This is most easily demonstrated by comparing the case of an industry in which overall demand is expanding with one in which it is stagnating or contracting. The cases of semiconductors and apparel come to mind. In a growing industry, a large potential job loss from trade may be easily absorbed, while in a stagnant industry, every potential job lost from trade may result in an actual displaced worker.

Using the standard methodologies for what they are best designed—namely, to identify sectors where trade has had a relatively large influence on the demand for domestic output and hence on potential job creation or job destruction—yields several conclusions. First, as chapter 2 indicates, through the end of the 1970s, trade destroyed potential job opportunities in U.S. manufacturing overall, but the number of jobs involved was relatively small compared to total U.S. manufacturing employment. The results surveyed by Dickens suggest that, at most, perhaps 100,000 job opportunities per year were lost as a result of trade, although this may be an underestimate given the underlying methodological difficulties discussed here and analyzed in greater depth by Dickens. Even Dickens's guesstimate of an upper bound of 300,000 jobs per year is small compared to total manufacturing employment of about 20 million full-time equivalent employees between 1973 and 1979.

Second, after 1980 the numbers begin to change perceptibly. The most recent input-output study of the employment effects of trade by the U.S. International Trade Commission (USITC) (1986) indicates that the 1984 trade deficit translated into a potential destruction of about 2.6 million jobs. According to this study, the deterioration in the trade balance from a position of surplus in 1980 to one of substantial deficit in 1984 potentially destroyed nearly 2.9 million jobs, or more than 3 percent of total 1984 employment. A recent Commerce Department study (1986) estimates that by 1986, every $1 billion of the trade deficit potentially destroyed 25,000 jobs, meaning that the 1986 deficit translated into potential lost job opportunities of four million, most of them in manufacturing.[11] Although one can fault such estimates on methodological grounds, the basic conclusion remains that the potential job loss from growing trade deficits has become disturbingly large in recent years. A related conclusion is that trade has had more devastating effects on job opportunities in manufacturing than in the rest of the economy.

What about the effects of trade on potential job destruction or creation in individual manufacturing industries? Again, the standard approaches yield some revealing conclusions. Using these approaches, industries where employment has been disproportionately threatened or fostered by trade can be identified. For the 1970s, job destruction was greatest in apparel, knitting, footwear, textiles, furniture and fixtures, motor vehicles and parts, radio and television, and electronic components and accessories, while job creation was greatest in office and computing equipment, chemicals and plastics, aerospace, construction and mining machinery, engines and turbines, and electrical machinery. The 1986 USITC study reveals that potential job losses were greatest in apparel, footwear and leather products, and miscellaneous manufacturing between 1980 and 1984, with large potential losses also occurring in a variety of other sectors, including primary nonferrous metals, radio, television and communications equipment, electronic components and accessories, and autos.

Significantly, the deterioration in the trade balance caused a potential loss of jobs in fifty out of fifty-two input-output manufacturing industries between 1980 and 1984. The only exceptions were petroleum refining and related industries and other transportation equipment. Between 1970 and 1980, in contrast, Lawrence (1984) found that the change in trade position actually caused a potential gain in jobs in thirty-one of the same fifty-two industries. By 1984 trade had a positive effect on domestic job opportunities in only nine manufacturing sectors, with the largest positive net effect on jobs in office and computing equipment, aircraft and parts, and engines and turbines.[12] Estimated jobs destroyed by trade in autos and apparel, two of the sectors discussed in this book, accounted for about 11 percent of the total number of jobs that were potentially destroyed by trade in 1984.[13]

Looking at the list of sectors where potential job destruction from trade has been the largest, two kinds of industries stand out—relatively labor-intensive industries with relatively unskilled labor, such as apparel and footwear, and relatively capital-intensive industries with relatively skilled labor, such as autos and primary steel. The former tend to be low-wage industries, while the latter pay wages that are among the highest in manufacturing. Potential job creation has been the greatest in technology-based industries, such as office and computing equipment, aircraft and equipment, electrical equipment, and scientific instruments, although the worsening trade balance in such industries in recent years has reduced, and in several cases even reversed, the positive effects of trade on employment opportunities. Such technology-intensive industries tend to pay wages that are close to the average for all manufacturing wages, with the exception of the aircraft industry, which is a high-wage industry.

A recent study by the OTA that uses an input-output methodology analyzes the effects of trade on potential employment opportunities between 1972 and 1984 in three categories of manufacturing industries—low-wage, medium-wage, and high-wage. The results indicate that a deteriorating trade balance during this period contributed to a decline in the share of each category in total full-time equivalent employment in the United States. Trade played the largest role in the decline of the share of the low-wage industries, which were predominantly comprised of the apparel, footwear, textile, and furniture industries. In medium-wage, mainly high-technology industries, improvements in labor productivity were the main reason why employment shares declined. These results are consistent with Kremp and Mistral's (1985) results on the effects of trade on low-, middle-, and high-technology industries. They are also reflected in this book's case studies of apparel and telecommunications equipment. Parsons argues in chapter 4 that in low-wage apparel industries, trade has been a major factor behind declining employment, while Stowsky argues in chapter 6 that in medium-wage telecommunications equipment industries, rapid changes in product and process technology, largely unrelated to international competitive pressure, have been the driving force behind employment declines.

Most of the existing studies of the effects of trade on employment agree that the average wages paid in industries that are large exporters, as measured by their export/sales ratio, are higher than the average wages paid in industries that are most import-sensitive. Even import-sensitive industries that have relatively low manufacturing wages, however, pay wages that are higher than the economy-wide average wage because the average includes the substantially lower wages that are paid in most service jobs. Existing studies also reveal that, on average, workers in the most import-impacted industries tend to be disproportionately female and minority group members who have relatively low levels of education. In contrast, industries that have high export/sales ratios tend to have disproportionately more educated and skilled workers and fewer black and female workers than import industries do. Dickens notes, however, that the differences between the average characteristics of workers in import-sensitive and export industries, although revealing, are not that large, especially when compared with the differences between the average characteristics of workers in manufacturing and those of workers in service jobs.

The case studies of the semiconductor and telecommunications industries confirm these general results about the kinds of jobs and workers that are helped or hurt by trade. Within each sector, the negative effects of trade have fallen disproportionately on low-wage production workers, many of them relatively low-skilled and with relatively low education levels, who produce the products that are most sensitive to import competition from cheaper labor sources abroad. In the semiconductor industry, most of the affected workers are female. In contrast, exports of more research-intensive product lines within both sectors have increased potential job opportunities for more skilled workers, especially those with engineering and scientific talent, who are disproportionately male. As the trade surpluses in such product lines have dwindled in these and other industries in recent years, the threat to such good jobs and skilled high-wage employees has increased.

The chapter by Dickens and Lang (Chapter 3) looks at the wages that are paid to workers in import and export sectors in greater detail. Within manufacturing, their results confirm the fact that sectors with large export/sales ratios pay higher wages than industries with large import/sales ratios do. Once nonmanufacturing exporting activities, such as agriculture, are included in the analysis, however, the results change. Jobs in sectors that have high import ratios on average pay more than jobs in sectors that have high export ratios, although the differences are not large. Both sectors pay wages that are in excess of the average wage in the economy.

According to the calculations presented by Dickens and Lang, balanced growth in U.S. trade by itself would leave the number of "good" jobs in the United States virtually unchanged, because the good jobs created by export growth would offset the loss of good jobs from import competition. By the same reasoning, unbalanced growth in imports, such as occurred between 1982 and 1986, would destroy good jobs. This conclusion is consistent with their finding that between 1976 and 1981, a period of approximate trade balance, the fraction of the labor force in good jobs remained more or less constant, while between 1981 and 1984, a period of rising trade imbalance, this fraction fell sharply.[14]

Dickens and Lang relate their findings to a growing body of literature by labor economists on the persistence of sectoral differences in wages that are paid to workers with similar skill and educational characteristics. This literature suggests that some kinds of jobs are "better" than others in the sense that they offer higher returns for the same set of worker characteristics. In the United States, such jobs are currently concentrated in sectors that produce goods that are traded and are subject to international competition.

Dickens and Lang argue that under such circumstances, many of the traditional policy prescriptions that result from classical trade theory must be reassessed. For example, in standard theory, a country cannot gain long-term advantage by subsidizing its exports. But with the sorts of persistent wage differences they document, this conclusion is no longer the case. If a foreign government subsidizes its exports of goods produced in high-wage sectors to the disadvantage of U.S. producers, the result may be a long-term gain in high-wage jobs abroad and long-term loss in such jobs at home. Similar considerations reinforce the conclusion from standard trade theory that barriers to U.S. exports put up by other countries can be very damaging, particularly when they target our high-wage export industries. Finally, Dickens and Lang present a simple model of trade that demonstrates that active trade policies in some domestic industries can improve domestic economic welfare and that such policies when responded to by other countries can actually lead to improvements in the economic well-being of both the United States and its trading partners.

Trade and the Aggregate Employment and Unemployment Rates

The preceding discussion suggested that trade is changing the composition of jobs within the manufacturing sector and within the economy as a whole. Yet we must be careful to distinguish the effects of trade on the composition of jobs from its effects on the number of employed people. As the experience of the last few years indicates, changes in the composition of employment are consistent with a rising level of total employment and a declining unemployment rate.

In the long run, most economists believe that trade will have little effect on the aggregate amount of employment in the United States. This belief rests on the view that in the long run, the amount of labor supplied is mainly determined by demographic and social forces and is relatively insensitive to the wages that employers pay. According to this interpretation, wages will adjust until employers are willing to employ the available labor supply; there is a set of wages at which all of those who wish to be employed will be able to find a job.[15]

According to this argument, if trade reduces the demand for U.S. labor, then U.S. wages must fall in the long run if the available supply of U.S. workers is to be employed. In other words, trade, like the other factors that determine the demand for labor, will affect U.S. wages, not U.S. employment levels. Of course, to the extent that wages do not adjust sufficiently to a change in demand that is caused by a change in trade, the level of employment will also be affected. But as long as the supply of labor does not change, and as long as there are no permanent barriers to wage adjustment, the effect on the level of employment will be transitory in the long run.

From this perspective, the real challenge that confronts the United States in an increasingly open and competitive world is not how to sustain employment opportunities for its population, but how to sustain employment opportunities with increasing real wages. As a nation, there is little solace in the fact that if U.S. wages fall far enough, U.S. workers will remain employed despite an intensifying onslaught of competition from lower wage producers.

The fact that the level of employment may not be affected by trade in the long run does not mean that trade will have no effect on the unemployment rate in the long run. Most economists believe that in the long run the unemployment rate does not depend on the level of aggregate demand; it depends on the rate at which people quit or are laid off and at which new people are hired.[16] And all of these rates are sensitive to the pace of structural change.

Even if there is sufficient aggregate demand (in the sense that the aggregate number of job vacancies equals the aggregate number of unemployed workers or the rate of new job creation matches the rate of job destruction), an economy that is undergoing more rapid structural change (in the sense that it is experiencing a more rapid change in the composition of its output and employment opportunities), is likely to have a higher rate of unemployment than that of an economy where the composition of output and employment is relatively constant. In the former economy, the quit, layoff, and hire rates will all tend to be higher, reflecting the greater turnover of labor among sectors, regions, and occupational categories.

This conclusion has an important implication for the possible effects of trade on the rate of unemployment. Greater openness tends to generate pressures for a faster pace of structural change in the domestic economy. This implies that, all other things being equal, the unemployment rate will tend to grow as the role of trade in the domestic economy expands. This argument is even stronger if trade is destroying relatively attractive job opportunities and if workers are reluctant to settle quickly for relatively less attractive job opportunities elsewhere in the economy.[17]

As noted earlier, there is evidence of a secular increase in the unemployment rate in the United States since the 1970s.[18] Many economists attribute most of this increase to so-called structural factors that have encompassed both changes in the composition of the available labor supply and changes in the composition of labor demand. There is a debate about the relative importance of these different structural factors. This debate is examined in chapter 2. The prevailing opinion is that much of the variation in the unemployment rate in the 1970s was the result of cyclical demand and that the gradual increase in the unemployment rate, after correcting for cyclical factors, was the result of structural changes in the labor supply that affected quits, layoffs, and hires. In particular, the growing importance of young and female workers in the labor force and the fact that these workers had higher quit rates, moved between jobs more frequently, and spent more time between jobs than the rest of the labor force are thought to have been major factors behind the trend increase in the unemployment rate.

In the 1980s, however, there are several reasons to believe that structural changes in the composition of labor demand, especially a shift in demand away from manufacturing and toward services, became a more important determinant of the continued upward trend in the unemployment rate. First, in a recent study, Summers (1986) finds that the changing age/sex composition of the labor supply toward groups with higher turnover rates actually explains little of the secular increase in the unemployment rate in recent years. Second, as noted earlier, during the 1979–1985 period, the decline in the number of manufacturing jobs and their share in total employment was especially large by past historical standards. Third, Summers also finds that the most dramatic increases in unemployment have occurred among prime-age males and that most of the increase has been concentrated among job losers. In addition, he documents that a large part of the observed increase in the unemployment rate is due to increases in the duration of unemployment. The incidence of long-term unemployment—people who report themselves out of work for more than twenty-seven weeks—has more than doubled since 1965. Taken together, these findings suggest that long-term job loss by men, the bulk of which is in manufacturing, is an important factor behind the upward trend in the unemployment rate.

A link between the unemployment rate and job creation or destruction in manufacturing is also suggested by evidence indicating that the higher the growth of industrial employment, the lower the unemployment rate. A recent study by Rowthorn and Glyn (1986) identifies such a relationship for all of the major industrial market economies, including the United States, between 1973 and 1983. Summers finds that the relationship between growth in relatively high-wage activities—manufacturing, construction, mining, and public utilities—and the unemployment rate is significantly stronger than the relationship between overall employment growth and the unemployment rate. He reports that between 1979 and 1985, for every one hundred jobs lost in high-wage activities, unemployment increased by twenty-five workers. This suggests that the more rapid pace of destruction of manufacturing jobs during this period was a factor behind the persistence of relatively high unemployment rates, despite a cyclical recovery after 1982.

If these results are combined with earlier evidence suggesting that trade has been an increasingly important factor in job displacement in U.S. manufacturing, then it is reasonable to conclude that the deteriorating trade position of the manufacturing sector has played an increasingly important role in keeping the unemployment rate high.

AN OVERVIEW OF THE CASE STUDIES

Apparel

The apparel industry provides the most straightforward illustration of the effects of trade on domestic employment and production. By any measure, apparel is a labor-intensive industry with relatively low skill requirements, low barriers to entry, and low transportation costs. Static comparative advantage theory predicts that such an industry will find itself confronted with a major threat from foreign producers who have a labor cost advantage relative to high-wage producers in the United States and other developed countries. The domestic industry's experience since the 1960s is consistent with this prediction. Several studies that were surveyed by Dickens (Chapter 2) and Parsons (Chapter 4) estimate that trade has contributed to a significant amount of potential job loss in the apparel industry. The rising value of the dollar has aggravated the cost disadvantage of American producers and magnified the effects of trade on potential job loss since 1980. For example, the recent (1986) USITC study shows that potential job loss from trade between 1980 and 1984 was larger in the apparel industry than in any other. And recent studies by Branson and Love (1986) and Eichengreen (1987) indicate that the dollar's appreciation had a significant dampening effect on apparel employment.

The behavior of returns to capital, real wages, and actual employment in the apparel industry is also consistent with the notions of comparative advantage. Low-cost foreign competition has reduced the returns to capital in apparel relative to the industrial average, has led to a steady erosion in real wages (both absolutely and relative to the industrial average since 1968), and has led to declining employment since 1973.

Significantly, all of these trends have developed despite a variety of protectionist measures designed to slow the pace of adjustment necessitated by foreign competition. These measures proved to have weak effects because of the form they took. As Chapter 4 indicates, given the ease of entry and exit in apparel production, foreign producers have been able to circumvent bilateral quotas by shifting production location. In addition, quotas that are expressed in quantity terms have encouraged foreign producers to shift into higher value items, thereby shifting the import threat from some subsectors of the industry to others. Finally, the rate of growth of imports of specific products allowed under the bilateral agreements has exceeded that of domestic production in recent years, allowing growing import penetration.

Many of the existing studies suggest that although trade effects on employment have been important, they have been swamped by the effects of technological change—indeed, the studies reviewed by Parsons suggest that the latter effects have been three times as large as the former. None of these studies, however, attempt to assess the extent to which technological change has been a response to foreign competition. Parsons argues that such competition has been a major incentive for innovation in both the technology and location of production. On the technology side, figures on production and employment trends show an increase in average labor productivity over time. This by itself is suggestive of labor-saving change in technology. A study for the 1972–1979 period confirms the labor-saving bias of technological change, supporting the view that low-cost foreign competition was an important factor behind this change (Richardson 1983).

Similarly, the physical location of U.S. production has changed in response to the threat of foreign competition. Producers have moved facilities offshore and subcontracted abroad. Such strategies have affected and will continue to affect both the productivity and the skill and occupational characteristics of labor employed at home.

As far as assessing future employment trends in the industry, two market options are possible for firms. One is a market niche strategy; since the advantage of foreign producers rests on substantial labor/cost advantages that translate into price advantages, American producers will be most successful in products where nonprice competition is important, especially in high-fashion, specialty items. As communications and design technology have improved, however, even these items have increasingly taken on the character of commodities in the sense that they can be mass-produced at foreign low-wage sites, far away from either the point of design or the point of sale.

The only potential long-run option for maintaining a significant portion of worldwide apparel production in the United States, aside from a costly protectionist strategy, would seem to be further automation in production, which the CAD/CAM revolution makes feasible, although it is very complex and economically uncertain. Such a strategy will not prevent the continued erosion of employment in the apparel industry because it is predicated on a major reduction in labor usage at all stages of the production process. Equally, many technologies diffuse quickly, and as long as a substantial labor component of production remains, production in a relatively low-wage location will continue to have a competitive advantage. Finally, the United States has not innovated in the production of the equipment that is necessary for automated apparel production. Consequently, the capital-intensive strategy in apparel is evolving elsewhere, especially in Japan and Europe.

Automobiles

The automobile industry, like the apparel industry, is one where trade has had a major impact on employment trends. In the auto case, however, trade did not become an important factor until the 1970s. The share of imports in the quantity of new automobiles that were purchased in the United States rose from about 22 percent to about 35 percent between 1970 and 1980. The estimates of potential job destruction from trade (reviewed in Chapter 5) differ depending on the time periods covered and reflect the extreme cyclical variability of the industry. But the estimates indicate that trade has reduced potential job opportunities and has been as important as changes in domestic demand have been in driving potential job opportunities in the industry since 1970. Like the apparel industry, the auto industry is a major employer—accounting for about 5.5 percent of total manufacturing employment in 1978—so that displacement effects from trade have been perceived as a major economic and social problem. In addition, there are substantial spillover effects between employment in the auto industry and employment in related supplier industries. Indeed, Scott (Chapter 5) cites estimates that for every work-year of labor that is displaced by trade in autos, two additional work-years are destroyed in supplier industries. This suggests that about 15 percent of U.S. manufacturing employment in 1978 was directly or indirectly tied to the production of automobiles.

Apart from the similarity in their sensitivity to trade, the apparel and auto industries have little in common. Auto production is capital-rather than labor-intensive and oligopolistic rather than competitive in terms of entry and exit. Competition is based not only on price, but also on quality, reliability, service, and product differentiation. Real wages have been persistently and significantly above the industrial average. Trade competition in autos has come almost entirely from producers based in other developed countries, especially Japan and Germany, while in apparel, trade competition comes mainly from low-wage Third World producers.

All of these characteristics suggest that a simple comparative advantage explanation that is based on implicit assumptions of product homogeneity, price competition, and free trade in competitive markets fails to explain patterns of trade in automobiles. In other words, while comparative advantage theory reasonably predicted that growing import pressure in the apparel industry would come from low-wage Third World countries, it could not have predicted that growing import pressure in the auto industry would come mainly from another developed country, namely, Japan. Several special factors played a role in the automobile case. They include: the effective closure of the Japanese market to U.S. and European producers; a sharp rise in gasoline prices and a shift in demand to smaller cars, where Japan had both a price and a quality/reliability advantage over the United States; the imposition of pollution controls and their effects on U.S. production costs; and the evolution of a superior organizational and technological production base in Japan, which, along with lower blue- and white-collar wages, combined to give Japan a significant manufacturing cost differential (MCD) in the production of small cars.

Chapter 5 suggests that the popular belief that excessively high wages of production workers in the U.S. auto industry were the most important factor behind its competitive difficulties is misguided. High wages mattered because the productivity performance of the American industry was relatively weak compared to that of the Japanese industry. In addition, Scott's evidence indicates that the relatively high wages of white-collar workers were as important a determinant of the MCD as were those of blue-collar workers.

The auto study examines the potential employment effects of the voluntary restraint agreement (VRA) on Japanese auto imports that was introduced in 1981. The VRA, like similar protectionist measures in apparel, was designed to slow the pace of import penetration, thereby reducing the pace of potential labor displacement and giving the domestic industry time to develop new products, technologies, and marketing strategies that would make it competitive at a later date. Like other voluntary quota arrangements, the auto quota program left decisions about employment and competitive strategies to the marketplace, even though its imposition distorted market incentives. Predictably, in keeping with past experience with similar arrangements in other industries, the prices and profits of both Japanese and American producers rose sharply, and Japanese imports moved toward higher value products.[19]

From the point of view of the issues of interest to this book, the critical concern is the VRA's effects on potential employment. Surprisingly, this issue has not been addressed very carefully, despite the fact that employment pressures were a major factor behind political support for the program. Scott argues that the critical question is what would have happened to the Japanese share of the U.S. auto market between 1980 and 1984 in the absence of the VRA.

Scott's analysis suggests that without the VRA, the Japanese might have gained 30–40 percent of the U.S. auto market by 1984, compared to an actual share of 22 percent in 1980. While it might seem unrealistic to assume such a large share increase in such a short period of time, it is instructive to note that the Japanese more than doubled their share between 1977 and 1980. In addition, in 1980 the Japanese had capacity expansion plans in place that would have allowed them to produce enough vehicles to double their share of the U.S. market by 1983. Finally, the U.S. competitive position relative to that of Japan had eroded sharply in the late 1970s and was reflected in an estimated MCD of between $1,500 and $2,000.[20] To make matters worse, by 1979 the quality of small cars sold by the Japanese in the United States was higher than that of domestic cars. And to weaken their competitive position still further, U.S. manufacturers had increased the prices of their small cars by 11 percent in 1980, prior to the imposition of the VRA.

If the Japanese had gained 30–40 percent of the U.S. market by 1984, the potential job destruction in the U.S. auto industry would have been in the range of 110,000 to 149,000 work-years. And these are only the direct effects. The indirect effects on jobs in supplier industries would have been two times as large. Scott's estimates of the employment effects of the VRA are much greater than those of other researchers, and they suggest that the cost of protection per job saved was much lower than the other studies suggest. Significantly, even with the VRA in place, the continued deterioration in the U.S. auto trade balance between 1980 and 1984 meant a further substantial reduction in potential auto jobs.[21] The USITC (1986) study estimates that almost 96,000 jobs, or about 11 percent of the 1984 level, were potentially destroyed by trade during this period.

The fact that the VRA may have eased trade pressure on job opportunities in the U.S. auto industry does not imply that it was a good policy. Although it may have saved a significant number of jobs in the short run, Scott argues that it did little to strengthen the competitiveness of U.S. producers in the long run. As he points out, the VRA allowed domestic producers to increase prices and did not restrain auto wages, especially white-collar wages. While the higher auto profits that were generated by the VRA might have been used to improve long-run competitiveness by financing more investment, the level of capital spending by the industry actually fell between 1980 and 1983.

Scott argues that a more appropriate policy to protect employment and enhance long-run competitiveness would have required a quid pro quo, such as granting temporary protection in exchange for price and wage restraint and the introduction of new cooperative labor/management efforts to improve productivity. He also argues, as most economists do, that tariff protection would have been preferable to quota protection for two reasons. First, it would not have had the effect of encouraging the Japanese to move aggressively toward the export of higher priced, higher value-added cars. Second, a tariff would have resulted in increased revenues for the U.S. government instead of increased profits for Japanese producers, as the VRA did.

Finally, Scott discusses the likely employment implications of future competitive strategies in the auto industry. At this point there is no evidence that the VRA improved the competitive ability of U.S. producers in the small car market, and the removal of the quota has led to continued growth in small car imports and continued job displacement pressures. These pressures have been mitigated to some extent by the decisions of Japanese producers to set up production in the United States, not because the customized nature of the product requires location near the point of sale, as in the telecommunications industry, but because of fear of future import restraints. According to the evidence cited by Scott, Japanese-owned plants will account for about 47,000 U.S. jobs by 1990, but each Japanese plant tends to employ significantly fewer workers than a similar American-owned plant because most of the parts used in Japanese assembly plants are imported.

U.S. car producers are emphasizing two strategies to become more competitive in the long run. Both of them will tend to reduce domestic employment prospects. The first is offshoring of component and final assembly. The second is greater automation of domestic production techniques. The offshoring option is more attractive for labor-intensive standardized components and vehicles, while the automation option is more attractive for components and vehicles where quality, reliability, and specialized features play a major role in competitive outcomes. Whatever combination of the two is finally adopted, under most foreseeable scenarios, total industry employment is likely to continue its secular downward trend.

Telecommunications Equipment

At an aggregate level, the telecommunications equipment industry stands in sharp contrast to the apparel industry in a variety of ways. It is a rapidly growing industry in terms of domestic output and domestic demand, it enjoys a rate of return on capital that is above the average for all industry, its workers receive real wages that are among the highest paid in the electronics-based industries and are above the manufacturing average, and it has never been a big employer of labor. Although the consumer premises equipment (CPE) segment of the industry is relatively labor-intensive, the industry is best classified as a high-technology one overall. Static comparative advantage theory predicts that trade in such an industry would be a source of growth for both production and employment in the United States.

There are no studies that directly test this hypothesis. In existing studies, the industry is traditionally aggregated with the radio and television equipment industry, where export and import patterns have been quite different. Import competition in radio and television equipment has been much greater than that in most types of telecommunications equipment. In 1984, for example, imports as a percentage of new supply (imports plus shipments) were about 52 percent in radio and television sets; they were only about 13–15 percent in telephone and telegraph apparatus, reaching about 40 percent in telephone instruments. As these numbers suggest, even within the telecommunications industry, there is great diversity in how different product lines have been affected by trade. The industry as a whole ran a net trade surplus in value terms through 1982, suggesting that until 1983 trade was a net source of potential job creation.[22] In low-end CPE products, the most labor-intensive segment of the industry, however, trade has been a net source of growing potential job destruction since the 1970s.

The erosion of the overall U.S. trade surplus in telecommunications equipment that began in the second half of the 1970s took place in the context of growing openness of the industry. As Stowsky (Chapter 6) indicates, it was only after the FCC allowed connection of non-AT&T equipment to the Bell System network that imports of most types of telecommunications equipment were allowed into the United States. Thereafter, imports began to increase. Import growth was given a further boost after 1980 as deregulation of the Bell System continued and as the value of the dollar increased. Overall, imports increased by about 29 percent in each year between 1972 and 1984, with the rate of increase doubling in the 1980s as compared to that of the 1970s. According to Stowsky, by 1984 the United States was the only major market for telecommunications equipment that was significantly free of government regulation, and it accounted for more than one-half of the exports of telecommunications equipment by the thirteen largest exporters.

On the export side, the continued regulation of telecommunications networks abroad limited export prospects for U.S. producers. Until the mid-1970s, exports represented less than 3 percent of the value of industry shipments. Thereafter the export/shipment ratio began to rise, hitting 6.2 percent in 1982 before beginning to decline.

Taken together, the rising importance of both exports and imports suggests that the potential effects of trade on industry employment have become much larger in recent years, while the shift from a trade surplus to a trade deficit suggests that potential job creation from trade has given way to potential job destruction. Behind these industry-wide trends, however, lie important differences in individual products. The divergences in product behavior are consistent with a static comparative advantage perspective that is applied within the sector. The CPE subsector includes private branch exchange (PBXs), handsets, and other products that are labor-intensive and require no customization for the user and no substantial after-sales service. Such products compete on price and are vulnerable to competition from low-wage producers. In contrast, switching equipment tends to be research-intensive, and U.S. producers can compete on design, service, and other nonprice criteria.

Even before the recent import challenge in all segments of the industry, employment levels began to stagnate and decline in the 1970s, especially among skilled jobs and craft occupations. Stowsky argues that these employment trends occurred despite rapid growth in demand and are best explained by rapid technological changes in production processes. He maintains that employment trends have been dominated by such changes, which in turn have been driven by innovation in the end-user characteristics of the products themselves rather than by a desire to save on labor costs, although the latter motivation has become more important as import competition has intensified. Stowsky's evidence suggests that changes in technology have had a disproportionate impact on production workers, resulting in a decline in the ratio of production workers to the total work force and a growing bifurcation between affluent programmers and engineers on one end and low-skilled production workers on the other.

Looking to the future, Stowsky argues that despite continued rapid growth in demand for telecommunications equipment, domestic employment is not likely to grow. There are two reasons for this: more offshoring of labor-intensive products and components and more automation in customized and service-intensive products and components.

Semiconductors

Between 1972 and 1987 the U.S. semiconductor industry was the fastest growing of all U.S. industries. The 1987 level of shipments in the industry was a staggering 5,094 percent higher than the 1972 level of shipments in real terms. Total employment in the industry grew at a compound annual rate of 5.8 percent per year between 1972 and 1984; it more than doubled by 1986. Behind the dramatic industry expansion was a rapid increase in total demand, driven by growing demand in the many electronic products that use semiconductors as a critical input. Besides being a growth industry, the semiconductor industry is a technology-intensive one, whether measured by the share of scientists and engineers in total employment, the share of R&D in total sales, or the pace of new product and process innovation. In the public imagination, the semiconductor industry has come to symbolize the quintessential high-technology industry—the kind of industry that will determine the future of American manufacturing.

During the last several years, however, the industry has also become the symbol of America's competitive decline. In 1980 fifteen American companies, all of them profitable, produced most of the semiconductors that were sold on world markets. In 1987 only three American companies were still producing and selling semiconductors for the merchant market, and all of them were running a loss. The domestic industry laid off approximately 65,000 workers between 1981 and 1987.[23]

Reflecting the industry's competitive difficulties, the U.S. share of the worldwide merchant market declined steadily from nearly 60 percent in 1975 to below 45 percent in 1986, and the U.S. share of the captive plus merchant market declined from 67 percent to 50 percent. The decline in the U.S. share was mirrored in the increasing share of Japanese producers, which went from 25 percent of the captive plus merchant market in 1975 to 39 percent by 1986 (Defense Science Policy Board 1987). And the erosion in the U.S. share of world markets was also reflected in a persistent erosion in the U.S. trade balance in semiconductors from a surplus position in the 1970s to a rapidly growing deficit beginning in 1981.

There are no precise estimates of the employments effects of the deteriorating trade position in the industry. In existing studies, the industry is traditionally aggregated with other electronic devices and accessories that have different trade patterns and in which the import penetration rate has been higher. Nonetheless, the available evidence that is presented in the chapter by Parsons (7) suggests some conclusions about the employment effects of trade.

The behavior of the trade balance indicates that trade had a positive net effect on potential job opportunities through 1980 and a growing negative effect thereafter. During the 1970s, imports grew much more quickly than exports, resulting in the gradual decline of the positive trade balance. This in turn caused a loss in job opportunities over time. In other words, although the level of trade had a positive effect on the level of industry demand and hence on job opportunities, the deterioration in the trade position reduced the level of industry demand and reduced potential job opportunities. Since total demand was growing dramatically during the 1970s, employment in the industry continued to grow rapidly, except during temporary cyclical downturns, despite the gradual deterioration in the trade position.

There was a significant change in the composition of imports during the second half of the 1970s. Through the end of the 1970s, the decline in the trade balance was mainly the result of growing imports from U.S.-owned assembly plants abroad under 806/807 tariff provisions. Therefore the question of the effects of trade on domestic employment is really a question of the effects of foreign direct investment by U.S. firms on domestic employment. The problem with answering the latter question is apparent in that such investment reduced costs and hence prices, thus increasing total demand for semiconductors. As a result, the answer is very sensitive to assumptions about how costs and prices would have been affected if domestic producers had chosen to keep production at home rather than offshore it. Parsons evaluates a range of estimates and concludes that in the 1970s, domestic assembly rather than assembly abroad would have meant a net gain in jobs, with a gain in assembly jobs more than offsetting a loss in nonassembly jobs.

In the 1980s the declining trade balance was increasingly the result of competition from Japanese producers. Under such competition, semiconductor prices fell dramatically, further stimulating demand, and the growth of total demand more than offset the negative effects of trade on U.S. employment, which hit a new peak during the cyclical boom in 1983–84. When the industry went into a slump in 1985, however, employment began to fall, reflecting both declining total demand and the onslaught of competition from the Japanese in U.S. and world markets.

The semiconductor industry demonstrates the extent to which factors other than the exchange rate were important in the deterioration of the U.S. trade balance after 1980. As Parsons demonstrates, and as the results of Branson and Love (1986) suggest, there is no simple relationship between the worsening trade balance in semiconductors and the appreciation of the dollar through 1985 or its gradual decline thereafter. Other factors were at work, including the continued offshoring of assembly jobs by domestic producers—two-thirds of the domestic industry's assembly employment was located abroad by 1983—and the relative productivity and quality gains by Japanese producers. In addition, there is strong evidence that Japanese producers have been dumping in world markets.

Over the longer run, it is difficult to predict the future of employment in the industry. The Bureau of Labor Statistics (BLS) predicts that employment levels will grow rapidly in the electronic components industry through 1995 in response to growing world demand. But the Japanese competitive threat shows no sign of abating. At the same time, technology is pushing toward greater automation in the production process. The composition of U.S. jobs will move still further toward fewer assembly jobs and more nonassembly ones. The workers that will be displaced by trade competition and technological change will not have the education and skills that are required for the nonassembly jobs that become available.

CONCLUSIONS

After two years of sustained decline in the dollar's value and a slowdown in U.S. economic growth, the U.S. trade balance is finally showing some sign of improvement. Exports are increasing and imports have begun to fall in real terms, although the overall deficit remains very very large. Most economists predict that the trade deficit will continue to decline, both absolutely and relative to U.S. GNP. During the next several years, the decline in the deficit will be a stimulus to demand for U.S. output, particularly the output of manufactured goods that make up the bulk of U.S. trade (Thurow and Tyson 1987). This does not mean, of course, that the adjustment in the U.S. trade deficit will bring the recovery of all U.S. manufacturing. Nor does it mean that a recovery in U.S. manufacturing output will lead to a recovery in U.S. manufacturing employment. Nor does it mean that the wages that are paid in manufacturing jobs will rise. But it does mean that at the aggregate level, the negative effects of trade on the demand for U.S. manufactured goods and on the workers who produce them have peaked and will continue to decline in the future.

The case studies that are contained in the following chapters indicate that the manner in which the output and employment levels of individual industries will be affected by the macroeconomic forces that underlie the improvement in the aggregate trade balance will vary depending on a number of industry characteristics. The results also confirm the general conclusions that arise from a comparative advantage perspective on how trade is likely to affect the composition of jobs in the future. Foreign competition from low-wage producers in developing countries will continue to threaten jobs in labor-intensive industries, such as apparel, and in the labor-intensive segments of capital- or technology-intensive industries, such as PBXs in the telecommunications industry and semiconductor assembly. Competition of this kind will lead to continued job displacement in the production of labor-intensive, easily transportable, relatively standardized products where competition is based mainly on price. Barring permanent protection, American producers of such products have essentially three strategies, none of which are likely to prevent further job erosion: they can exit from the industry, they can offshore production, or they can automate to reduce labor use in production. The types of workers that are most susceptible to job displacement from foreign competition of this sort are the relatively unskilled, low-wage production workers, a disproportionate number of whom are often minority and female.

On balance, trade is likely to be a source of growth to domestic production and employment in technology-intensive industries, such as integrated circuits, most telecommunications products, and computers, which compete on the basis of design, quality, and customized service. The actual impetus to job creation from trade in these sectors will depend both on the pace of growth in world demand and on the share of U.S. producers in world markets.

Although the size of the potential job creation effects from trade in high-technology products is uncertain, the types of jobs and labor skills that are likely to be involved are not. Such jobs will require highly skilled and educated labor, often commanding high levels of scientific and engineering training, and will tend to be highly paid and relatively secure. At the present time, a disproportionate number of such jobs are held by white males, and in the absence of basic changes in the educational system and the educational goals of different groups, this is likely to continue to be the case.

Three policy conclusions emerge from the analysis that is presented in this book. First, in the future, U.S. policymakers must be more sen-(1) sitive to the effects of their decisions on the U.S. trade position. The United States is now an open economy in which trade plays a much greater role in determining production and employment levels than in the past. Policy choices that fail to sustain our competitive position in technology and productivity over the long run and that generate unsustainable macro imbalance over the short run now impose greater costs on our manufacturing industry and jobs than they did when the United States was more closed to foreign trade and had a greater lead over its foreign competitors. America can no longer afford another bout of the "American disease" of the first half of the 1980s—adopting macroeconomic policies that push the dollar up and undermine the competitive health of the manufacturing sector.

Second, as a result of greater openness, the United States is now more (2) sensitive to the stress and strain of structural change that is induced by changing patterns of trade competition. As the pace of structural change quickens, the need for a broad-based worker retraining and relocation program becomes more pronounced. It is neither equitable nor efficient for workers who lose a job as a result of the changing composition of the economy to bear all of the costs of moving to another job. The fact that the kinds of workers that are displaced by trade competition are not apt to have the requisite skills or training for the jobs that are created by trade makes the need for such a program even more critical.

Third, in the future, U.S. manufacturing will be increasingly high (3) technology in both basic industries, such as apparel and autos, where high-technology inputs will transform production techniques, and in the high-tech industries themselves. A high-tech America requires a work force that has the skills and training that are needed to use the new technologies. The U.S. educational system from kindergarten through college must be modified to meet these new requirements if American workers are to be able to compete in the world economy with rising rather than falling wages.

NOTES

1. For a series of case studies on the effects of trade on production and employment levels in labor-intensive industries in the United States during the 1960s and 1970s and resulting protectionist responses, see Zysman and Tyson (1983).
2. This conclusion has also been suggested by Kremp and Mistral (1985). They find evidence of an increase in the income elasticity of import demand in the U.S. economy. They interpret this increase to be the result of a relative loss in product and production advantage by U.S. producers. All other things being equal, a gradual increase in the income elasticity of import demand in the United States would require a gradual decline in the dollar's value to prevent a deterioration in the trade balance. A more recent study by Krugman and Baldwin (1987) also finds a long-term trend of deterioration in the U.S. trade position in nonagricultural goods, which they attribute to "declining competitiveness." Given such a trend, a dollar depreciation would have been required to prevent growing import penetration during the 1980–1985 period.
3. The trade balance figures in the text reflect recent corrections for undocumented U.S. exports to Canada and were provided by the Department of Commerce.
4. The figures on full-time equivalent employment in manufacturing between 1979 and 1985 and earlier are taken from Cremeans (1985) and from an update provided by Cremeans to the authors.
5. This figure is based on a recent report by the Office of Technology Assessment (1987). See Cohen and Zysman (1987) for an illuminating discussion of the links between manufacturing and services.
6. These figures are taken from a report by the Economic Policy Institute (1986).
7. Significantly, from the point of view of the effects of trade on domestic employment opportunities, manufacturing jobs in sectors that export or compete with imports are higher paying than those in the rest of the economy. See the evidence in Chapter 4 and the research by Katz (1986) and Abowd and Freeman (1986).

8. This is the rate of growth from the fourth quarter of 1982 to the fourth quarter of 1986. See Bryan and Day (1987).

9. For an extended discussion of the input-output approach and its weaknesses in evaluating the employment effects of trade, see Chapter 2.

10. The OTA results discussed in this paragraph are based on the standard input-output assumption of unchanged technology. The OTA study also examines how observed changes in input-output coefficients between 1972 and 1984 affected production levels in different industries. Overall, the study finds that changes in production processes are about as important as changes in total demand—both domestic and foreign—in determining changes in output level. However, for an industry, such as automobiles, that is not a major supplier of inputs to other sectors, changes in the production process are not significant determinants of changes in output level, while for semiconductors and telecommunications equipment, which are major suppliers of inputs to other industries, such changes in production processes are much more important. See Office of Technology Assessment (1987).

11. Thurow and Tyson (1987) reach a similar estimate of 4 million jobs lost as a result of trade in 1985–1986, using a slightly different methodology.

12. The USITC numbers and the numbers cited from Chapter 2 include both direct and indirect effects. Indirect effects include the labor required to produce all of the intermediate inputs embodied in the production of traded goods. Direct effects include the labor directly employed in the production of traded goods. For more on this distinction, see Chapter 2. The USITC numbers are reported in work-years or full-time equivalents, not in terms of the number of workers actually employed.

13. Because the input-output analysis reported by the USITC is not done at the four-digit industrial classification level, the effects of trade on potential job opportunities in semiconductors and telecommunications equipment cannot be distinguished. Semiconductors are included in the broader classification of electronic components and accessories, while telecommunications equipment is included in the broader classification of radio, television, and communications equipment. Both broader classifications include labor-intensive product lines, where the effects of trade on job opportunities have been much greater than in the narrow, more technology-intensive product lines of interest in the case studies contained in the remainder of this book.

14. Dickens and Lang note that they cannot directly assess how much of the decline in the fraction of the labor force in good jobs after 1981 was the result of the growing trade imbalance and how much was the result of the 1982–1983 recession. They also emphasize that although a growing trade imbalance may destroy good jobs, it may also produce beneficial effects—at least in the short run—in the form of lower prices for U.S. consumers and possible gains in efficiency due to enhanced competition.

15. These arguments are consistent with U.S. economic performance in recent years. The level of employment and the ratio of the number of people employed to the working-age population have reached new peaks, mainly as a result of the social forces behind the rising labor-force participation rates for women. At the same time, U.S. wages in real terms have fallen from the peak levels that were realized in the first half of the 1970s.

16. This long-run rate of unemployment has come to be called the "natural rate" of unemployment because it is the rate to which the economy converges as wages adjust. When unemployment gets above this level due to an insufficiency of demand, wage growth slows. This increases the incentives for employees to hire new workers, which in turn causes the unemployment rate to move back to its natural level.

17. Unemployment resulting from the unwillingness of workers who have been laid off from high-paying jobs to take available lower wage jobs has recently drawn the attention of labor economists. Such unemployment is called "transitional" unemployment. See Summers (1986).

18. This increase has occurred along with an increase in the level of employment and an increase in the employment ratio.

19. For a discussion of how similar forms of protection affected market performance in other industries, see the chapters by Yoffie and Aggarwal and Haggard in Zysman and Tyson (1983).

20. This cost differential in dollars developed despite a sharp decline of the dollar in terms of the yen between 1976 and 1978.

21. The studies by Branson and Love (1986) and Eichengreen (1987) suggest that the dollar's appreciation was a major factor behind the continued deterioration in the auto trade balance during the 1980–1984 period.

22. To be certain that this conclusion is correct, it would be necessary to have estimates of the trade balance in real rather than nominal terms.

23. These figures are taken from Reich (1987).

REFERENCES

Abowd, John, and Richard Freeman. 1986. "Internationalization of the U.S. Labor Market." National Bureau of Economic Research, Cambridge, Mass., August. Mimeo.

Aggarwal, Vinod, and Stephan Haggard. 1983. "The Politics of Protection in the U.S. Textile and Apparel Industry." In *American Industry in International Competition,* edited by John Zysman and Laura D'Andrea Tyson. Ithaca: Cornell University Press.

Bluestone, Barry, and Bennett Harrison. 1987. "The Great American Jobs Machine Takes a U-Turn," *Washington Post,* April 25.

Branson, William, and James Love. 1986. "Dollar Appreciation and Manufacturing Employment and Output." National Bureau of Economic Research Working Paper No. 1972, Cambridge, Mass., July.

Bryan, Michael, and Ralph Day. 1987. "Views from the Ohio Manufacturing Index." *Economic Review,* Federal Reserve Bank of Cleveland, First Quarter.

Cohen, Stephen, and John Zysman. 1987. *Manufacturing Matters: The Myth of the Post-Industrial Society.* New York: Basic Books.

Council on Competitiveness. 1987. *America's Competitive Crisis: Confronting the New Reality.* Washington, D.C.

Cremeans, John. 1985. "Three Measures of Structural Change." In *The Service Economy: Opportunity, Threat or Myth?*, edited by the U.S. Department of Commerce, Economic Affairs. Washington, D.C.: U.S. Department of Commerce.

Defense Science Board. 1987. *The Report of the Defense Science Board Task Force on Defense Semiconductor Dependency.* Washington, D.C.: Department of Defense. February.

Economic Policy Institute. 1986. "Family Incomes in Trouble." Briefing paper, Washington, D.C., October.

Eichengreen, Barry. 1987. "International Competition in the Products of U.S. Basic Industries." National Bureau of Economic Research Working Paper No. 2190, Cambridge, Mass., March.

Kremp, Elizabeth, and Jacques Mistral. 1985. "Commerce exterieur americain: d'ou vient ou va le deficit." *Economie prospective internationale,* 22 (Paris: Centre d'Etudes Prospectives et d'Informations Internationales).

Krugman, Paul, and Richard Baldwin. 1987. "The Persistence of the U.S. Trade Deficit." *Brookings Papers on Economic Activity,* no. 1: 1–56.

Katz, Lawrence. 1986. "International Trade and the Wage Structure in U.S. Manufacturing." Harvard University. December. Mimeo.

Lawrence, Robert. 1984. *Can America Compete?* Washington, D.C.: Brookings Institution.

Lund, David C. 1986. "Employment Effects of U.S. International Trade Changes." Working paper, U.S. Department of Commerce.

Office of Technology Assessment. 1987. *Technology and the American Economic Transition.* Washington, D.C., forthcoming.

Reich, Robert. 1987. "The Rise of Techno-Nationalism." *The Atlantic Monthly,* May, pp. 63–69.

Richardson, J. David. 1983. "Worker Adjustment to U.S. International Trade: Progress and Prospects." In *Trade Policy in the 1980s,* edited by William Cline. Washington, D.C.: Institute of International Economics.

Rowthorn, Bob, and Andrew Glyn. "The Diversity of Unemployment Experience since 1973." Paper prepared for research program on Global Macro Economic Policies of the World Institute of Development Economic Research, Helsinki, July 1986.

Summers, Lawrence. 1986. "Why Is the Unemployment Rate So Very High Near Full Employment?" *Brookings Papers on Economic Activity*, no. 2: 339–83.

Thurow, Lester, and Laura Tyson. 1987. "The Economic Black Hole." *Foreign Policy* 67 (Summer): 3–21.

United States International Trade Commission. 1986. *U.S. Trade Related Employment: 1978–84*. USITC Publication No. 1855. Washington, D.C.: USITC, May.

Yoffie, David. 1983. "Adjustment in the Footwear Industry: The Consequences of Orderly Marketing Agreements," in *American Industry in International Competition*, edited by John Zysman and Laura D'Andrea Tyson. Ithaca: Cornell University Press.

Zysman, John, and Laura Tyson, eds. 1983. *American Industry in International Competition: Government Policies and Corporate Strategies*, Ithaca, N.Y.: Cornell University Press.

2 THE EFFECTS OF TRADE ON EMPLOYMENT
Techniques and Evidence
William T. Dickens

Although the study of trade has concerned academic economists for many years, a large body of practical work on the effect of trade on U.S. employment has begun to develop only recently. The growing importance of trade has no doubt stimulated this interest. As a new literature, applied trade studies have some major drawbacks: Much of the work is piecemeal, and there are no comprehensive models of the effects of trade. These studies also tend to focus more on that which is easy to do than on topics and approaches that might be more useful for dealing with practical problems.

What follows is a review of the economics literature as it bears on a number of questions that are relevant to the effects of trade on U.S. employment. Six questions are considered:

1. What have been the effects of trade on employment in the recent past?
2. What has been the effect of U.S. direct investment abroad?
3. What has been the effect of foreign direct investment on employment in the United States?
4. Have high union wages made U.S. industries less competitive and caused their decline?
5. Have changes in the composition of U.S. trade contributed to macroeconomic instability in the recent past?

6.   What are the characteristics of workers who find jobs in industries that are expanding due to export demand and what are the characteristics of jobs and workers in declining import industries?

A conclusion that summarizes the major findings and considers what needs to be done to improve our knowledge of how trade affects employment closes the chapter.

MAJOR ISSUES

What is the Employment Impact of U.S. Trade?

There are a wealth of studies that address the question of the employment effects of trade. These studies are sometimes undertaken to ascertain the effects of trade on the displacement of currently employed workers. Most have concluded that the effects of past changes in trade patterns and potential changes from tariff reductions are relatively small. However, nearly all of them consider employment effects by examining the effects of trade on labor demand. Not a single study considers displacement explicitly. It is immediately obvious that labor demand and employment are not necessarily equivalent. One needs only to consider the likely displacement effects of a trade-induced reduction in demand of one job in a fast growing as opposed to a declining industry. In the growing industry, the lost job opportunity will only reduce the pressure on a strained labor market, while in a rapidly declining industry, a lost job opportunity can mean that a worker loses a job and has very dim prospects for reemployment. Displacement is not directly considered in these studies because there is little data on the extent and nature of displacement. The types of studies that will be reviewed are divided into three categories. The first contains the accounting studies that attempt to break down the changes in employment in an industry into their proximate "causes," including changes in demand that are due to changes in trade. The second category includes studies that take the basic accounting approach and extend it to consider the indirect effects of changes in demand for the products of one industry on the demand—and, consequently, employment—for the products of other industries that provide inputs for the first industry. These are referred to as input-output studies. The third category contains a number of different types of studies. What they have in common is their use of a more complicated economic behavioral model of either the production process and/or the demand for traded goods. These are referred to as model-based studies.

Four conclusions can be drawn from the review of these studies:

1. As noted in the introduction, these studies tell us nothing about the level of employment in the economy as a whole in the long run.

2. The studies do tell us something about the changing composition of employment. In particular, most studies agree that trade has increased employment in chemicals, plastics, engines, turbines, generators, construction and mining machinery, office and computing machinery, aircraft parts, and scientific instruments. Trade has decreased employment in apparel, furniture and fixtures, leather products, screws and stamping, and radio and televisions. Trends in all of these industries have been much the same from the mid-1960s to the early 1980s. In the mid-1980s, the list of industries that are negatively affected by trade has become much larger due to the large trade deficit. Chapter 3 discusses the possible effects of these changes on the productivity of the economy and our economic well-being.

3. Even very large tariff reductions (50 percent or 60 percent) are unlikely to cause the displacement of more than 200,000 workers; they will probably cause far fewer.

4. The short-run effects of trade on the aggregate unemployment rate were small in the 1970s, with fewer than 300,000 workers displaced each year. This number is probably a substantial overestimate. This situation changed markedly during the 1980s as the appreciation of the dollar led to a flood of imports and a drop in U.S. exports. Over 500,000 job opportunities were lost in 1982 and 1983, and about 1.5 million were lost in 1984. There may have been substantial dislocation during this period that may have contributed to the depth of the 1982 recession and the slow recovery of the unemployment rate since then.

Accounting Studies.   The point of departure for all of these studies is the change in employment in an industry that takes place over the study period. Using an equation called an accounting identity, it is possible to partition the change in employment into the changes that are associated with the demand for the product, the changes in labor productivity, and an interaction effect. If $YA = E$, where Y is output demand, E is employment, and A is the number of workers required to produce d dollars worth of output, then $\%\Delta E = \%\Delta Y + \%\Delta A + (\%\Delta Y)(\%\Delta A)$. The change in demand can be further partitioned into the changes that are due to increased consumer demand and those that are due to changes in the quantity of imports. Further, changes in consumer demand are sometimes partitioned into changes in domestic and export demand. Given this identity, researchers take the changes in imports and either the changes in demand or labor productivity and then compute the remaining major category as a residual. For the case where the researcher explicitly computes the changes in imports and productivity (Cable 1977), demand is calculated as the residual. When demand is explicitly calculated, productivity is calculated as the residual (Frank 1977; Krueger 1980a, 1980b, 1980c; Marsden and Anderssen 1978). The interaction between productivity growth and changes in demand is ignored and assumed to be small in both cases.

Table 2–1 presents estimates from a number of these studies. The computed employment effects of trade are found to be very small in general. Krueger argues that since the rate of employment loss due to imports is less than 3 percent in almost every industry, that loss could be absorbed through quits and slower hiring without causing any dislocation. Her analysis dealt with fairly aggregate industries. When she performed the analysis at a more detailed level, she found a few industries that had very high levels of employment loss due to imports, but, of course, fewer workers were involved.

Input-Output Studies.   A major problem with the accounting studies is that they ignore the indirect effects of trade on demand. For example, an accounting study of the effects of trade on employment in the steel industry would treat changes in the demand for steel that originate from the auto industry as a result of changes in domestic demand, despite the possibility that some of the decline in the demand for autos is due to increased foreign competition. To remedy this problem, input-output studies (see Table 2–1b for examples) take historical data on the amount of the output of each industry that is used as input in each of the other industries and construct estimates of the indirect effects of changes in the demand for imports or exports in one industry on the changes in demand in all of the other industries. These demand numbers are divided by average labor productivity in each industry to get employment effects. For comparison, several studies perform the same exercise to find the employment effects of changes in domestic demand for final products.

Table 2–1. Studies in Trade and Employment.

a. Accounting Method.

Type	Growth in Employment Due to Trade, 1963–1976 (average percent per year)[1]		Growth in Employment Due to Trade, 1970–1976 (average percent per year)[2]	
	Exports	Imports	Imports	Net Trade
Food products	.1	−.4	−.02	−.13
Tobacco products			−.05	−.38
Textile mill products	.1	−.2	.09	.43
Apparel	0.0	−.8	−.96	−.77
Lumber products	.1	−.6	−.18	−.19
Furniture and fixtures	0.0	−.5	−.24	.09
Paper products	1.2	−4.7	−.13	−.01
Printing and publishing	.1	−1.5		
Chemicals	.6	−.7	−.20	−.08
Petroleum and coal products	0.0	−1.5	−.43	.59
Rubber and plastic products	−1.5	−1.0	−.30	−.06
Leather products	0.0	−1.8	−1.51	−1.27
Stone, clay, and glass products	.3	−.6	−.11	−.05
Primary metals	−.1	−1.4	−.23	−.42
Fabricated metal products	.6	−.8	−.16	−.18
Nonelectric machinery	.7	−.9	−.32	−.55
Electrical and electronic machinery and supplies	.7	−1.8	−.90[t] −3.20[n] −1.82[q]	−.14
Transportation equipment	1.0	−.7	−.64	−.23
Instruments	1.2	−1.2	−.56	−.28
Miscellaneous manufacturing	.4	−1.3	−.58	.01

Table 2-1. (continued).

b. Input-Output Method.

Type	Effect (including secondary adjustments) of $1 Million in 1958 Trade to Developing Countries (number of jobs)[3]		Job Opportunities Embodied in Competitive Imports, 1960 (thousands of jobs)[4]		Change in Total Job Opportunities Embodied in Exports, 1963–1972 (thousands of jobs)[5]	Change in Net Total Trade-Related Job Opportunities (thousands of jobs)[6]		Net Employment Effects of Trade with Developing Countries (thousands of jobs)[7]
	Exports	Imports	Direct	Indirect		1964–1972	1972–1974	
Food products	1.8	119	12.7	7.8	−4			5.04
Tobacco products			1.6	.5	−2			
Textile mill products	4.0	192	48.9	26.6	1			
Apparel	1.4	189	37.0	8.8	0	−95.04	−1.63	−78.95
Lumber products	7.1		13.6	12.8	8			−78.95
Furniture and fixtures			2.7	1.4	1	−8.17[b] −11.93[c]	.06[b] −2.44[c]	
Paper products	7.1[hh]	153[hh]	3.8	11.8	14			
Printing and publishing			2.1	11.5	9			
Chemicals	6.2		12.4	27.9	23			
Petroleum and coal products	.4		1.2	2.4	0			

Industry								
Rubber and plastic products	1.2		12.8	7.2	10	−40.70[t]	−5.90[t]	−32.56[f]
Leather products			13.3	4.1	−2	−31.58[e]	4.62[e]	
Stone, clay, and glass products	1.8		23.3	10.4	8			
Primary metals	8.7	.120	18.8	50.2	−32	−90.66[f]	−10.67[f]	28.56[f]
Fabricated metal products			12.8	18.4	41	−25.77[g]	−2.03[g]	8.63
Nonelectric machinery			22.8	17.3	75[t] 4[h] 10[j] 25[k]	33.199[j] 35.46[k]	29.58[j] 19.35[k]	8.57[h] 13.87[j] 15.45[k]
Electrical and electronic machinery and supplies			23.5	12.5	67[t] 1[n] 2[o] 32[p]	−40.19[n] −9.00[r] 6.99[q]	.29[n] 8.16[r] 5.39[q]	.28[n]
Transportation equipment	7.7		25.0	11.7	102[t] 23[s] 74[u]	−116.49[s] 117.52[u]	−11.53[s] 85.84[u]	33.38[s] 55.88[u]
Instruments			14.3	5.1	12[t] 4[v] 6[w]	5.58[x]	5.11[x]	
Miscellaneous manufacturing	33.4[ii]	132[ii]	29.5	8.2	9			

Table 2-1. (continued).

Type	Net Job Changes Due to Trade, 1970:1 to 1971:1 (thousands of jobs)[8]		Growth in Employment Due to Net Trade (average percent per year)[9]		Job Opportunities Embodied in Trade (thousands of jobs)[10]		Job Opportunities Embodied in Trade (thousands of jobs)[11]	
	Direct	Indirect	1970–1980	1973–1980	Exports	Imports	1984 Net	Change 1978–1984
Food products	23.3	63.7	.19	.34	−9	−7	−51	−26
Tobacco products			.38	.46	0	1	4	−1
Textile mill products	−3.6	−4.7	−.63[a]	−.54[a]	−1[t] / 5[a]	51[t] / 52[a]	−151	−114
Apparel	−15.3	−13.6	−.16	−.06	−4	2	−52	−226
Lumber products			.01[y]	.69[y]	26	−24	−41	−57
Furniture and fixtures			.05[b] / −.45[c]	.06[b] / −.30[c]	4[t] / 2[b] / 2[c]	3[t] / 3[b] / 0[c]	−43	−23
Paper products			.15[z]	.36[z]	3	−12	−57	−37
Printing and publishing			.04	.09	5	−1	−6	−14
Chemicals			.54[d] / .44[aa]	.80[d] / .79[aa]	45[t] / 38[aa]	−6[t] / −1[aa]	−8	−53

Industry								
Petroleum and coal products			-.06	.60	4	-27	-65	13
Rubber and plastic products			-.05	.21	7	-17	-113	-82
Leather products			-1.59[e]	-1.73[e]	1[t]	47[t]	-208	-120
					1[e]	42[e]		
Stone, clay, and glass products			-.13[bb]	.04[bb]	3	-9	-64	-36
Primary metals	-60.3	-56.5			42[t]	48[t]	-253	-175
			-.29[f]	0.0[f]	17[f]	22[f]		
Fabricated metal products	.1	.1			17[t]	7[t]	-135	-87
			-.37[g]	-.21[g]	2[g]	4[g]		
Nonelectric machinery	34.9	30.4			148[t]	67[t]	-8	-186.4
			1.78[h]	1.76[h]	18[h]	0[h]		
			1.99[j]	2.20[j]	24[j]	-2[j]		
			1.61[k]	2.76[k]	87[k]	41[k]		
Electrical and electronic machinery and supplies	-9.9	-11.0			56[t]	54[t]	-261	-338
			-.57[m]	-.22[m]	0[m]	1[m]		
			-.78[p]	-.59[p]	36[p]	47[p]		
Transportation equipment	16.3[t]	-19.9[t]			-18[t]	22[t]	170	-147
	-22.1[s]	-53.3[s]	-1.11[s]	-.91[s]	-23[s]	-5[s]		
			1.28[u]	2.09[u]	-9[u]	30[u]		
Instruments					28[t]	6[t]	-3	-36
			-.16[v]	.04[v]	28[v]	6[v]		
			.03[w]	.03[w]	0[w]	0[w]		
Miscellaneous manufacturing			-.50	-.64	-10	35	-226	-108

Table 2-1. (continued).

c. Model-Based Studies.

Type	Employment Effects of 50% Linear Tariff Cut (for detailed SIC industries impacted by at least 5%) (thousands of work years)[12]	Change in Employment due to 50% Linear Tariff Cut, by Exchange Rate Regime (1970 data base) (percent change)[13]		Net Direct Effects of 60% Tariff Cut (1971 data base) (thousands of jobs)[14]	Simulated Increase in 1979 Employment if Import Competition Held Constant at 1967 Level over 1967–1979 (percent change)[15]	Employment Effects of a 40% Exchange Rate Appreciation (approximately the appreciation between 1980 and 1984) (thousands of jobs)[16]
		Fixed	Flexible			
Food products		−.11	−.12	−1.7		−32.8
Tobacco products	10.23					−3.1
Textile mill products	−.54	−.14	−.14	−37.0		−56.3
Apparel		−.09	−.08			−54.2
Lumber products	−1.79	.09	.09	−.7		1.2
Furniture and paper products	−1.66	.09	.10			3.0
Paper products	−1.54	−.01	−.00			−5.0
Printing and publishing		−.01	−.01			57.4
Chemicals		.44	.46	3.3		−42.7

Petroleum and coal products	−5.88	−1.47	−1.42			−17.2
Rubber and plastic products		.28	.28	−.5		−27.5
Leather products	−.923	.17[jj]	.11[jj]	−3.5[dd]	5.0[ee]	−21.9
Stone, clay, and glass products	−5.04	0.04[bb]	−.03[bb]		−23.9[cc]	−46.6
Primary metals	−4.38	.39[f] / .21[kk]	.43[f] / .16[kk]	−4.4		−262.7
Fabricated metal products	−.33	.35	.35		13.5[gg]	−180.1
Nonelectric machinery	6.58[k]	.43	.46	16.9		−432.3
Electrical and electronic machinery and supplies	−2.98[n] / 5.14[q] / 2.38[r]	.27	.28		71.3[n]	20.3
Transportation equipment	4.13[u]	.42	.43	0.0		−139.6
Instruments		.36	.39	1.6		−47.9
Miscellaneous manufacturing						−45.1

Table 2-1. (continued)

Notes:
a Knitwear
b Household furniture
c Nonhousehold furniture
d Plastics and synthetic materials
e Footwear
f Iron and steel
g Screw machine products and stampings
h Engines, turbines, and generators
i Construction, mining, and oil field machinery
k Office, computing, and accounting machinery
m Radio, TV, and communications equipment
n Radio and TV sets only
o Communications equipment only
p Electronics components and accessories
q Semiconductors
r Electronic tubes and components (excluding semiconductors)
s Motor vehicles and parts
t Sector total
u Aircraft and parts
v Professional, scientific, and controlling instruments and supplies
w Optical, opthalmic, and photographic equipment
x Photographic equipment and supplies only
y Lumber products excluding containers
z Paper products excluding paperboard
aa Chemicals and selected products
bb Stone and clay products
cc Pottery only
dd Leather hides only
ee Leather tanning only

ggNuts and bolts only
hhIncludes other wood products
iiIncludes machinery
jjLeather and fur products
kkNonferrous metals

Sources:

1. Frank (1977: Table 3–4).
2. Krueger (1980b: Tables 1 and 2).
3. Lydall (1975: Tables 27 and 28).
4. Jacobs and Kutscher (1962: Table 2).
5. Eldredge and Saunders (1973: Table 4).
6. Bureau of International Labor Affairs (1978: Table 2A).
7. U.S. International Trade Commission (1983: Table 3).
8. Krause (1971: Table 2).
9. Lawrence (1983: Table 4–3).
10. U.S. International Trade Commission (1983: Table 3).
11. U.S. International Trade Commission (1986: Table 4).
12. Baldwin and Lewis (1978: Table 7).
13. Deardorff et al. (1977: Tables 3 and 4).
14. Cline et al. (1978: Table 8).
15. Grossman (1982b: Table 2).
16. Branson and Love (1986: Table 6).

Once again, these studies find relatively small employment effects in most industries, although a few industries are identified as being seriously affected. Table 2–1 presents a review of these estimates for several industries.

Model-Based Studies.   The input-output studies represent an improvement over the accounting studies, but they are still subject to a great deal of criticism. The model-based studies represent attempts to deal with many of the problems that are inherent in input-output and accounting studies.

The input-output studies take quantities of imports and exports as given. This makes them of little use for evaluating the effects of tariffs since one cannot know a priori the effects of tariff reductions on the quantity of exports and imports demanded. Baldwin and Lewis (1978) and Deardorff, Stern, and Baum (1977) assemble general equilibrium[1] models of world trade to determine the effects of tariff changes on import and export demand. The approach of these researchers is to specify simple models of how each country's demands for its own home goods and the imports of all foreign countries are dependent on the prices of those goods. Assuming that any country can produce any amount of any good at a constant price, it is then possible to compute the effects of a change in tariffs on the level of demand for each industry. These initial changes are then used as input for an input-output model that determines final employment effects. Both studies find very small effects in nearly all industries, even for very large tariff reductions.

A potential problem with the accounting, input-output, and general equilibrium studies is that they assume that a dollar's worth of imports displaces a dollar's worth of U.S. production. But we would only expect this to happen if the imported goods were exactly the same as the domestically produced goods. On the other hand, it is possible that some imported goods, such as a unique type of houseware, are so different from anything that is produced domestically that they do not displace any domestic production. A number of studies examine this possibility. Grinols and Thorbecke (1978) perform an input-output study of the effect of a hypothetical increase in U.S. trade on employment. They then go on to examine an alternative model where domestic production does not vary one-for-one with foreign imports. Instead they calculate regression[2] estimates of the extent to which domestic production is depressed by increases in imports. They do not report the results of their regression analysis, but argue that the small change between the results of their input-output study and model-based study indicates that imperfect substitutability is not an important consideration. Pelzman and Martin (1981) also consider this issue. They estimate separate demand equations for imported and domestic textiles and find that domestic production declines nearly one-for-one when imports increase. Finally, Grossman (1982b) examines a wider range of industries. Although he does not explicitly consider employment effects, his estimates for the degree of substitutability between U.S. goods and those that are produced by less developed countries (LDCs) support the conclusions that imports and domestically produced goods are close substitutes. Thus it seems likely that the results of input-output studies are not badly biased when this problem is ignored.

Two final model-based studies are worthy of mention. These were done by Grossman (1982c, 1984). Grossman notes that accounting studies and input-output studies are generally inadequate for assessing trade impacts for a number of reasons (1982a). First, these studies take the quantities of exports, imports, and domestic demand as given and they treat changes that are due to changes in domestic demand as not being related to trade. However, if lower import prices increase domestic demand, this would be an incorrect assumption. Changes in prices that are due to trade may also induce changes in the way goods are produced, which would show up as changes in labor productivity in the accounting methodology. Thus a change that was caused by trade would be misattributed to autonomous technological change.

Grossman specifies a very general behavioral model of both production and demand to deal with these problems. He then assumes specific algebraic forms for each of the behavioral relations and manipulates these equations to obtain the employment levels in each industry purely in terms of variables that are assumed to be outside the control of decisionmakers in the industry. These variables include energy prices, the overall price level, capital stock and labor force for the economy, time trends, seasonal effects, and import prices, including tariffs. The last of these—import prices—is taken to represent the effects of trade. Grossman goes on to estimate the equations for each industry by using multiple regression and simulates the effects on employment if there had been no change in the real price of imports in each industry. Price changes are assumed to have had their full impact on employment by the end of eighteen months.

Of the ten industries he studies (five are shown in Table 2–1) only one shows substantial trade effects in the late 1960s and the 1970s. Employment in pottery and related products is increased by about one-third, and employment in radio and television is decreased by nearly one-half.

Steel shows substantial effects in the 1980s, but these are almost entirely due to changes in exchange rates rather than basic competitiveness.

Analysis.   The accounting studies have one important problem that is peculiar to them. They do not count changes in demand that are caused by trade that originates in other industries as trade induced. The input-output studies solve this problem. But it is minor when compared to the more basic problems that are shared by the accounting and input-output studies. As was noted in the discussion of model-based studies, there is no reason to assume that the level of domestic consumption of final goods is not affected by trade. A change in the price of imports could increase or decrease domestic demand. The most likely scenario is that decreased import prices lead to increased domestic demand, causing trade effects on employment to be overestimated. Another problem is that both types of studies measure import competition in terms of the dollar value of imports rather than their actual quantity. Thus if foreign prices are lower than domestic prices, true effects may be understated. For example, if foreign shoes are half the price of domestic shoes, then $100 worth of imported shoes could displace $200 worth of domestic shoes, doubling the employment effects. One study suggests that this could be an important factor in some industries (U.S. International Trade Commission 1983). However, to the extent that the market allows domestic prices to differ from foreign prices, domestic goods cannot be perfect substitutes for foreign goods. Thus imports will not displace domestic goods on a one-for-one basis, and using dollar comparisons may provide a reasonable estimate of job impacts.

A final problem is potentially of considerable importance. All of the accounting studies suggest that improved labor productivity accounts for a great deal of falling employment in trade-impacted industries. It is possible that trade competition causes rationalization of production and induces labor-saving technical change. At the very least, by driving marginal firms out of business, it will increase average industry productivity. Correlation studies of the relation between productivity increases and import competition provide mixed results,[3] but one could not expect a clear relation in cross section data, at least not in the United States, where it is often argued that our comparative advantage lies in products in their early stages of development where productivity growth is likely to be highest. Even if import competition induces technical change, if autonomous technical change gives U.S. industries an export advantage, then the correlation between import penetration and labor productivity growth could be zero, negative, or positive. To the extent that trade increases labor productivity, employment effects will be understated.

Although the general equilibrium studies solve the problem of taking quantities as exogenous, they are not a complete solution to the problems of the accounting and input-output studies. They do not address the problem of how changes in trade, apart from those caused by tariff reductions, affect employment. Also, they make extremely simple assumptions about the nature or demand and production technologies. Most of these assumptions are probably not very important, but two of them are critical and work in opposite directions. The first is the assumption of dollar-for-dollar substitution of imports for domestic products of the same industry. The second is the assumption that the use of regression studies can determine the sensitivity of demand to import prices. Since the United States is a large country, its demand almost certainly affects international prices. Since increased demand would be associated with higher supply prices, demand estimates that are based on assumptions of fixed prices would most likely underestimate the effects of prices on domestic demand and, consequently, employment. This would happen because increased prices that are caused by increased demand would be correlated with a demand for increased quantities rather than with reductions, as would be the case if price changes were not affected by the level of demand. In the worst case, if all price movements were caused by changes in demand, one would find that increased prices seem to lead to greater demand. Thus the general equilibrium models do not completely solve the problem that they set out to solve. Further, they are subject to the most important criticism of the accounting and input-output studies—that competition may induce increases in labor productivity.

Grossman's work represents a major improvement over these other studies in one dimension. By estimating the relation between employment and import prices by using econometric methods and historical data, his analysis solves, to some extent, the problem of not attributing changes in labor productivity that are induced by trade to changes in trade patterns. To the extent that rationalization, factor substitution, and induced technical change take place within eighteen months of changes in import prices, they will be correctly attributed to trade causes. However, to the extent that they take longer, they will not. Changes in production processes in particular could be expected to take longer. Some evidence of the potential importance of this problem can be found in Grossman's study of the steel industry, which attributes the overwhelming bulk of employment decline to long-term trends, including productivity growth and the downsizing of U.S. cars. To the extent that those long-term trends have been induced by foreign competition, Grossman's analysis fails to correctly attribute the employment effects to that competition.

This points to another problem with Grossman's analysis. Like the accounting studies, it does not properly attribute the changes in demand that are caused by changes in trade patterns in other industries. Thus the estimated employment effects of trade in a particular industry may be under- or overestimates, depending on the relative importance of imports and exports in the demand of the industries that buy the products of the industry in question.

Grossman claims that his approach avoids the problem of assuming that changes in the levels of imports and domestic demand are given. In fact, all he does is substitute the assumption of given foreign prices for given quantities. The U.S. economy is large, and changes in domestic demand could be expected to affect international price levels, leading to both over- and underestimates of trade effects. For example, if U.S. demand for a good contracts, the world price may fall. At the same time, U.S. production and employment will fall, leading Grossman to underestimate the effects of imports on employment since the statistical procedure he uses projects future employment responses to changes in import prices on the basis of the average response in the past. Similarly, an increase in U.S. demand could lead to an overestimate.

What can we conclude about the relative merits of these different approaches? The input-output studies are clearly preferable to the accounting studies. However, as noted above, they suffer from a number of problems that complicate the interpretation of their results. Since some of the problems bias the estimate down and others bias them up, the results cannot even be interpreted as upper or lower bounds. The failure to attribute employment loss due to trade-induced rationalization properly is a major problem that biases estimates downward. Measuring imports in dollar value also leads to an underestimate. Ignoring the effects of changes in world prices on domestic demand could be producing either upward or downward biases. Assuming that all output that is produced abroad would be produced domestically biases employment effects upward. Since there are effects in both directions, it is tempting to conclude that they cancel out, but in the absence of evidence on the relative sizes of the effects, this would be irresponsible.

The general equilibrium studies allow the input-output methodology to be applied to the question of the effects of tariffs, but they do not solve the problems of induced changes in labor productivity or the extent to which foreign goods substitute for domestic goods. Grossman's work solves some but not all of the problem with the productivity effects, but it introduces the new problem of interpreting the changes in price levels as opposed to changes in quantities. His work also assumes away the indirect effects of trade from one industry to another. Once again there are biases working in both directions so that it is impossible to interpret Grossman's estimates as upper or lower bounds. Specifying the likely range of error is impossible without more quantitative analysis of the effects of trade on productivity and the forces that cause the price dynamics that Grossman takes as given.

Apart from these problems that complicate the estimation of the employment figures, there is a more basic problem in interpreting their meaning. First, as noted in the introduction, the net gain or loss of jobs that is computed in these studies says nothing about the effects of trade on the aggregate level of employment or unemployment. In the long run, labor supply is far more important than demand. In the short run, it will not be the net level of job creation in the economy as a whole, but the amount of displacement that is created by trade that will most affect the level of employment and unemployment. Creating new jobs with trade will, of course, reduce unemployment in the short run, but increasing displacement and new job creation equally would probably cause an increase in unemployment in the short run because of the increased turnover in the labor market. Despite these problems, the large effects of trade on job opportunities starting in 1982 suggest that it may have contributed somewhat to the severity of the 1982 recession and to the slow recovery.

Second, the studies are probably of some use for determining the effects of trade on the long-run composition of employment. Although the levels may not be reliable, the directions of change probably are. From Table 2–1, chemicals, plastics, engines, turbines, generators, construction machinery, aircraft parts, and scientific instruments can be identified as industries that have seen relatively consistent increases in export demand. On the other hand, autos, apparel, furniture and fixtures, leather products, screws and stamping, and radio and televisions are industries where employment has been lost. The types of workers that are employed in these industries are examined later. The next chapter discusses the implications of these changes for our economic well-being.

Third, the use of these studies for evaluating the employment displacement effects of tariff reductions seems reasonable except for the objections that concern the estimates of substitution and demand elasticities and induced technical change. Since the employment effects that were found are fairly small—less than 200,000 workers, even for 50 percent or 60 percent across-the-board tariff reductions—it seems unlikely that tariff changes would substantially affect aggregate unemployment rates.

This brings us to the fourth and most important use of these studies: estimating the number of workers who lose their jobs as a result of foreign trade and the effects of displacement on the unemployment rate. Even if we had very accurate estimates of potential employment gains or losses from trade, we would still know very little about the likely displacement effects. In a growing industry, large losses of job opportunities that are due to trade could be easily absorbed, but in a declining industry, every lost job could result in a displaced worker. In a stagnant industry, the normal levels of turnover might or might not be enough to absorb changes in the number of job opportunities. Further, if employers perceive the drop in demand that results from trade as being permanent, they may quickly adjust their work force to completely accommodate the lower level of demand. But if employers are not sure whether the change is permanent, they may not lay off skilled or white-collar workers who would be hard to replace if demand increased again. This can be an important factor. In the economy as a whole, it takes a 2.5 percent to 3 percent reduction in demand to produce a 1 percent drop in employment over the business cycle. (This is known as Okun's law.)

· Another problem that is posed by the level of aggregation in these studies is that a broadly defined industry could show no increase in imports if imports of one product increased while another declined. If different firms produced the two types of goods, then the displacement effects could be substantial. The problem could be even worse if instead of considering employment effects of imports alone, one considered the net effects of imports and exports. On the other hand, considering only imports could bias displacement estimates upward if the product of the industry really is homogeneous.

A final complication is pointed out by Brechling (1978). Taking figures on total employment gain and loss in an industry and comparing them to normal attrition figures will not allow one to compute the displacement effect because the amount of attrition that takes place depends on both the state of the economy and the state of the industry under analysis. Brechling shows that while normal attrition (which includes quits, firings for cause, and retirement) could absorb about 79 percent of displacements in the iron and steel industries if output demand were to drop by 12 percent over one year, if the effect of industry conditions on quits is taken into account, then less than 43 percent of the reduction in force could be accomplished by turnover (in depressed industries, workers are much less likely to quit).

All this suggests that estimating displacement effects from employment effects is quite difficult. This difficulty could be avoided if there existed any accounting that was kept of workers displaced by trade. If the United States's trade adjustment assistance (TAA) program was widely known, easy to apply for, had screening that would insure that all of those who get in have been permanently displaced by trade, and kept good records, all we would have to do to find the number of workers who were displaced by trade would be to look at the agency's records. Unfortunately, the TAA program does not meet these needs. Before the changes that were made in 1974, it was widely acknowledged that requirements for admission to the program were very strict. Thus the 45,000 people who received adjustment assistance in the twelve years the program was in operation are a lower bound on the number of trade-displaced workers. Since requirements for participation in the program have been liberalized, the number of people receiving the assistance has grown to more than 100,000 per year. However, a study by Corson and Nicholson (1981) finds that over 70 percent of those who received trade adjustment assistance in the mid- to late 1970s were not permanently displaced and eventually returned to their original employers. Thus one might think that 30,000 per year represents an upper bound on displacement. But because many workers and employers do not know about the existence of TAA, and because a group of workers must still file a fairly involved application, only workers whose union or employer files for them are likely to receive assistance. Many trade-displaced workers may never even apply for assistance because they do not recognize their displacement as being caused by trade, because they do not know about the program, or because they do not have the resources to file an application.

Given all of these complications, it is probably impossible to say much at all about the amount of displacement that is caused by trade. When taken together, all of the evidence suggests that the TAA number of 30,000 a year in the late 1970s is probably an underestimate. An upper bound is much more difficult to establish. With some estimates (reviewed in Table 2–2) as high as 100,000 job opportunities lost a

Table 2-2. Estimates of Trade Impact at the Aggregate Level in the United States

a. Accounting Method.

Scope of Estimate	Years	Total Employment Growth	Decomposition of Employment Growth into Portions Due to:				
			Domestic Demand	Productivity	Exports	Imports	Net Trade
Components of growth in employment in selected import-competing industries, 1963–1971 (average percent rate of growth)[1]	1963–1967	2.6%	6.0%	−2.9%	0.3%	−0.8%	−0.5%
	1967–1970	−1.6	1.3	−2.5	0.6	−1.1	−0.4
	1970–1971	−0.0	4.2	−3.8	−0.1	−0.3	−0.4
	1963–1971	0.7	4.0	−2.9	0.4	−0.9	−0.5

b. Input-Output Method.

Scope of Estimate		
Employment effect (including secondary adjustments) of $1 million increase in 1958 exports to developing countries (number of jobs)[2]	Exports:	130.5
Job opportunities embodied in competitive imports, 1960 (number of jobs)[3]	Direct	502,200
	Indirect	570,700
	Total	1,072,900
Change in total job opportunities embodied in merchandise exports, 1963–1972 (number of jobs)[4]	1963–1969	5,100
	1963–1972	3,600
	1969–1972	800
	1970–1971	−5,200
	1971–1972	−200

Total job opportunities related to manufacturing trade (number of jobs)[5]

Year	Exports	Imports	Net
1965	2,126,000	1,684,000	442,000
1970	2,783,000	2,810,000	−27,000
1975	4,103,000	3,372,000	731,000

Employment changes for sectors undergoing change in net trade balance of over $175 million between 1963 and 1975[6]

	Exports	Imports	Net
Total job gains		346,678	
Total job losses		126,367	
Net job gains		219,311	

Employment changes due to trade, 1970:1 to 1971:1 (number of jobs)[7]

	Exports	Imports	Net
Net direct		−500	
Net indirect		17,100	

Employment due to foreign trade (number of jobs)[8]

Year	Exports	Imports	Net
1970	1,570,000	−1,620,000	−50,000
1972	1,450,000	−1,910,000	−45,000
1973	1,780,000	−2,120,000	−34,000
1980	2,930,000	−2,980,000	−6,000

Net labor content of exports and imports, by direct and total domestic measures (thousands of work years)[9]

Year	Exports/Imports	Direct	Total Domestic
1978	exports	2,571	4,846
1978	imports	2,438	5,222
1980	exports	3,322	6,291
1980	imports	2,444	5,566
1982	exports	2,822	5,395
1982	imports	2,521	5,638

Table 2-2. (continued).

Net labor content of exports and imports, by direct and total domestic measures (thousands of work years)[10]

Year	Exports/Imports	Direct	Total Domestic
1978	exports	2,531	5,220
1978	imports	2,423	6,276
1978	net		-1,055
1979	exports	2,883	6,047
1979	imports	2,442	6,386
1979	net		-337
1980	exports	3,225	6,727
1980	imports	2,470	6,412
1980	net		315
1981	exports	3,156	6,549
1981	imports	2,509	6,478
1981	net		70
1982	exports	2,830	5,899
1982	imports	2,830	5,899
1982	net		-615
1983	exports	2,670	5,545
1983	imports	2,560	6,620
1983	net		-1,075
1984	exports	2,606	5,529
1984	imports	3,166	8,090
1984	net		-2,561

c. *Model-based Studies.*

| | Total employment | | −19.8 to −21.0 |
| Net employment effects of 50 percent linear tariff cut (thousands of man years)[11] | Manufacturing employment | | 33.9 to 34.7 |

Exports/ Imports	Total Excluding Oil	Total Excluding Oil and Textiles
imports	97,300	55,700
exports	61,800	57,200
net	−35,600	1,400

Direct employment effects of 60 percent tariff cut, 1971 data (number of jobs)[12]

Nondurable	−203,200
Durable	−1,130,300
Total	1,333,500

Direct employment effects of 40 percent appreciation of dollar[13]

Sources:
[1]Frank (1977).
[2]Lydall (1975).
[3]Jacobs and Kutscher (1962).
[4]Eldridge and Saunders (1973).
[5]Bureau of International Labor Affairs (1978).
[6]Grinols and Thornbecke (1978).
[7]Krause and Matheison (1971).
[8]Lawrence (1983).
[9]U.S. International Trade Commission (1983).
[10]U.S. International Trade Commission (1986).
[11]Deardorff, Stern, and Baum (1977).
[12]Cline et al. (1978).
[13]Branson and Love (1986).

year, and the possibility that even these numbers could be underestimated by a substantial amount, it is conceivable that as many as 300,000 workers per year lost their jobs due to trade changes during the 1970s. However, it must be stressed that this is a guess, reflective more of our ignorance about trade effects than the effects themselves. With these difficulties in identifying the displacement rate, it is hard to say anything about unemployment. However, given that this is an extreme estimate and that over half of the unemployed displaced workers are likely to find a job within a year during normal times, it is very likely that trade raised the unemployment rate much less than one percentage point on average during the 1970s. Again, the story is different for the 1980s; as many as 1.5 million job opportunities were lost due to trade in 1984 (U.S. International Trade Commission 1986). A displacement of this magnitude could contribute significantly to the unemployment rate.

What is the Effect of Direct Investment Abroad?

The effect of direct investment abroad by U.S. corporations is a very controversial subject. Despite this, it has been subject to very little careful analysis. Two nearly polar positions exist on the role of direct foreign investment (DFI). On the one hand, the U.S. labor movement, which is most concerned with the detrimental effects, argues that foreign investment amounts to nothing more than shipping U.S. jobs overseas to take advantage of low-wage labor in developing countries. The opponents of such investment also argue that foreign investment involves not only the direct export of jobs, but also the export of U.S. technology, which is argued to be our major source of advantage in trade. By making foreign workers more competitive, this further exacerbates job losses.

On the other side of the argument are those who defend U.S. investment abroad. They argue that overseas investment not only does not cause a loss of jobs, but acts to increase domestic employment. U.S. corporations go abroad to reach new markets and protect old ones. It is argued that in the absence of foreign investment, U.S. corporations would be in danger of losing foreign markets to competitors. By investing abroad to remain competitive, they increase domestic employment by creating increased demand for managerial and support personnel in the home office and for U.S. capital exports. They argue that technology transfer is a necessary component to such investment since it gives them an advantage in entering foreign markets. Further, if technology transfer were limited, U.S. corporations would lose business to foreign providers of similar technology.

We will examine these two competing claims, first in light of the basic facts of U.S. investment abroad, and then by considering the results of what little analytic work has been done on the subject.

The value of the stock of U.S. direct foreign investment has risen from $75 billion in 1970 to about $228 billion in 1981. That amount has gone up and down since then and was at $233 billion in 1985—the last year for which data are available (U.S. Department of Commerce 1986: 40). This may explain why interest in this problem has declined so much in recent years while interest in the effects of trade on employment has been rising. The most likely explanation for the lack of growth in foreign investment is the increased return on capital invested in the United States.

The composition of U.S. foreign investment is very suggestive of its importance for domestic job displacement. In 1985 the stock of U.S. investment abroad was $233 billion, of which only $96 billion was invested in manufacturing. The rest of U.S. foreign investment was in mineral extraction, banking and finance, wholesale and retail trade, and other industries that are unlikely to produce products that would displace domestic employment (U.S. Department of Commerce 1986: 72). Since the domestic capital stock is certainly larger than the GNP, which is in excess of $3 trillion, the ratio of the stock of total U.S. investment abroad that could compete with domestic production to domestic capital is certainly far less than .05. By itself this argues for the likely insignificance of aggregate employment effects of direct investment. The data that are presented by the Department of Commerce do not allow us to examine the significance for small sectors since they are insufficiently disaggregated.

Detractors of DFI have often presented it as U.S. employers moving factories to less developed countries to take advantage of cheap labor. An examination of the division of DFI between developed and underdeveloped countries shows this characterization to be inaccurate. Of the stock of U.S. direct foreign investment in 1983, less than one-fourth was in developing countries, and less than 9 percent of the total was in manufacturing in developing countries.[4] Further, manufacturing investment in developing countries has declined faster in recent years than all direct foreign investment combined (U.S. Department of Commerce 1986: 29, 40).

Despite the relative unimportance of direct foreign investment, we might wish to know what the impact has been on employment. This could serve as a guide to what could happen if conditions change and it begins to increase again. Unfortunately, the studies of this phenomenon provide little insight.

Detractors of direct foreign investment have presented two types of studies that are meant to demonstrate the negative effects of DFI. The first type is comprised of case studies of plant closings where the plant's work was shipped abroad (for example, see AFL-CIO 1973). The problem with these studies is that they give us no idea of the magnitude of job displacement. Nor do they allow us to judge whether the job loss could have been prevented if the DFI had not been made. We have no way of knowing from these studies if the plants would have been closed anyway because of foreign competition. The second type of study—those that show the differential growth rates of employment between industries that do a great deal of DFI and those that do not—also tells us nothing about employment effects. It has been noted that at least during some periods, employment growth in those industries that engage in DFI has been slower than those that do not (Jager 1975). Of course, this does not imply anything about displacement since the reason for the slow employment growth is never established as DFI. Further, other studies show that faster domestic employment growth is associated with DFI (Kraseman and Barker 1973; Hawkins 1972a; Business International Corporation 1972). Equally unpersuasive are the case studies that were done by supporters of DFI. For example, a group from the Harvard Business School analyzed nine foreign investment decisions that were made by nine different firms in the nine major industries in which DFI takes place. They concluded that foreign competition necessitated the investments and that no jobs would have been saved by a prohibition on overseas investment (Stobaugh et al. 1972). However, because the group used confidential corporate data to reach these conclusions, there is no way to independently evaluate them or even the extent to which the projects they examined are representative of the universe of DFI projects.

Also unpersuasive are surveys of businessmen who are asked why their companies engage in DFI. They inevitably stress the need to defend markets (Business International Corporation 1972; Polk, Meister, and Veit 1966; National Foreign Trade Council 1971). But these people were certainly aware of the potential political impact of their answers, and they should be discounted accordingly.

Quantitative analysis of net job loss or creation has been attempted by a number of authors. The U.S. Tariff Commission conducted a study, published in 1973, in which they analyzed the net employment effects of DFI under a number of different assumptions. Under those that were least favorable to DFI, they found that it had caused the loss of 2.4 million jobs and the creation of 1.1 million new jobs through 1970. In this case it was assumed that all production that was done overseas could have been done domestically with no loss of demand. Under the alternative assumption that corporations would have lost half of the sales made from goods produced abroad if they had continued to produce these goods at home, net job loss was just over 400,000. Finally, under the assumption that the U.S. share of world trade did not change during the 1960s, U.S. DFI produced a net job gain of 500,000. The authors of the report expressed a belief that the latter figures were probably more accurate. A study by Hawkins (1972b) reaches similar conclusions about the range of possible estimates. He suggests that the best estimate from the range would be no net job creation or destruction.

The most commonly cited problem with these studies is the wide range of estimates of the potential employment effects. Even more discouraging is the analysis done by Frank and Freeman (1978a, 1978b), which suggests that by not taking into account the secondary employment effects of DFI, existing studies underestimate the size of the range. The reason for the wide range of estimates in all of these studies is that different assumptions are made about the degree to which foreign production substitutes for domestic production. Frank and Freeman (1978a, 1978b) and Adler and Stevens (1974) attempt to remedy this problem. Lacking the necessary data to statistically evaluate substitutability, they instead attempt to identify it by using economic theory. They derive formulas that yield estimates of the substitution parameter as a non-statistical function of observable data, such as the volume of home production relative to foreign production and relative costs. The estimates obtained by this method are suggestive at best since the values that are arrived at are dependent not only on the extreme assumptions of the theory, such as static demand curves and equilibrium in all markets, but also on the exact functional form assumed for the production technology and for foreign demand for the goods that are produced by DFI. Since the range of estimates that Frank and Freeman arrive at are not very much smaller than those of the other studies, it is doubtful that this approach contributes much. Several studies have attempted to use statistics to establish the relationship between domestic and foreign investment and between exports and foreign investment (Herring and Willett 1973; Lipsey and Weiss 1969; Horst 1972, 1974, and 1978). In all cases the authors interpret their evidence as indicating that foreign investment increases demand for domestic production and, consequently, domestic labor. But there is no way of knowing from these studies whether the correlation between DFI and exports or domestic investment results from the causal relation that is suggested by the authors or some other factor. For example, if an industry has a product for which demand is growing both at home and abroad, we might see their foreign and domestic investment increasing, but it would not be the case that the foreign investment was creating the demand for the domestic investment.

Of all the studies surveyed, only those done by the Tariff Commission, Hawkins, and Freeman and Frank provide any insight at all into the likely employment effects of DFI. Even these studies have serious faults. As mentioned above, the wide range of estimates of net job creation suggests only the extent of our ignorance about this phenomenon. Going further, there is little sense to examining net job creation. As explained in the introduction and the previous discussion of the effects of trade on employment, such numbers are difficult to interpret. For the most part, they do not tell us much about employment.

The authors of the studies of the employment effects of DFI present disaggregated estimates of job losses and gains. As with those authors who study the effects of trade, they conclude that DFI increases employment for skilled and white-collar workers and decreases employment for unskilled production labor. But many of the problems that were discussed earlier complicate the interpretation of these figures. There are additional problems as well. If it was assumed that demand for the goods that were being produced by DFI was fixed, then any amount that was produced abroad would mean a smaller demand for domestic production, a loss of domestic jobs, and displacement of employed workers. However, if DFI is undertaken to meet expanding demand, then the "job loss" is an abstract one. Some workers who might have been employed in the domestic production of the good are not, but no one has been displaced. If it were not for the argument that most DFI is defensive in nature, undertaken to protect competitive advantage, one might suspect that the overwhelming majority of DFI was new production capacity to meet new demand in foreign markets. Because these arguments do seem credible, it is impossible to guess the degree to which the job losses that are calculated in these job-counting studies result in displacement. To the best of my knowledge, no one has considered this question.

In conclusion, however much of a problem for domestic employment DFI has been in the past, it cannot be a major contributor to our current problems since there has been no substantial increase since the beginning of the 1980s. It could still be that DFI is contributing to employment problems in some narrowly defined industries, but it cannot be a major contributor to aggregate problems. The facts of DFI also suggest that the picture painted by its detractors is far removed from reality. Very little DFI is in manufacturing in developing countries. The studies that have attempted to examine the employment effects of DFI are all badly flawed to the point that they provide no useful estimate of the extent of displacement that is caused by direct foreign investment. Taking the numbers from the Frank and Freeman study and considering the objections raised above, a safe guess would be that the total displacement effect of $1 billion (1984) of new DFI would be less than 40,000 jobs but greater than zero. However, this is only a guess since we have no quantitative evidence on the magnitude of many of the potential biases. Thus if DFI were to begin increasing again at rates such as those that prevailed in the early 1970s, it could cause considerable dislocation, but the exact extent of that dislocation is impossible to judge from existing studies. Also, none of the studies give us any believable quantitative estimate of the impact of the technology transfer that goes hand in hand with DFI. In the absence of this information, it is impossible to assess the claims that this was or ever again could be a major factor contributing to U.S. job dislocation.

One last point is worth noting. For DFI to dislocate employed workers, it would have to result in foreign production that substituted for exports or was imported to substitute for domestic production. In either case the displacement would be attributed to changes that were due to trade by any of the methods that were analyzed above. Thus adding the effects of DFI to those of foreign trade would be double counting.

What are the Employment Effects of Foreign Investment in the United States?

If little study has been made of direct foreign investment by the United States, far less has been made of foreign direct investment in the United States by other countries (FDI). We are aware of no academic studies of the employment consequences. All we have are tabulations of the magnitude of FDI that were made by the Department of Commerce and some journalistic accounts of the reasons for the investment. We review this information here and present some speculation on its relevance for U.S. employment.

According to figures from the Department of Commerce, FDI in the United States amounted to over $182 billion in 1985, the most recent year for which figures are available (U.S. Department of Commerce 1986: 74). That number has been increasing steadily since at least 1970, when FDI amounted to only $13 billion. The rate of investment has increased considerably in the recent past, with the level of investment more than tripling since 1979 (Belli 1984; U.S. Department of Commerce 1986: 74). Nonbank affiliates of foreign companies had assets of $292 billion in 1980 (a year in which FDI was $83 billion) and employed just over 2 million workers. Further, while those firms accounted for less than 3 percent of total employment for similar enterprises, they accounted for one-fourth of all U.S. exports and one-third of all U.S. imports (Belli 1983: 25).

While FDI that originates in Japan and OPEC countries has received a great deal of attention in the press, most FDI continues to originate in Europe—primarily in the United Kingdom and the Netherlands. Only 2.5 percent of FDI originated in OPEC nations in 1985, and only 9.8 percent originated in Japan. OPEC's share increased in 1981 and again in 1982 and has fallen off since then. Japan's share has been growing in recent years (Belli 1984b: 37–38; U.S. Department of Commerce 1986: 79).

Several reasons have been suggested for the recent surge. Reich (1984) has argued that U.S. firms that attempt to maintain their position against foreign competition have been developing more joint ventures with foreign investors. Others have suggested that the fear of losing U.S. markets in the event of protectionist legislation is a major spur for FDI ("How Overseas Investors Are Helping to Reindustrialize America" 1984). Still another factor may be the relatively high rate of return on U.S. investments in the last several years. In an interesting twist on the argument that U.S. firms go abroad to find docile labor, some have suggested that European firms find the United States an attractive place to invest because the lack of restrictive labor laws makes it easy to lay workers off when demand is low ("How Overseas Investors Are Helping to Reindustrialize America" 1984).

This last reason suggests one reason FDI may be an important consideration, particularly for problems of displacement. If foreign countries are exporting their more volatile demand industries to the United

States, this could contribute to the cyclical sensitivity of the U.S. economy and could increase the normal rate of unemployment by increasing the normal flow into the pool of unemployed workers.

Another consideration is the role of FDI in providing jobs for displaced workers and in particular workers that are displaced by foreign competition. One celebrated example of this is the Toyota/GM joint venture in Fremont, California, which has reopened a plant that was closed by GM in reaction to reduced demand. With possibly 2 million jobs attributable to FDI nationwide, the potential contribution of this source of new jobs is considerable. However, there is no evidence that even a substantial fraction of FDI is going to industries and localities where there are unemployment problems.

Except for these two possible roles, FDI cannot be expected to have substantial impact on domestic employment. Once again, in the long run, employment levels depend more on labor supply than on labor demand. Of course, FDI should affect incomes by reducing the earnings of capital, increasing the earnings of labor, and increasing tax revenues. But current levels of FDI are too small to have large effects, and growth would have to be considerable before much of an effect would be felt.

Have High Wages and Unions Caused the Decline of U.S. Industry?

A commonly heard argument is that U.S. unions are causing a loss of competitiveness in many manufacturing industries and, consequently, a loss of employment. The steadily declining percent of the work force that is organized by unions is cited as evidence of this effect. Despite some very strong opinions on the subject, little research has been done. What evidence there is suggests that high wages are not the cause of the relatively poor performance of unionized industries.

If the interaction of trade and high labor costs had actually caused the decline of the union sector, then we would expect that the rate at which unions lost members due to such factors as plant closings and layoffs would have increased considerably in the 1970s relative to the 1950s, when trade was not a major consideration. Indeed there is much anecdotal evidence suggesting that this is the case. We hear a great deal about union plants shutting down and union workers losing their jobs. However, the one study that has been done of the total loss of union members due to these causes (Dickens and Leonard, 1985) shows that while there had been a greater loss of union members in the 1970s, if one takes out the effects of the business cycle, there is no evidence of any trend increase in loss of membership due to other economic causes and no evidence of any major change in the relationship between the loss of members due to economic causes and the business cycle. Instead, the authors find that the major cause of the drop in the percent of the work force that is organized by unions is their lack of success in organizing.

One of the industries that is often cited as being a prime example of the negative effects of unions on employment is the steel industry. Grossman (1984) examines the role that is played by union wages in determining the level of employment in that industry from 1976 to 1983. He claims that of the over 200,000 jobs lost in that industry during that period, less than 2 percent were due to wage increases. Further, he finds that between 1979 and 1983, union wage concessions should have led to an increase in employment had it not been for the effects of the business cycle, appreciation of the dollar, and long-term structural changes in productivity and the demand for steel.

Grossman's study can be faulted in that it only considers the immediate effects of wages on employment and not the long-term effects. The important role that he finds for long-term structural change may reflect the effects of wages on labor-saving technical change. Since Grossman's study begins in 1976, it is possible that employment in the steel industry was already substantially depressed by the existing high wages.

Thus all of the evidence that we have points to the same conclusion. First, the performance of manufacturing industries and trade can be readily explained by the behavior of domestic demand and foreign exchange rates. We do not need to appeal to high union wages for an explanation. Further, the two studies that were cited above both suggest that high labor costs due to high union wages cannot account for the changes that have occurred in employment in the heavily unionized industries.

Have Changing Trade Patterns Caused the Large Fluctuations in the Unemployment Rate of the Last Fifteen Years?

Several recent studies suggest that displacement due to trade may have macroeconomic significance. Lilien (1982a, 1982b) and Neumann and

Topel (1984) claim to show that sharp changes in the sectoral composition of employment in the 1970s were responsible for much of the fluctuation in unemployment rates during that period. Lilien claims that because this type of unemployment is structural in nature, standard aggregate demand policies could not have attacked it without producing significant inflation. If trade problems are responsible for these disruptions, then it could be that the reallocations caused by changing comparative advantage were responsible for most of the macroeconomic woes of the last decade.

To begin with, there is a major problem in relating those results to trade. All of the studies reviewed in the section on the employment impact of U.S. trade attribute most of the changes in the composition of employment to changes in the pattern of domestic demand rather than to trade. This suggests that even if Lilien and Neumann and Topel are right about dislocation being the source of our macroeconomic problems, the dislocation is probably not due to trade. Since Lawrence's (1984) analysis separates the effects of trade from the effects of domestic demand by looking at the changes in the quantities of each, there may be some reason to question his analysis. For example, importing foreign cars that are more reliable and last longer could reduce the domestic demand for new cars. More generally, changes in domestic relative prices that are induced by changes in world prices could affect the quantities demanded domestically. However, with one exception, it is hard to think of a significant example of this type of development. The one exception is oil prices. The increases caused by the 1973 war in the Middle East and the 1979 revolution in Iran may have caused domestic demand to shift away from cars, particularly large cars. It is possible that these dislocations precipitated the 1974 and the 1980 recessions, though most economists believe that it it was the combined effect of these price increases on the general price level and the response of the Federal Reserve to the general price increases that brought on these recessions.

There are also good reasons to be suspicious of Lilien's and Neumann and Topel's claims about the importance of changes in the composition, as opposed to the level, of demand. A study by Weiss (1984) shows that Lilien's results could be consistent with the standard view that the variations of unemployment in the 1970s were due to variation in demand, which occurs when firms hire workers more slowly in response to an upswing than they lay off workers in a downturn. Abraham and Katz (1986) show that Lilien's results could also be reconciled with the standard view that employment in sectors that are contracting over time is more sensitive to the business cycle than it is in sectors that are expanding. Both Weiss and Abraham and Katz present empirical evidence that supports their alternative interpretations of Lilien's results. Further, Abraham and Katz suggest that if it is changes in the composition rather than changes in the levels of demand that have caused the recessions of the last decade, then Lilien's measure of changes in composition should be positively correlated not only with unemployment but also with job openings. They show that this is not the case.

Neumann and Topel's paper is more recent and has not been subjected to the same scrutiny as Lilien's. Since they use a different measure of changes in employment composition, it is not clear whether their effort is subject to the same criticism as Lilien's. However, since it is highly correlated with Lilien's, it is doubtful that their results would pass the test of being positively correlated with job vacancies.

None of these studies considers the 1982 recession. Given the large changes in job opportunities that took place due to trade from 1982 on, it is conceivable that trade contributed substantially to the depth and length of this most recent downturn.

What Types of Jobs are Created and Destroyed by Trade?

Several studies (Abowd and Freeman 1986; Aho and Orr 1980, 1981; Mitchell 1975; Lawrence 1984; Katz 1986) have attempted to determine the characteristics of workers who are displaced by trade and those who have obtained employment in the industries that are expanding due to trade. The often stated concern is that highly skilled production workers (such as steel and auto workers) are being displaced, are suffering large income losses, and are then unable to get high paying new jobs since these jobs require skills that the displaced do not have and are located in different parts of the country.

Mitchell (1975) examines the demographics of workers in jobs in export and import industries. His method is to determine the industrial location of those jobs from input-output tables and then to compute the average characteristics of the workers in these locations from the averages for all workers in the industry. He finds that there are small but not inconsequential differences between the two groups of workers. He finds that export industry workers earn more and that import-impacted industries employ relatively more women, blacks, union members, part-time workers, Northeasterners, Southerners, and production workers and employ fewer college-educated workers and Westerners.

One might draw two implications from this study. The first is that the popular image of the displaced workers as Northern, well paid, highly skilled union production workers is only partially correct. Those in the import-competing industries do not tend to be the relatively advantaged. On the contrary, it seems to be the more disadvantaged groups that are most at risk. It is the Southern textile worker rather than the Northern auto worker who best represents those affected by import competition. On the other hand, the popular view of the representative worker in the export industry does not appear to be far off. However, the numbers also suggest that it may be a mistake to focus too much on the representative worker. Overall, one should also be impressed by the similarity of the workers in the import and export industries. They differ by less than three-tenths of a year in their median education, there is less than a 4 percent difference in the percent of total employment located in each region of the country, and average annual compensation differed in 1970 by less than 10 percent. Thus there are differences between those who are likely to be affected by import competition and those who benefit from increased exports, but the differences are not what we might expect, nor are they as large as we might expect.

Of course Mitchell's method shares all of the flaws of the input-output assessments of trade impact on which it is based. To the extent that the input-output method misidentifies the affected industries and their relative importance, Mitchell's averages are flawed. Going further, Mitchell's analysis assumes that the workers who are displaced by imports or work producing exports are representative of the industry as a whole. This is unlikely to be the case. A decrease in the demand for imports is most likely to affect the least senior workers first. It may also be more likely to affect the least advantaged workers most if they are those most recently hired and therefore the ones who will be first fired. Those affected by imports could be either the higher paid workers (if firms with high labor costs are affected most by import competition) or the lowest paid workers (if the industry's product is not homogeneous and low-paid workers produce the version that competes most directly with foreign imports). Finally, Mitchell looks at the characteristics of all workers in import-competing industries and export industries. Even if these workers share the average characteristics of all workers in these industries, there is no reason to suspect that the recent increases in export demand have been spread proportionally across all export industries or that the losses in import supply have been distributed proportionally among import-producing industries. There is certainly no reason to believe that future changes will be distributed proportionally. In the extreme, some import-competing industries could flourish while some export industries perish due to increased competition.

Studies by Aho and Orr (1980, 1981) and Lawrence (1984) are a partial answer to the last of these problems. Aho and Orr use the input-output method to identify the twenty industries that have gained the most employment because of recent changes in international trade and those that have lost the most. They then compare the average characteristics of workers in the two sets of industries. The results of their study are qualitatively similar to those of Mitchell. The losers are, on average, the disadvantaged. There is a higher proportion of skilled workers, white-collar workers, and scientists and engineers that are employed by the industries that have gained from trade, but the differences are not extreme. For example, 78.1 percent of the jobs in the industries that were hurt by trade are in production—63.7 percent of the jobs in the industries that were helped by trade are in production.

Aho and Orr do not consider geographic distribution, but Lawrence does (1984: 77–79). His results complement those of Mitchell and Aho and Orr. He first compares the characteristics of workers in the auto and computer industries; their characteristics are indeed very different. However, when he considers a class of industry—high-tech—that has been helped by trade and a class—low-tech—that has been hurt by it, he finds results that are similar to those of other studies. There are differences, but the differences are not large. Abowd and Freeman (1986), who use better trade data, also find few differences in net trade impact by region.

We might also hope to learn whether trade is causing an increase in the variance of workers' incomes by eliminating middle-income jobs and creating many high- and low-income jobs. From the results that were just presented, it appears that trade is eliminating low-wage jobs and creating relatively high-wage jobs. If this were the case, then trade might even be narrowing the income distribution, though the relatively small differences in the averages do suggest that the effect could not be large. The problem is that we are looking at averages, and the results that are reported in these studies tell us little about the dispersion of workers' characteristics. However, the small differences in the occupational composition of these industries suggest that even if there are fewer middle income jobs being created than are being lost, the effect cannot be an important one.

A final study by Katz (1986) is worthy of mention. Using the same trade data that Abowd and Freeman did, he replicates the findings of other studies with respect to the characteristics of employees in the export and import industries. Using a data set on workers' wages and industry characteristics created by Dickens and Katz (1987), he shows that both union and nonunion workers in import industries have substantially lower wages and those in export industries have substantially higher wages than average, even after taking into account their education and work experience, their personal backgrounds, and their geographic location. These findings have important implications for the potential welfare effects of trade, which will be discussed in the next section.

CONCLUSIONS

In summary, the major conclusions to be drawn from above are: First, while much effort has gone into studies of the employment effects of trade, they tell us little about either the short- or long-run effects of trade on the level of employment or unemployment. They do have some value for determining the effects of trade on the composition of employment, and this may be important for determining the effects of trade on our economic well-being. What these studies have to say about the level of unemployment is obscured both by the form in which the information is presented and by a large number of methodological issues that prevent us from moving from the calculated job opportunity losses to the actual number of displaced workers and the severity of their displacement problems. It is impossible to interpret these figures as giving a reasonable range for the number of workers that are displaced by trade each year or in any given year. For example, in the 1970s it could be as few as 30,000 a year or as many as 300,000 a year. What this does say is that it is very unlikely that trade changes had a substantial effect on the U.S. unemployment rate in the 1970s. As noted above, the story for the 1980s is very different; possibly millions of workers were displaced by trade in at least some years.

But, even if the numbers were not large enough to matter for the unemployment rate, displacement could still be a major social problem given the severe consequences of permanent job loss. The studies of the employment effects of trade probably do allow us to identify some industries as having benefited from or been hurt by trade. Industries in which trade appears to have increased employment include chemicals, plastics, and office and computing machinery. Industries that have been hurt by trade include apparel, furniture and fixtures, autos, leather products, nuts and bolts, radio and televisions, and, in more recent years, steel.

Second, the stock of U.S. direct investment in foreign countries has not increased since the beginning of the 1980s and thus does not currently have any substantial effect on U.S. employment. Further, less than half of such investment is in goods that compete with domestic employment.

Third, foreign investment in the United States, which is increasing, plays a negligible role in the determination of domestic employment. Although the numbers of workers hired are not insignificant when compared to estimates of trade displacement, there is no reason to believe that any substantial amount of this investment is going to create jobs for displaced workers.

Fourth, what little evidence we have suggests that high union wages have not been a major contributor to the decline in employment in the highly unionized industries. Rather, it appears that other factors are responsible.

Fifth, despite recent studies that suggest that changes in the composition of industrial demand have caused large fluctuations in the unemployment rate in the last fifteen years, there is little evidence to suggest that trade changes were a major cause of the composition changes in the 1970s. Further, the studies have been criticized, and it seems likely that standard explanations for employment fluctuations are preferable, with the possible exception of the 1982 recession.

Sixth, the popular view of the worker who finds a job in an expanding import industry is fairly accurate. Such workers tend to be well paid, more educated, more skilled, more likely to be white collar, and less likely to be union members than the average worker in the economy. However, the popular image of the trade-displaced worker as being a well paid, skilled, Northeastern white male industrial worker turns out to be incorrect. Workers in industries with the biggest estimated losses in employment due to imports tend to be disproportionately black, female, poor, unskilled, and located in the South. Although there are substantial differences between the two groups, focusing attention on their differences distracts from another surprising fact—the differences are mostly marginal, a few percent in each category. Since all of the studies focus on averages and not dispersion, it is difficult to use the figures to assess the claims of a disappearing middle, but the lack of very large differences in such categories as clerical and production workers suggests that whatever effect there is cannot be too large.

Of all the results surveyed here, the most disappointing are those on the amount of displacement caused by trade and its contribution to the level and fluctuations in the unemployment rate. A deliberate effort to remedy this problem is called for. Most of the technical flaws that were identified in the preceding analysis can be dealt with by building models of industry labor markets along the lines of the work done by Brechling (1978). These models could be linked with such trade models as Grossman's to obtain estimates of trade impacts on employment opportunities and then on employment and unemployment. Additional work would also need to be done on the relation between import competition and labor productivity. How important a factor is import competition in inducing rationalization of production and technical change? Hopefully, such studies could identify mechanisms that could be incorporated into the employment models. They could at least suggest what types of sensitivity analysis should be done to determine displacement and labor market effects.

REFERENCES

Abowd, John M., and Richard B. Freeman. 1986. "Internationalization of the U.S. Labor Market." National Bureau of Economic Research, Cambridge, Mass., August. Mimeo.

Abraham, Katherine, and Lawrence Katz. 1986. "Cyclical Unemployment: Sectoral Shifts or Aggregate Disturbances?" *Journal of Political Economy* 94, no. 3 (June): 507–22.

Adler, Michael, and Guy V.G. Stevens. 1974. "The Trade Effects of Direct Investment." *Journal of Finance* 29, no. 2 (May): 655–76.

AFL-CIO. 1973. "A Program to Build America's Jobs and Trade in the Seventies." Testimony of I.W. Abel before the House Ways and Means Committee. Washington, D.C.: AFL-CIO, May 17.

Aho, C. Michael, and James A. Orr. 1980. "Demographic and Occupational Characteristics of Workers in Trade-Sensitive Industries." Economic Discussion Paper 2, Office of Foreign Economic Research, Bureau of International Labor Affairs, U.S. Department of Labor, April.

——. 1981. "Trade-Sensitive Employment: Who Are the Affected Workers?" *Monthly Labor Review* 104, no. 2 (February): 29–35.

Baldwin, Robert E., and Wayne E. Lewis. 1978. "U.S. Tariff Effects on Trade and Employment in Detailed SIC Industries." In *The Impact of International*

Trade and Investment on Employment: A Conference of the U.S. Department of Labor, edited by William G. Dewald. Washington, D.C.: U.S. Government Printing Office.

Belli, R. David. 1983. "Foreign Direct Investment in the United States: Highlights from the 1980 Benchmark Survey." *Survey of Current Business* 63, no. 10 (October): 25–35.

————. 1984. "Foreign Direct Investment in the United States in 1983." *Survey of Current Business* 64, no. 10 (October): 26–36.

Branson, William H., and J.P. Love. 1986. "Dollar Appreciation and Manufacturing Employment and Output." National Bureau of Economic Research Working Paper No. 1972, Cambridge, Mass., July.

Brechling, Frank. 1978. "A Time Series Analysis of Labor Turnover." In *The Impact of International Trade and Investment on Employment: A Conference with the U.S. Department of Labor,* edited by William G. Dewald. Washington, D.C.: U.S. Government Printing Office.

Bureau of International Labor Affairs. 1978. "The Impact of Changes in Manufacturing Trade on Sectoral Employment Patterns—Progress Report." In *Trade and Employment,* edited by The National Commission for Manpower Policy, Special Report No. 30, November.

Business International Corporation. 1972. *The Effects of U.S. Corporate Direct Foreign Investment 1960–1970.* New York: Business International Corporation.

Cable, Vincent. 1977. "British Protectionism and LDC Imports." *Overseas Development Institute Review* no. 2 (October): 29–48.

Cline, William R., Nororu Kewanabe, T.O.M. Kronsjo, and Thomas Williams. 1978. "Multilateral Effects of Tariff Negotiations in the Tokyo Round." In *The Impact of International Trade and Investment on Employment: A Conference with the U.S. Department of Labor,* edited by William G. Dewald, Washington, D.C.: U.S. Government Printing Office.

Corson, Walter, and Walter Nicholson. 1981. "Trade Adjustment Assistant for Workers: Results of a Survey of Recipients Under the Trade Act of 1974." In *Research in Labor Economics,* Vol. 4., edited by Ronald G. Ehrenberg. Greenwich, Conn.: JAI Press.

Deardorff, A.V., R.M. Stern, and C.F. Baum. 1977. "A Multi-Country Simulation of the Employment and Exchange-Rate Effects of Post-Kennedy Round Tariff Reductions." In *Trade and Employment in Asia and the Pacific,* edited by N. Akrasanee, S. Naya, and V. Vichit-Vadakan. Honolulu: University of Hawaii Press.

Dickens, W.T., and Lawrence F. Katz. 1987. "Interindustry Wage Differences and Industry Characteristics." In *Unemployment and the Structure of Labor Markets,* edited by Kevin Lang and Jonathan Leonard. New York: Basil-Blackwell.

Dickens, William T., and Jonathan Leonard. 1985. "Accounting for the Decline in the Percent of the Workforce Organized, 1950 to 1980." *Industrial and Labor Relations Review* 38, no. 3 (April): 323–34.

Eldridge, Donald P., and Norman Saunders. 1973. "Employment and Exports, 1963–72." *Monthly Labor Review* 96, no. 8 (August): 16–27.

Frank, Charles R. 1977. *Foreign Trade and Domestic Aid.* Washington, D.C.: Brookings Institution.

Frank, Robert H., and Richard T. Freeman. 1978. "Distributional Consequences of Direct Foreign Investments." In *The Impact of International Trade and Investment on Employment: A Conference of the U.S. Department of Labor,* edited by William G. Dewald, Washington, D.C.: U.S. Government Printing Office.

Grinols, Errol, and Erik Thorbecke. 1978. "The Effects of Trade Between the U.S. and Developing Countries on U.S. Employment." Working Paper No. 171A, Cornell University.

Grossman, Gene M. 1982a. "Comment on Eric Verreydt and Jean Waelbroeck, 'European Community Protection against Manufactured Imports from Developing Countries: A Case Study in the Political Economy of Protection.' " In *Import Competition and Response,* edited by Jagdish N. Bhagwati. Chicago: University of Chicago Press.

——— . 1982b. "The Employment and Wage Effects of Import Competition in the United States." National Bureau of Economic Research Working Paper No. 1041, Cambridge, Mass., December.

——— . 1982c. "Import Competition from Developed and Developing Countries." *The Review of Economics and Statistics* 64, no. 2 (May): 271–81.

——— . 1984. "Imports as a Cause of Injury: The Case of the U.S. Steel Injury." National Bureau of Economic Research Working Paper No. 1494, Cambridge, Mass., November.

Hawkins, Robert G. 1972a. "U.S. Multinational Investment in Manufacturing and Domestic Economic Performance." Occasional Paper No. 1, Center for Multinational Studies, Washington, D.C., February.

——— . 1972b. "Job Displacement and the Multinational Firm: A Methodological Review." Occasional Paper No. 3, Center for Multinational Studies, Washington, D.C., June.

Herring, R., and T.D. Willett. 1973. "The Relationship Between U.S. Direct Investment at Home and Abroad." *Rivista Internazionale de Scienze Economiche e Commerciale* 20, no. 1 (January): 72–82.

Horst, Thomas. 1972. "Firm and Industry Determinants of the Decision to Invest Abroad: An Empirical Study." *Review of Economics and Statistics* 54, no. 3 (August): 258–66.

——— . 1974. "American Exports and Foreign Direct Investments." Discussion Paper 362, Harvard Institute of Economic Research, Cambridge, Mass., May.

——— . 1978. "The Impact of American Investments Abroad on U.S. Exports, Imports and Employment." In *The Impact of International Trade on Investment and Employment: A Conference of the U.S. Department of Labor,* edited by William G. Dewald. Washington, D.C.: U.S. Government Printing Office.

"How Overseas Investors Are Helping to Reindustrialize America." 1984. *Business Week*. June 4, pp. 103–4.

Jacobs, Eva E., and Ronald E. Kutscher. 1962. "Employment in Relation to U.S. Imports." *Monthly Labor Review* 85, no. 7 (July): 771–73.

Jager, Elizabeth R. 1975. "U.S. Labor and Multinationals." In *International Labor and the Multinational Enterprise,* edited by Duane Kujawa. New York: Praeger.

Katz, Lawrence F. 1986. "International Trade and the Wage Structure in U.S. Manufacturing." Harvard University, Cambridge, Mass., December. Mimeo.

Kraseman, Thomas W., and Betty L. Barker. 1973. "Employment and Payroll Costs of U.S. Multinational Companies." *Survey of Current Business* 53, no. 10 (October): 36–44.

Krause, Lawrence B., and John A. Matheison. 1971. "How Much of Current Unemployment Did We Import?" *Brookings Papers on Economic Activity* no. 2: 417–28.

Krueger, Anne O. 1978a. *Foreign Trade Regimes and Economic Development: Liberalization Attempts and Consequences.* Cambridge, Mass.: Ballinger Publishing Co. for the National Bureau of Economic Research.

———. 1980a. "Impact of Foreign Trade on Employment in the United States." In *Current Issues in Commercial Policy and Diplomacy—Papers of the Third Annual Conference of the International Economics Study Group* (Sussex, 1978). London: Macmillan for the Trade Policy Research Center.

———. 1980b. "LDC Manufacturing Production and Implications for OECD Comparative Advantage." In *Western Economies in Transition,* edited by Irving Leveson and Jimmy W. Wheeler. Boulder: Westview Press.

———. 1980c. "Protectionist Pressures, Imports and Employment in the United States." *Scandinavian Journal of Economics* 82, no. 2: 133–46.

———. 1980d. "Restructing for Import Competition from Developing Countries, I: Labor Displacements and Economic Redeployment in the United States." *Journal of Policy Modeling* 2, no. 2 (May): 165–84.

Lawrence, Robert Z. 1984. *Can America Compete?* Washington, D.C.: Brookings Institution.

Leontief, Wassily. 1953. "Domestic Production and Foreign Trade: The American Capital Position Re-examined." Reprinted in 1968. *Readings in International Economics,* edited by Richard E. Caves and Harry G. Johnson. Homewood, Ill.: R.D. Irwin.

Lilien, David M. 1982a. "Sectoral Shifts and Cyclical Unemployment." *Journal of Political Economy* 90, no. 4 (August): 777–93.

———. 1982b. "A Sectoral Model of the Business Cycle." Working Paper No. 8231. University of Southern California Economic Department, Los Angeles, December.

Lipsey, R.E., and M.Y. Weiss. 1969. "The Relation of U.S. Manufacturing Abroad to U.S. Exports: A Framework for Analysis." *American Statistical Association Proceedings—Business and Economic Statistics Section,* pp. 497–508.

Lydall, H.F. 1975. *Trade and Employment: A Study of the Effects of Trade Expansion on Employment in Developing and Developed Countries.* Geneva: International Labour Office.

Marsden, J.S., and H. Anderssen. 1978. "Structural Change: Exploring Some Perspectives." Paper presented to the Conference on the Economics of Structural Adjustment, University of Newcastle, November 15–16.

Mitchell, Daniel B. 1975. "Recent Changes in the Labor Content of U.S. International Trade." *Industrial and Labor Relations Review* 28, no. 3 (April): 355–75.

National Foreign Trade Council. 1971. *The Impact of U.S. Direct Foreign Investment on U.S. Employment and Trade.* New York: National Foreign Trade Council, Inc., November.

Neumann, George R., and Robert H. Topel. 1984. "Employment Risk, Sectoral Shifts and Unemployment." Mimeo.

Pelzman, Joseph, and Randolph C. Martin. 1981. "Direct Employment Effects of Increased Imports: A Case Study of the Textile Industry." *Southern Economic Journal* 48, no. 2 (October): 412–26.

Polk, J., I. Meister, and L. Veit. 1966. *U.S. Production Abroad and the Balance of Payments.* New York: The Conference Board.

Reich, Robert B. 1984. "Japan Inc., U.S.A." *The New Republic* no. 3645 (November 26):P 19–23.

Stobaugh, Robert B. and Associates. 1972. "U.S. Multinational Enterprises and the U.S. Economy: A Research Study of the Major Industries That Account for 90 Percent of U.S. Foreign Direct Investment in Manufacturing." In *The Multinational Corporation: Studies on U.S. Foreign Investment, Volume 1,* edited by the U.S. Department of Commerce, Office of International Investment. Washington, D.C.: U.S. Bureau of International Commerce.

U.S. Department of Commerce. Bureau of Economic Analysis. 1986. "Foreign Direct Investment in the U.S.: Detail for Position and Balance of Payment Flows, 1985." *Survey of Current Business,* 65, no. 7 (August): 74–88.

U.S. International Trade Commission (USITC). 1983. *U.S. Trade-Related Employment.* USITC Publication No. 1445. Washington, D.C.: USITC, October.

———. 1986. *U.S. Trade-Related Employment: 1978–84.* USITC Publication No. 1855. Washington, D.C.: USITC, May.

Weiss, Lawrence. 1984. "Asymmetric Adjustment Costs." Working Paper, University of Chicago Business School.

Wragg, R., and J. Robertson. 1978. "Post-War Trends in Employment, Productivity, Output, Labour Costs and Prices by Industry in the U.K." Research Paper No. 3, Great Britain Department of Employment, June.

3 WHY IT MATTERS WHAT WE TRADE
A Case for Active Policy

William T. Dickens and Kevin Lang

In the simplest theory—the source of the "free-trade" preference of most economists—the goods that a country trades do not matter for its welfare. With markets unencumbered by tariffs, subsidies, or other forms of government intervention, the country will export goods that it can produce relatively cheaply and import those that it finds expensive to make and, as a result, will be better off. However, if wages are not determined in the manner described by the simple competitive model, this prescription may not be relevant. We argue that noncompetitve wage differentials are an important feature of the U.S. economy and are of serious consequence for the formation of trade policy.

In the standard trade theory, it is assumed that firms that are producing different products pay the same wage to workers with similar characteristics such as education, training, and years of job experience. This occurs because a firm that pays a higher wage than other firms will attract many workers. The firm will recognize this excess supply of labor as a signal that it can lower its wage. Similarly, a firm that pays a low wage will find it difficult to attract enough workers and will either

The authors thank Philip Bokovoy and Rachel Friedberg for their able research assistance and the Institute of Industrial Relations at Berkeley for generous research support. This work was also supported by the National Science Foundation under grant SES-8606139. Lang's work has been supported by an Olin Fellowship at the National Bureau of Economic Research.

have to raise its wage or go out of business. These actions by workers and firms will lead all firms to pay the same wage for similar workers.

Since firms will never hire an additional worker if the wage they must pay is greater than the value of the goods the worker will produce, and will always try to hire more workers when it is less, the productivity of the "marginal worker" (one more or one fewer) will equal the wage and thus be equal across all firms if they pay the same wage for similar workers. In this case, shifting workers from one industry to another does not alter the productivity of the economy.

On the other hand, if firms producing export goods pay more than those producing import goods for identical workers doing similar jobs, the marginal worker in the export industry must be more productive. If the amount of goods that are traded increases, then jobs will be eliminated in import industries and increased in export industries. Workers will happily leave the import industry for jobs in the higher paying export industry, and the economy as a whole will be more productive as a result of the change. In general, if there are wage differences for similar workers between firms that are producing different products, it will be in the country's interest to encourage increased employment in the high-wage/high-productivity industries. One way to do this would be to encourage the export of products made in industries that pay high wages and to discourage the import of such products.

This argument is presented in more detail in the next section, and the sorts of conditions that could give rise to wage differences are described. We then present evidence that suggests that at least some of the conditions do exist and consider the impact of trade on the productivity of the U.S. economy. The last section gives the policy implications of the analysis.

WHY IT MIGHT MATTER WHAT WE TRADE

The key to the argument is that, under certain circumstances, moving workers from low-wage to high-wage industries will increase the productivity of the economy and could make some workers better off without making any others worse off. To see how this might happen, consider the following hypothetical example.[1]

A country with 240 million people produces two types of goods: agricultural goods, or "bushels," and manufactured goods, or "widgets." Each agricultural worker produces one bushel, and each worker in manufacturing produces one widget. Next let us assume that people always spend half of their income on bushels and half on widgets. If they do, then as the price of a good goes up, people will buy less of it. Finally, we make the assumption of standard economic analysis that the price of all goods is set equal to their marginal cost. These assumptions are not intended to be realistic but to provide a simple example of an economy that will behave in much the same way as a real one.

For contrast, we begin with the situation in which wages are set competitively so that workers in agriculture earn the same wages as those in manufacturing. A little algebra (see the Appendix) shows that in the absence of trade, half of all workers will be employed in agriculture and half in manufacturing. The cost of bushels will equal the cost of widgets, and therefore the prices will also be equal. With equal prices, people will consume equal amounts of both goods, so that 120 million bushels and 120 million widgets will be consumed.

Now let us assume that there is another smaller country with less land per worker and less access to raw materials. This country of 40 million people requires two workers to produce a widget and one and two-thirds to produce a bushel. In the absence of trade, the cost of producing widgets, and therefore the price, would be 20 percent higher than that for bushels. Consequently, the population would consume 20 percent more bushels. Again, some simple algebra shows that for the country to consume according to this rule, and to consume only what it can produce with its available work force, it will produce and consume 12 million bushels and 10 million widgets.

With free trade, the small country will specialize in the production of bushels, since it can get one widget for each bushel it trades with the large country but can produce less than a widget with the labor it takes to produce a bushel. If it does this, it will produce 24 million bushels and trade 12 million of them for 12 million widgets. It now consumes the same 12 million bushels it did before, but consumes 2 million more widgets. It has clearly benefited from trade.

The large country will be unaffected. It will produce 12 million more widgets and 12 million fewer bushels, but since labor is equally productive in both activities, transferring the workers between the two industries does not affect well-being. The consumers in the large country still buy 120 million widgets and 120 million bushels. In a more realistic model that allowed the increase in the demand for widgets in the large country to cause their price to increase slightly, both countries would share the gains from trade. This is the standard argument for free trade.

However, if wages in manufacturing are greater than those in agriculture for comparable workers, trade need not be beneficial. If manufacturing paid twice as much for equivalent workers, our two economies would behave quite differently. In the absence of trade, the cost and price of widgets in the large country will be twice that of bushels. Consequently, consumers will demand fewer, and fewer will be produced. To be exact, we would expect the large country to produce and consume 160 million bushels and 80 million widgets.

The situation would be similar in the small country. With manufacturing wages twice the wages in agriculture, and with manufacturing workers more productive, the cost and price of widgets will be 220 percent of the price of bushels. Consumers in the small country will purchase 16 million bushels and 6⅔ million widgets.

If we allow trade, the small country will again find that it can purchase widgets from abroad at below the domestic price. In the small country, one must pay more than twice as much for a bushel as for a widget that is produced domestically. However, a widget can be bought from abroad in trade for only one bushel. Therefore the country will again specialize in the production of bushels. It will produce 24 million bushels and trade 12 million of them for 6 million widgets and consume fewer widgets and bushels than in the absence of trade! The large country will produce 152 million bushels and 88 million widgets, trade 6 million widgets for 12 million bushels, and consume 164 million bushels and 82 million widgets, more of both than without trade.

How did this happen? Why is this outcome so different from the one in which the two countries had equal wages in agriculture and manufacturing? The answer lies in the changes in the productivity of the work force in the two economies that result from trade. Workers in the manufacturing sector produce a product that is worth twice as much as the product they would produce if they were working in agriculture. (Widgets are worth twice as much because fewer are being produced, and people value scarce goods more. Alternatively, the cost is higher so people want fewer. Both statements are true.) When a worker is moved from manufacturing to agriculture, the economy loses productivity. The people in the small country find it cheaper to buy their widgets from abroad than from domestic producers. Consequently, jobs are lost in the manufacturing sector. Although the cost of manufactured goods is more than twice that of bushels, the real cost to the economy in terms of forgone output of bushels is much lower. So while it is individually rational for the people in the small country to buy their widgets from abroad, it may not be in the best interest of the country as a whole.

The workers originally in the agricultural sector end up better off because they get the same wage in terms of bushels and pay a lower price for their widgets. However, the workers who originally produced widgets lose their higher paying jobs and work for half as much in terms of bushels. It is a very small consolation that they now pay a slightly lower price for their widgets. Their loss of income is so large that even if we were to give them the gain experienced by the lower income workers, it would not compensate fully for their loss. The winners are in the large country. Workers who start off in the high-wage industry are unaffected by trade. Those who start off in the low-wage industry and stay there are also unaffected. The big winners are the agricultural workers who get the new manufacturing jobs when the large country switches to producing more widgets for export.

Of course, this situation could be easily reversed. If the small country were even less productive in bushels than in widgets, it would produce widgets. In this case, the former agricultural workers in the small country would gain from the wage increase, and all workers in the small country would benefit from the new lower price of agricultural goods. The workers who lost their manufacturing jobs in the large country would be the big losers.

What happens in either case is that productivity is lost when workers move from the high-wage/high-productivity manufacturing jobs to agriculture. It is important to note that when we refer to high-wage jobs, we do not mean jobs that require unusual skills or that are unusually dangerous or unpleasant. When wages are high for any of these reasons, they compensate workers only for the expense of training or for the displeasure caused by the bad working conditions. When higher wages are paid only for these reasons, productivity is not gained by moving workers to high-wage jobs since the higher productivity of the worker is offset by the loss of productivity in training or the loss of welfare from exposure to the bad working conditions. In the next section we will detail other reasons that might lead firms to pay high wages.

Given that trade may reduce welfare, what policies should countries pursue? In answering this question, it is helpful to begin by considering policy in the absence of trade. It may be sensible for government to subsidize the wages of workers in the widget industry. Let us assume that the after-tax wages of workers in manufacturing must be twice those of workers in agriculture. Then, if all workers paid an income tax of one-third bushel, and manufacturing employers received a wage subsidy of two-thirds bushel per employee, the manufacturing employers cost would be only one bushel per worker—the same as in agriculture.

Since costs would be equal in the two industries, so would prices, and given our assumptions about demand, the large country would produce 120 million bushels and 120 million widgets. The subsidy returns prices and production to what they would be in the absence of the wage distortion.

How has each type of worker fared? With the subsidy, manufacturing workers would each consume two-thirds bushels and two-thirds widgets. Each agricultural worker would consume one-third of each product. Without the subsidy, each manufacturing worker would consume one bushel and one-half widget, and each agricultural worker would consume half that amount. Formal analysis (see the Appendix) can demonstrate that both types of workers are made worse off by the subsidy, but that workers who are shifted from bushel to widget production are made substantially better off. On average, workers are consuming one-sixth less of a bushel and one-sixth more of a widget each. Valued at current prices, that is a fair trade. Valued at the prices that prevailed before the tax and subsidy, that is a good trade. The expected value of a randomly chosen workers consumption is either the same or greater, depending on which prices are used to evaluate it. In this sense, the country is better off.

What happens if we allow trade? Consider the following scenario. Suppose that the small country is not happy with its losses from trade and decides that it would be better off producing the high-wage good for export; the government adopts a policy of encouraging the production of widgets. The policy could involve wage subsidies, low-interest loans, tax incentives, or any combination of policies that would reduce the cost of producing widgets relative to bushels. Suppose that the subsidy is sufficient that it becomes cheaper to produce widgets at home than to buy them from the large country. Then the small country will switch its labor force over to widget production and will make 20 million of them. It will ship 10 million widgets abroad in exchange for 20 million bushels. It is now consuming more widgets and more bushels than it did before it began to engage in trade.

The situation is different in the large country. Its production of the high-wage widgets has now declined. It will produce only 66⅔ million widgets along with 173⅓ million bushels. After trade it will consume 153⅓ million bushels and 76⅔ million widgets. The large country is now worse off than it was in the absence of trade.

What can the large country do? It could put a prohibitively high tariff on widgets. That would make it somewhat better off because the economy would be returned to its pre-trade position. But it has other alternatives that can make the average consumer even better off.

Suppose that the large country decided to adopt a policy of subsidizing the export of widgets with the subsidy paid for with a proportional tax on wages. If the subsidy is small, then the small country will ignore it and continue to produce widgets. However, if the subsidy is large enough, the small country will revert to producing only bushels, and the average consumer in both countries will be better off. In particular, if the large country offers to sell widgets to the small country for 1.1 bushels each, then the small country will specialize in producing bushels. The large country will produce slightly more than 91 million widgets and slightly less than 149 million bushels. It will trade slightly less than 11 million widgets for 12 million bushels and will consume slightly fewer than 161 million bushels and 80.4 million widgets.

In the large country, those who continue to work in their old jobs lose the value of the tax—about .013 bushels per agricultural worker and .017 bushels per manufacturing worker. But those who get the new jobs in manufacturing gain so much that, on average, citizens of the large country are now consuming more of both goods than they were in the absence of trade. The citizens of the small country are also better off, though it is harder to tell, as they are consuming more widgets but fewer bushels. The key is to note that at the existing price of slightly less than 1.2 bushels per widget, consumers could buy the $6\frac{2}{3}$ million widgets that they consumed in the absence of trade and still have some bushels left over. Thus they are better off than they were before trade. The large country gains its advantage from being able to produce the high-wage good. As long as it is getting more than one bushel for each widget that it produces, it is benefiting from the arrangement because it would have to transfer a worker from the widget industry, and thus forgo the production of a widget, in order to get the bushel via domestic production. The small country gains from exploiting its comparative advantage. As long as it does not have to pay more than 1.2 bushels for its widgets, it is better policy for it to produce bushels and trade for widgets since it would have to give up 1.2 bushels in order to produce another widget. The two countries could negotiate where, within the range of 1 to 1.2 bushels, the price would be set. Obviously, the higher the price of widgets, the better off the large country is.

WHY SIMILAR WORKERS MAY
NOT BE PAID SIMILARLY

It makes sense that if identical workers are paid more by one firm than another to do similar jobs, the low-paid workers will want to work for the higher paying firm, and the high-paying firm should lower its wages. Alternatively, the loss of workers to the high-paying firm would lead the low-paying firm to raise its wages. Why would a high-paying firm continue to pay workers high wages, even when there are job applicants who would be willing to work for less?

Several answers to this question have been suggested.[2] The first is that some firms may pay high wages in order to keep their workers from shirking. If workers can quickly get another job at the same wage, firms cannot discipline workers by threatening to fire them. However, if the firm pays a premium wage, workers will be afraid of losing their jobs, and employers will have greater control over them. Similarly, some firms may have to invest a great deal in hiring and training their workers and may not want to risk losing them to another employer offering a higher wage. Such employers may choose to pay a high wage instead. Workers who offered to work for less would be turned down because they would be likely to leave after the employer had paid for their training.

Another possibility is that it may not be easy for firms to determine how capable workers are, but workers may have a good idea of their capabilities. High-quality workers may apply only for high-paying jobs. Therefore a firm may have to offer high wages to all of its employees in order to get at least some good workers.

It has often been suggested that workers care a great deal not only about the amount of money they earn but also about the feeling that they are getting paid what they are worth. If this is the case, and workers who are paid less than they believe they are worth will not work as hard, then employers may be forced to pay high wages to meet these expectations. Traditional industry wage differences may play a role in determining what workers feel is a fair wage, so that firms in some industries must pay more than those in others. Even if some workers were willing to work for less, they would be turned down since they might soon become disaffected when they discovered what other workers in the industry were being paid.

Yet another reason that some firms may pay higher wages than others is the influence of unions. Most studies find that unions raise wages by about 15 percent (Freeman and Medoff 1984). A firm may also pay higher wages to prevent unionization. More generally, workers may be able to get a share of profits and the return on capital earned by firms through implicit bargaining. While such rent-sharing need not result in workers with high wages being more productive than similar workers elsewhere, there is considerable evidence that they are.[3]

Of course, trade may affect the wages that are paid. If for example, the wage differentials were due to unionization, the manufacturing workers in the small country in the example above might be willing to take a large enough wage cut to preserve their jobs and to make the widgets they were producing cost slightly less (in terms of bushels) than those of the large country. In this case, the manufacturing workers in the large country would lose jobs. If they took a wage cut, they could then compete again with the workers in the small country.

Thus it is important to establish not only *whether* similar workers are paid differently for similar work but also *why*. If wages are high in order to promote work discipline, it is unlikely that trade would have a substantial effect on the wage premium. On the other hand, if trade destroys a domestic monopoly, it may be impossible for workers to continue to capture the same level of rents.

ARE THE WAGES OF SIMILAR
WORKERS DIFFERENT?

It is impossible to establish with certainty whether workers in some industries receive wages that are higher than those of similar workers in other industries.[4] This is because it is impossible to define exactly what constitutes similar workers. Workers with the same number of years of education and experience could still be very different—they could have gone to very different schools or have different levels of ambition and productivity. However, a great deal of very suggestive evidence has been collected recently, to which we will now turn.

Wage differences across industries are very large. A 50 percent difference in average wages exists between a typical high-paid industry and a typical low-paid industry. The gap between the highest and lowest paid industries in Table 3–1 is $7.17, or nearly 200 percent. Further, a number of studies (reviewed in Dickens and Katz 1987b) have found that the pattern of which industries pay high wages is remarkably similar across countries. Obviously, these industries do not employ the same types of workers. However, even when we restrict the comparison to workers with similar characteristics, the differences are very large.

Table 3–1.   Industry Wages and Wage of Average Worker.[a]

		Average Industry Wage	Wage of Average Worker
1–4	Agriculture	4.81[b]	5.63[c]
5&6	Metal mining	10.26	9.39
7	Coal mining	10.86	9.91
8	Gas and oil extraction	8.59	9.16
9	Stone and clay mining	7.52	7.84[d]
10	Chemical mining	7.52	7.84[d]
11&12	Construction	9.96	7.84
13	Ordnance	8.26	8.84
14	Food and kindred	6.85	6.99
15	Tobacco manufacture	7.74	8.62
16	Fabric, yarn, and thread	5.13	6.74
17	Miscellaneous textiles	5.39	7.13
18	Apparel	4.52	5.89
19	Miscellaneous fabricated textiles	5.12	6.09
20&21	Lumber and wood products	6.58	6.65[d]
22	Household furniture	5.12	6.53[d]
23	Other furniture	6.25	6.53
24	Paper products	8.16	8.00
25	Paper containers	6.94	6.99
26	Printing and publishing	7.53	6.95
27	Chemicals	8.80	8.70
28	Plastics	8.21	8.08
29	Drugs and cleaners	7.68	8.09
30	Paints	7.39	7.66
31	Refining	10.10	9.37
32	Rubber and plastic products	6.52	7.30
33	Leather	6.10	6.83
34	Footwear	4.45	6.33
35	Glass	7.81	7.24
36	Stone and clay	7.21	7.16
37	Iron and steel	8.36	7.77
38	Nonferrous metals	8.77	7.62
39	Metal containers	9.84	7.16[d]
40	Heating and plumbing products	7.18	7.16[d]
41	Screw machine products	7.94	7.16[d]
42	Other fabricated metal	6.82	7.18
43	Engines and turbines	9.73	8.67
44	Farm and garden machinery	8.78	7.70
45	Construction and mining machinery	8.92	8.09[d]
46	Material handling equipment	7.68	8.09[d]
47	Metalworking machinery	8.18	7.66

Table 3–1. *(continued)*

		Average Industry Wage	Wage of Average Worker
48	Special industrial machinery	7.51	7.41[d]
49	Machinery and equipment	7.98	7.41[d]
50	Miscellaneous machinery	7.80	7.41[d]
51	Office and computing machinery	6.74	8.75
52	Service industry machinery	7.23	7.41
53	Electrical industrial equipment	7.13	7.50
54	Household appliances	6.95	7.64
55	Electric lighting and wire	6.42	7.50
56	Radio, T.V., and communications equipment	7.58	8.06
57	Electronics components	6.05	7.50[d]
58	Miscellaneous electrical machinery	7.96	7.50[d]
59	Motor vehicles and equipment	9.86	7.95
60	Aircraft and parts	9.28	8.43
61	Other transport equipment	8.29	7.72
62	Scientific instruments	6.25	7.66
63	Optical and photo equipment	7.64	7.72
64	Miscellaneous manufacturing	5.46	6.72
65	Transport and warehouse	9.01	7.54
66	Communications except radio and T.V.	8.70	8.82
67	Radio and T.V. broadcast	7.44	7.14
68	Electric, gas, and sanitary	8.90	8.67
69	Wholesale and retail	5.48	6.15
70	Finance and insurance	5.79	7.46
71	Real estate and rental	5.79	6.50
72	Hotel, personal, and repair services	6.71	5.68
73	Business services	6.71	6.99
74	Eating and drinking places	3.69	4.89
75	Auto repair and service	6.10	6.39
76	Amusements	6.03	5.87
77	Medical, educational, and nonprofit	6.20	6.55

[a]Average wage data are from the Bureau of Labor Statistics monthly wage data for 1983. Computation of wage of average worker is described in text. The surplus numbers used in calculations are these numbers minus 4.89, the estimated wage for the average worker in the lowest paid industry (#74).

[b]Computed from average weekly earnings for all farming and other agricultural occupation weekly earnings, *Monthly Labor Review*, September 1986, p. 32. Deflated using CPI from the 1986 *Economic Report of the President*.

[c]Not computed in the same manner as other wage surplus estimates. Estimated using a regression of wage surplus estimates on average wages.

[d]Similar industry codes grouped together to resolve incompatibility between census industry codes and input-output industry codes.

To do this, we construct a statistical model of the amounts that different types of workers earn, taking into account their age, education, sex, race, city, state, whether they are union members, occupation, part-time or full-time status, and the industry in which they are employed. We then compute the average wage of an average worker in each industry based on the model. These figures are presented in the second column of Table 3–1.[5] The highest average wage is now only $5.02 (about 100 percent greater than the lowest).

Why would workers with all of the above characteristics in common, except that they are employed in different industries, make such different wages? One possibility is that there has been a recent increase in demand for the products of high-paying industries, and that these industries demand certain skills that are consequently in short supply. Workers with those skills could earn high wages. If this is a major reason, then the wage differences should not last very long, but they do. All studies of industry wage differences have found them to be remarkably stable over time. Cullen (1956) found that fourteen of the twenty-one highest paying industries in 1880 were still among the highest paying in 1949, and fifteen of the lowest paying twenty-one in 1880 were still among the lowest paying in 1949. More recently, Krueger and Summers (forthcoming) found that the correlation between industry-average wages for comparable workers between 1970 and 1984 is .91 and between 1984 and 1900 is .616. It seems very unlikely that these wage differences are due in any large part to temporary high demand for certain types of workers.

Another possibility is that it is differences in jobs, not differences in workers, that explains the high wages. In particular, if a job is unpleasant or dangerous, then an employer will have to pay more to attract the same quality of worker. For example, a number of the highest paying jobs are in mining, a demanding, dirty, and dangerous industry. Attracting workers to these jobs requires high wages. However, the same cannot be said of other very high-paying jobs. Communications workers' jobs, for example, are no more dangerous and hardly seem less pleasant than working in a hotel or doing personal services or repair work. Yet service workers earn $3.14 less each hour.

Systematic evidence can be brought to bear on this point. Krueger and Summers (1987) report an attempt to explain the large industry differences in wages by looking at a number of job characteristics. They find that taking into account differences in job quality actually exacerbates differences rather than explaining them. Further, if workers in high-paid industries were merely being compensated for bad working conditions, they would be unlikely to value their jobs any more than the low-paying jobs—they get good pay, but it is just enough to get them to leave the lower paying, but more pleasant, jobs. Yet there is evidence that workers who have the higher paying jobs value them very highly. Many studies have shown that people are much less likely to quit jobs in high-paying industries.

In a series of papers on the structure of the labor market (see, for example, Dickens and Lang 1985a and b), we have developed complementary evidence of noncompetitive wage differences. It has long been suggested that it is conceptually useful to think of jobs as being of two types: primary jobs that are high paying, offer pleasant working conditions, reward education, and give workers opportunities for advancement, and secondary jobs that offer none of the amenities of primary jobs. Our work has shown that a statistical model that allows for two different types of jobs fits available data much better than one that does not. Further, the characteristics of the two types of jobs are exactly those described above—good jobs and bad jobs—and there is evidence in our work that at least some people are not able to choose which type of job they get. In particular, the wage premium earned by workers in primary jobs is so large that it is hard to believe that similar people in the secondary sector are there by choice. One explanation for these findings would be noncompetitive wage determination in the primary sector.

So if some workers receive noncompetitively high wages, which of the many reasons that were mentioned previously is the explanation? Two pieces of evidence suggest that it is unions, the threat of unions, or some other form of rent-sharing that may be responsible for interindustry wage differences. First, nearly all of the studies that have considered the relation of wages and profits have found them to be positively associated.[6] Second, the wages of workers in all occupations in high-paying industries seem to be higher than those of similar workers in other industries. If any set of workers is paid more, all workers are paid more. When secretaries' wages are higher, so are those of managers, laborers, and truck drivers. The result holds for both union and non-union workers.

However, the union and union-threat results are inconsistent with the fact that the pattern of industry wage differences is very similar across a wide variety of countries with very different economic systems. In some, unions are quite strong; in others, they are virtually nonexistent.

It seems as if workers obtain a share of the return on fixed capital as well as a return on profits even when formal unionization is difficult. Perhaps this is because of wage norms or the ability of workers to act collectively even in the absence of unions.

As we have noted, if wage differentials reflect rent-sharing, international trade may affect the differentials. The most careful study of the relation of wages and changes in trade patterns to date is Katz (1986b). He finds, for manufacturing industries, that there is a negative correlation between the change in the level of import penetration between 1960 and 1984 and the wage change in the industry over the same period. He also finds a positive correlation between wage change and the ratio of exports to shipments. However, the predicted changes in wages are small. For example, the share of imports in the motor vehicles market rose from 11.9 in 1972 to 21.5 in 1984. For this doubling of import share, Katz's analysis predicts less than a 2 percent decline in wages. This, coupled with the evidence discussed before—that industry wage differences are very persistent over time—suggests that trade has not had a large impact on wages in the past. Thus, ignoring the effects on wages in calculating the welfare impact may not be a serious problem.

WHAT TYPES OF JOBS DOES TRADE CREATE AND DESTROY?

If we accept the possibility of noncompetitive wage differences, then trade would be most damaging to the U.S. economy if imports replaced production in industries that pay equivalent workers more than other industries do. The effect would be attenuated to the extent that export industries also paid high wages or to the extent that trade caused wages in high-wage import industries to be lowered to protect employment.

Bulow and Summers (1986) suggest that the U.S. economy may be suffering from a loss of good high-paying jobs because of trade. As a test of this proposition, we have estimated our dual labor market model on a representative sample of workers for each year from 1976 to 1984. We find that, after remaining fairly constant from 1976 to 1981, the fraction of the labor force working in good—primary sector—jobs has fallen dramatically from 61 percent in 1981 to 55 percent in 1984.[7] Thus, there appears to have been little or no change during the period of balanced increases in trade, but a large drop-off in the fraction of primary jobs since 1981, when the United States began to develop its large trade deficits. Whether these changes are due to trade or to the 1982 recession is impossible to determine from this analysis, so we turn now to a direct examination of the employment effects of trade.

With our current trade deficit, imports may be eliminating more high-wage jobs than exports are creating. Someday, however, we will probably have to run a trade surplus to compensate for our current deficit. If we do this by producing high-wage export goods, the net effect could be to increase productivity. The studies reviewed in the preceding chapter all found that the wages of workers in jobs lost to imports were lower than those of workers in exports. If production of the exports required the creation of as many jobs as imports eliminated, overall we would have an increase in productivity. Although data are not available for a thorough analysis of whether or not this type of increase can be expected, we present some results that suggest the importance of these considerations.

The first step is to estimate the "wage surplus" in each industry; that is, how much more or less is earned by equivalent workers in each industry. To do this, we use the technique described above. We use the seventy-seven input-output industry codes, since we wish to match these wage estimates with trade and employment data from the USITC's 1986 input-output study. Once the wage-predicting equation is estimated, we construct the wage surplus in each industry as the difference between the predicted wage for a worker with average characteristics in each industry and the predicted wage for that worker in the lowest paying industry—eating and drinking places.

Having estimated these industry wage surpluses, we can now estimate average surplus in import-displaced and export-created jobs. To do this, we multiply the USITC's estimates of the number of export-created job opportunities in each of the seventy-seven input-output industries by the computed wage surplus for that industry. We then take the sum and divide it by the sum of the number of jobs created. For 1984 we arrive at an average wage surplus of $2.21. By performing a similar calculation that uses the number of job opportunities lost to imports, we estimate the average wage surplus of workers displaced by imports to be $2.28. These figures can be compared to an average wage surplus of $1.86 for the entire labor force.

Two things are notable about these two numbers. The first is that they are very similar. The second is that they are large relative to the average wage surplus for all workers. Both import and export workers are highly paid. This fits with the evidence on the changes in the fraction of good and bad jobs in the labor force. Balanced increases in trade have little effect since imports and exports both employ a high, and similar, fraction of high-wage workers. However, when imports increase and exports do not (as has been the case since 1982), high-wage jobs are lost.

A difference between these results and those cited in the preceding chapter is that the wage surplus is slightly larger for import workers than for export workers. These results are not too different from those of Mitchell's. He found higher wages in export industries, but they were very close to the import wages.

Katz found very large differences. What might explain the differences between his findings and ours? First, our use of the wage surplus measure does not explain them. When we repeat our procedure using average industry wages instead of surpluses, we find that the average wage of import-displaced workers is five cents higher than that of export industry workers. The differences in the time period may account for the small difference between our finding and Mitchell's, but they cannot explain the large difference between ours and Katz's. Using data from every year from 1978 to 1984, we find that the import wage surplus is nine to thirteen cents higher. The results are similar for average wages.

Finally, the difference cannot be explained by our use of input-output techniques to take into account both the direct and the indirect effects of trade on employment. When we perform the same calculations for the average wages and wage surplus of workers in the industries that are directly affected by trade, we find the same pattern of results.

What does explain the difference between our results and those of Katz is that he looks only at trade in manufactured goods. The seventy-seven input-output industries also include two industries in which the United States has a large trade surplus: agriculture and wholesale. No doubt, the latter reflects manufactured goods that pass through wholesale warehouses before being shipped abroad, but that activity has large employment effects, and the workers are relatively low paid. The agriculture sector is also low paid. When we restrict our average wage calculations to the manufacturing sector, we find that the wage surplus for export workers is about thirty-six cents higher than that for import workers, and the average wage is about sixty-five cents higher.

Table 3–2 presents nine estimates of the gain in productivity to the economy if all trade were eliminated. Several cautions are in order in interpreting these numbers. In addition to the problems with input-output analysis mentioned in the previous chapter, there are additional

Table 3-2.   Estimated Losses of Output from Trade Induced Changes in the Composition of Output (in $ millions).

	Workers Filling Import Jobs Come from:		
	Unemployment or Jobs Earning No Surplus	Jobs Earning an Average Surplus	No Additional High-Wage Jobs Created
Trade deficit as in 1984	12,394	2,874	728
Trade deficit eliminated by increasing exports	6,787	1,979	895
Trade deficit eliminated by decreasing imports	5,522	1,610	728

Computations described in text.

considerations unique to this analysis. First, the wage surplus calculations are based on the assumption that the trade-affected workers are the same, on average, as other workers in the industry. Second, and more important, these calculations ignore all of the effects of trade except those on the types of jobs workers held. For instance, if trade disciplines domestic monopolies, then the efficiency losses that would result from the loss of that discipline are ignored. The gains from trade that result from other countries having comparative advantages in some goods are ignored as well. Also missing from this accounting is the cost of reallocating resources from their current use to new uses.

The first line of Table 3-2 shows the estimates of the effect of a complete elimination of trade on the productivity of labor under three sets of assumptions about the labor and product markets. In the first column, the effect is estimated assuming that all goods that are currently purchased from abroad would be produced domestically, and that all workers that are currently employed in export jobs would find work in the newly expanded import-competing industries. Further, because of the trade deficit, and because it requires a greater number of workers to produce $1 million worth of import goods than $1 million worth of export goods, there will be many more jobs created in the import sector than are lost in the export sector.[8] In this case, we assume that the additional workers come from unemployment or from jobs with no wage surplus. Under these assumptions, the economy would undergo a $12,394 million increase in productivity as a result of the reallocation of labor from lower wage industries and unemployment to the import sector. This assumption is extremely optimistic.

Estimates in the second column are computed on the assumption that the extra workers that are needed to fill jobs in the import industries earned an average-wage surplus in their former employment. The third column presents estimates based on the assumption that workers who are displaced from export jobs would take employment in the import industry, but that no additional jobs are created—the economy simply goes without the imports. In the last case, the gain is $700 million, very small relative to the total value of exports, which was in excess of $400 billion in 1984.

Even this analysis exaggerates the impact of trade, because it includes the benefit of getting rid of a large trade deficit. To evaluate the impact of trade on productivity in the absence of a trade deficit, the next two lines of the table perform the same calculations as did the first line but assuming that trade was balanced. In the second line, it is assumed that balance is achieved through an equal proportional increase in export of goods from all industries. The third line shows the calculations under the assumption that trade has been balanced by an equal proportional decrease in the purchase of exports in all industries.

All nine numbers are positive. Because of the slightly higher wage in import industries, and because a greater number of jobs are displaced by a dollar's worth of imports than are created by a dollar's worth of exports, elimination of trade would increase the productivity of the economy. However, these numbers are all small. Even the $12 billion, which probably exaggerates the expected productivity impact of trade, is less than 3 percent of the total value of imports in that year. If we were able to buy the imported goods we bought abroad for 3 percent less than we could have made them at home, we came out ahead. It seems likely that the actual comparative advantage of foreign producers was larger than that—despite the considerations analyzed here, trade is welfare-enhancing for the U.S. economy.

One important consideration that is ignored by the previous analysis is the effect of trade on wages. This could be quite important, but there is little evidence that it is, at least in the United States. As noted above and in Chapter 1, some industries that are facing foreign competition have seen wages decline, while others have seen wage growth. The overall effect is very small.

CONCLUSION

When equivalent workers are paid similar wages (and when a large number of other conditions also obtain), free trade is to be preferred as the way to make people as well-off as possible with existing resources. But in a world where workers in some industries earn more than equivalent workers in other industries, this simple prescription may not be the best. As the above examples show, free trade can benefit some countries at the expense of others, and policies that are self-destructive in the case of the standard economic model of trade can work to a country's benefit.

In examining the trade position of the United States, there is no evidence that we are either big winners or big losers regarding the composition of our trade. We import goods made in high-wage industries, but our exports are also very high wage goods. Only pennies separate the average wage surplus in import and export industries. Even with our large trade deficit, the lost productivity due to losing jobs to imports is certainly small relative to consumers' gains of being able to buy imported goods at lower prices than it would cost to manufacture them domestically. This suggests an important conclusion to be drawn from this work: Despite the potential for gains from an active trade policy, the United States should be careful not to start a trade war that could reduce the volume of trade. Besides the loss to consumers of low-prices imports, the cost of adjusting to the lost jobs in export industries would also be substantial.

Does this mean that the United States should never use tariffs or subsidies? Obviously the answer is no. Even in standard trade theory free trade is not necessarily best unless all countries practice it. The above analysis suggests that some seemingly harmless practices may not be. In standard trade theory, a country cannot gain long-term advantages from subsidizing its exports. But with the sorts of wage differences we have discussed, that is no longer the case. The United States should be wary of high-wage imported goods that are competitive only because the government of the exporting country has subsidized the industry. We should be alert not only to direct subsidies such as export credits but also to indirect subsidies such as research and development support, low-cost loans, and investment credits.

If we find that we are losing high-wage employment to countries that engage in such policies, we have several options. One possibility is to cut off trade with them, but we would not want to do this if the prices of their goods were so low that, even if domestic workers were not earning a surplus, we could produce the good as cheaply ourselves. Alternatively, we could take any of a number of less drastic steps. Bilateral trade negotiations would be one possibility. First we would want to determine which country can produce what goods at the least expense. We should then seek an agreement whereby each country exports that good in which it has a comparative advantage and neither country is denied productivity gains by lost high-wage employment. The example above, in which the large country subsidized its exports to the small country, is a model of how both countries can benefit from such agreements. We want other countries either not to subsidize their high-wage exports or to subsidize them enough so that we gain more from the low cost of the good than we lose in worker productivity from the loss of the high-wage jobs. If negotiations fail, the example also suggests how a series of unilateral actions by two countries can arrive at a result that benefits both.

Subsidies are not the only policies that require caution. We must guard against being in a situation where other countries are exporting high-wage goods to us but are blocking our exports of high-wage goods with tariffs or other restrictive trade policies. This is true even in the standard trade model, but doubly true when we introduce the consideration of interindustry wage differences. Our policy in telecommunications is one example of this. We have opened our domestic market up to international competition, something few other countries have done. The manufacture of telecommunications equipment offers high-wage employment, and the United States has lost many such jobs to imports. The countries providing these goods have gotten something for nothing. Even if we decided it was in our best interest to import this equipment rather than produce it domestically, we should at least try to negotiate some quid pro quo from the countries providing it—large subsidies on the sales of the equipment or concessions in other areas.

Finally, the United States need not relegate itself to a position of reacting to the acts of other countries. As illustrated in one of the examples above, a policy of supporting high-wage industries can increase domestic productivity even in the absence of trade. The problem with such an industrial policy is its distributional consequences—many people pay to increase the well-being of a few who get the new high-wage jobs. It is possible that similar ends can be accomplished using trade policies with less of a distributional cost.

With large interindustry wage differences, there is a great potential both for gain and loss in managing our trade relations with other countries. These issues must be considered in formulating trade policy.

APPENDIX
THE EFFECTS OF TRADE IN A SIMPLE MODEL

First let us establish what happens in the large country when wages are equal in the two industries. Since labor is the only factor of production with wages equal and each worker producing one bushel or one widget, the cost of the two goods will be equal. If the cost is equal, by assumption the prices will be equal, and if the prices are equal, people will consume equal quantities of both goods. Denoting the price of bushels as Pb and the number consumed as Cb, the price of widgets as Pw and the amount consumed Cw, by assumption the amount spent on each good is equal, so

$$Pb \times Cb = Pw \times Cw. \tag{3A-1}$$

If $Pb = Pw$, then $Cb = Cw$. In the absence of trade, production must equal consumption, so denoting the amount of each good produced as Nb and Nw and the amount of labor used as Lb and Lw, we have

$$Nb = Nw = Lb = Lw. \tag{3A-2}$$

Since there are 240 million people, and all will be employed in one of the two industries, it must also be that

$$Lb + Lw = 240 \text{ million}, \tag{3A-3}$$

so putting 3A–2 and 3A–3 together, we know that $Lb = Lw = Nb = Nw = Cb = Cw = 120$ million.

For the smaller country, with the higher cost of producing both goods we get the following equations (denoting the small country's quantities using lower case letters):

$$pb = wb \times 5/3 \text{ and } pw = ww \times 2, \tag{3A-4}$$

since the wages in the two industries (ww and wb) are equal,

$$pw = pb \times 1.2, \tag{3A–5}$$

and therefore since $pw \times cw = pb \times cb$,

$$pw/pb = cb/cw = 1.2. \tag{3A–6}$$

Since $cb = nb = lb \times 3/5$ and $cw = nw = lw/2$, and since $lw + lb = 40$ million,

$$
\begin{aligned}
cb = cw \times 1.2 &= lw \times .6 = (40 \text{ million} - lb) \times .6 \\
&= (40 \text{ million} - cb \times 5/3) \times .6 = (24 \text{ million})/2 \\
&= 12 \text{ million}, \tag{3A–7}
\end{aligned}
$$

and that and 3A–6 imply $cw = 10$ million, which by 3A–7 implies $cb = 12$ million.

In the presence of trade, the large country's prices will prevail since it will be producing both goods. To see this, note that the small country can buy all the widgets or bushels it wants from the large country without creating a demand for more than can be produced. But if the large country tries to buy bushels for widgets from the smaller country, it will exhaust the small country's capacity for producing bushels and then bid the price up until it is equal to the price in the large country (that is, the same as the price of widgets).

With prices of the two goods equal in the small country, only bushels will be produced since they are cheaper. Now

$$pw = pb \text{ so } cw = cb. \tag{3A–8}$$

Since the country can not consume more bushels than it can produce or more widgets than it can get in trade,

$$cb = nb - cw = lb \times 3/5 - cw = 24 \text{ million} - cw, \tag{3A–9}$$

which together with 3A–8 implies that $cw = cb = 12$ million. The large country will simply cut the output of bushels by 12 million and increase the output of widgets by 12 million, and nothing else will change.

However, if we assume that the manufacturing wage is twice that of the agricultural wage, then in the large country

$$Pw/Pb = Cb/Cw = 2. \tag{3A–10}$$

Since it still takes only one of each worker to produce either good, in the absence of trade

$$Cb + Cw = Nb + Nw = Lb + Lw = 240 \text{ million}, \tag{3A–11}$$

which together with (3A–10) implies that Cb = 160 million and Cw = 80 million.

Using the same approach for the small country, only noting that

$$pw/pb = cb/cw = 2.4, \qquad (3A\text{–}12)$$

because of the differences in the physical productivities in the two industries and

$$cb = lb \times 3/5, \; cw = lw/2, \text{ and } lb + lw \\ = 40 \text{ million}, \qquad (3A\text{–}13)$$

We can conclude that in the absence of trade cb = 16 million and cw = 6.67 million.

With trade it will again be the large country's prices that prevail. Since widgets are still relatively cheaper in the large country, the small country will specialize in the production of bushels. As in the case when the wages were equal, the small country will produce 24 million bushels and trade 12 million to the large country for widgets. But since the price of widgets is now twice what it was in the other example, the small country will get only 6 million. So cw = 6 million and cb = 12 million, which is less of each than before trade.

In the large country, we have (3A–10) as above, but instead of (3A–11) we have

$$Cw = Lw - 6 \text{ million}, \; Cb = Lb + 12 \text{ million}, \\ \text{and } Lw + Lb = 240 \text{ million}, \qquad (3A\text{–}14)$$

which together imply Cw = 82 million and Cb = 164 million. Both are larger than in the absence of trade.

If in the absence of trade the large country puts a tax on all of its workers of ⅓ bushel and uses the tax to pay a subsidy of two bushels per worker to manufacturing employers, then employers in agriculture will pay their workers enough to buy one bushel (since wage must equal marginal product), and after tax they will have enough left to buy ⅔ bushels. Manufacturing employers must pay their workers so that their after-tax wage is twice that of agricultural workers so it must be be enough to buy ⅝ bushels (2 × ⅔ + ⅓). With manufacturing employers receiving a ⅔ bushel subsidy per worker, their labor costs are the same as those of employers in agriculture—enough to buy one bushel per worker. With cost equal, prices will be equal and the quantities produced and consumed will be the same as in the case where there is no trade and no wage distortion.

If the small country subsidizes its manufacturing industry, this can be reversed. If the subsidy is large enough that it is cheaper to buy domestic widgets than foreign widgets, the small country will specialize in the production of widgets. It will produce 20 million and trade 10 million for 20 million bushels. Now $cw = 10$ million and $cb = 20$ million, both larger than in the absence of trade. Going through calculations for the large country like those above, only modifying (3A–14) so that

$$Cw = Lw + 10 \text{ million}, \quad Cb = Lb - 20 \text{ million}, \quad (3A-15)$$

we get the result that $Cw = 76.67$ million and $Cb = 153.33$ million. Both are smaller than before.

If the large country subsidizes the small country's purchases of widgets, the trade-off the small country faces between widgets and bushels changes as does the consumption pattern. If the large country sets the price of widgets so that the small country can get a widget for only 1.1 bushels, then

$$pw/pb = cb/cw = 1.1, \quad (3A-16)$$

so if the small country produces only bushels,

$$cb = 24 \text{ million} - cw \times 1.1, \quad (3A-17)$$

which gives us $cw = 10.909$ million and $cb = 12$ million.

In the large country, (3A–15) becomes

$$Cw = Lw - 10.909 \text{ million and } Cb$$
$$= Lb + 12 \text{ million}, \quad (3A-18)$$

so with domestic prices unaffected by the subsidy $Lw = 91.27$ million, $Lb = 148.73$ million, $Cb = 160.73$ million, and $Cw = 80.36$ million.

NOTES

1. Several more theoretical treatments of this argument exist in the economics literature. Bulow and Summers (1986) consider the effects of subsidies on welfare in greater detail in a more general model. Bhagwati and Srinivasan (1983) consider the ranking of policy alternatives in a number of models with sectoral wage differences.
2. Yellen (1984) and Katz (1986a) survey all the reasons discussed here, give more thorough discussion of them, and provide references to the development of the arguments in the economic literature.

3. Freeman and Medoff (1984) review a large literature that strongly suggests that productivity increases with unionization. Theoretically, if unions bargain efficient contracts then the existence of a union should not affect the number of workers hired by a firm nor the productivity of workers. Brown and Ashenfelter (1986), Card (1986), and Svejnar (1986) find evidence inconsistent with the efficient contract view. Only Abowd (1987) finds support for it. MaCurdy and Pencavel (1986) find evidence inconsistent with the view that union firms choose wages and employment on the labor demand curve. This finding is consistent with the efficient contract view but not inconsistent with some models of union behavior in which contracts are not efficient. In the case where firms are not unionized but pay high wages to prevent unionization, Dickens (1986) shows that the higher wages may go with either higher or lower productivity for the marginal worker; however, he argues that the most likely case is higher productivity.

4. This section draws heavily on Dickens and Katz (1987a and b) and the papers cited therein.

5. For a more complete description of the method, see Dickens and Katz (1987a).

6. The effect is present for both union and nonunion workers. In fact, Dickens and Katz (1987a) find the effect is stronger for nonunion workers.

7. In an earlier study (Dickens and Lang 1987), we reported that the percent of the workforce in primary jobs rose from 1973 to 1983. We now believe that finding resulted from our forcing the 1973 and 1983 years to share the same wage equation. It is possible that the percent primary was very low in 1973, but more likely our earlier results are an artifact of the constraints put on the model. So far, we have been unable to estimate the model for 1973 without the constraint.

8. From the previous discussion it may seem contradictory that the average labor productivity in import industries is lower but wages are higher. This is not a problem, however, since the average productivity of labor need not equal the marginal product, which is what wages must equal.

REFERENCES

Abowd, John M. 1987. "Collective Bargaining and the Division of the Value of the Enterprise." NBER Working Paper #2137, January.

Bhagwati, J.N., and T.N. Srinivasan. *Lectures on International Trade.* Cambridge, Mass.: MIT Press

Brown, J.N., and O. Ashenfelter. 1986. "Testing the Efficiency of Employment Contracts." *Journal of Political Economy* 94 (June): 540–87.

Bulow, J.I., and L.H. Summers. 1986. "A Theory of Dual Labor Markets with Application to Industrial Policy, Discrimination and Keynesian Unemployment." *Journal of Labor Economics* 4 (July): 376–414.

Card, David. 1986. "Efficient Contracts and Costs of Adjustments: Short-Run Employment Determination for Airline Mechanics." *American Economic Review* 76: 1045–71.

Cullen, D. 1956. "The Interindustry Wage Structure, 1899–1950," *American Economic Review* 46 (June): 353–69.

Dickens, W.T. 1986. "Wages, Employment and the Threat of Collective Action by Workers." NBER Working Paper #1856, March.

Dickens, W.T., and L.F. Katz. 1987a. "Interindustry Wage Differences and Industry Characteristics." In *Unemployment and the Structure of Labor Markets,* edited by K. Lang and J. Leonard. New York: Basil-Blackwell.

––––––. 1987b. "Interindustry Wage Differences and Theories of Wage Determination." NBER Working Paper, June.

Dickens, W.T., and K. Lang. 1985a. "A Test of Dual Labor Market Theory." *American Economic Review* 75 (September).

––––––. 1985b. "Testing Dual Labor Market Theory: A Reconsideration of the Evidence." NBER Working Paper #1670.

––––––. 1987. "Where Have All the Good Jobs Gone?" In *Unemployment and the Structure of Labor Markets*, edited by K. Lang and J. Leonard. New York: Basil-Blackwell.

Freeman, R.B., and J. Medoff. 1984. *What Do Unions Do?* New York: Basic Books.

Katz, L.F. 1986a. "Efficiency Wage Theories: A Partial Evaluation." In *NBER Macroeconomics Annual 1986*, edited by S. Fischer. Cambridge, Mass.: MIT Press.

––––––. 1986b. "International Trade and the Wage Structure in U.S. Manufacturing." Harvard University. Mimeo.

Krueger, A.B., and L.H. Summers. 1987. "Reflections on the Inter-Industry Wage Structure." In *Unemployment and the Structure of Labor Markets*, edited by K. Lang and J. Leonard. New York: Basil Blackwell.

––––––. Forthcoming. "Efficiency Wages and the Inter-Industry Wage Structure." *Econometrica*.

MaCurdy, Thomas E., and John Pencavel. 1986. "Testing Between Competing Models of Wage and Employment Determination in Unionized Markets." *Journal of Political Economy* 94 (June): 530–39.

Svejnar, Jan. 1986. "Bargaining Power, Fear of Disagreement and Wage Settlements: Theory and Empirical Evidence from U.S. Industry." *Econometrica* 54 (September): 1055–78.

Yellen, J. 1984. "Efficiency Wage Models of Unemployment." *American Economic Review Proceedings* 74 (May): 200–5.

4 THE DOMESTIC EMPLOYMENT CONSEQUENCES OF MANAGED INTERNATIONAL COMPETITION IN APPAREL

Carol A. Parsons

The future looks bleak for the domestic apparel industry. With a $17.6 billion trade deficit in 1986 and a set of foreign competitors that hire labor at wages that are often no more than 15 percent of U.S. wage levels, it is easy to be pessimistic about the employment prospects of workers in the domestic apparel industry. Innovative production and marketing strategies notwithstanding, the labor intensity of apparel production in combination with the enormity of the wage disparity between the rich and the poor countries means that domestic employment in apparel production will almost certainly continue to fall.

UNDERSTANDING FOREIGN TRADE AND DOMESTIC EMPLOYMENT IN APPAREL

This chapter approaches the question of how international trade affects domestic employment in the apparel industry. It begins by reviewing the effects of trade on domestic employment. While most macroeconomic studies conclude that trade has had a relatively small effect on employment when compared to productivity improvements, these studies are generally unilluminating. By insisting on a formal separation between the effects of trade and those of productivity improvements, these studies

113

miss the obvious connection between the two: imports increase and domestic firms attempt to reduce the labor content of their products in order to compete with their low-wage developing country competitors. Input-output analyses provide a useful counterweight to this approach. By estimating the labor content of imports, these studies generate estimates of the reduction in labor demand and conclude that imports have dramatically reduced domestic "job opportunities," particularly for female, minority workers.

The chapter then briefly describes the institutions that have arisen to manage international trade in the textile-apparel business. Rather than reciting the history of the Short-Term Agreement, the Long-Term Agreement, and the Multifiber Agreement, the discussion will be limited to identifying the most frequent ways in which these agreements break down.[1] In particular, the use of quotas has had and continues to have the unfortunate effect of forcing trade regimes to continually widen their span of control to include more products and more types of fiber. Furthermore, even as the scope of managed trade has expanded, the structure of trade management has encouraged participants to escape from the controls in two ways. On the one hand, quotas encourage producers to shift production into uncontrolled categories; on the other hand, quotas induce producers to shift production toward more valuable output and thus maximize the value of the product mix within quota categories. MFA quotas thus have a doubly perverse effect: the value of controlled imports increases, as does the range of controlled categories.

Finally, the chapter examines the strategic responses open to domestic apparel producers and evaluates their economic and political efficacy as competitive responses to international competition. This is a critical part of assessing the impact of trade on employment because in a market economy the demand for labor is derived from demand for the product. The competitive success of firms is a crucial determinant of employment levels. Generally, there are three strategies that apparel firms can pursue: (1) the maintenance of some level of protection; (2) a shift out of apparel manufacturing; or (3) a breakthrough in the automation of the apparel production process. Taken together, the possible responses—from international free trade to a wave of large-scale automation—imply one certain outcome: employment in apparel will not increase. Put more bluntly, the best that labor can hope for is a set of responses by governments and firms that will slow the rate of domestic job loss.

THE DOMESTIC APPAREL INDUSTRY

The U.S. apparel industry is a good approximation of the atomistic competition described by Adam Smith. There are over 15,000 firms in the industry, and the top four firms in almost all product segments account for less than 25 percent of total shipments (see Table 4–1). Work clothing for men and boys, a highly concentrated and heavily capitalized industry segment, is the exception, with the top four firms delivering 49 percent of total shipments. This segment, which is primarily comprised of blue jeans, is dominated by the two largest apparel firms in the country, Levi Strauss and Blue Bell. In its standard product, size, and market power, the work clothing segment differs sharply from the norm.

Since production has relatively low capital requirements, outside of these concentrated industry segments, firms enter and leave the industry easily. Capital per apparel worker was $599 in 1981—up 75 percent from $341 in 1974, yet still quite low compared to the textile industry, where capital per worker increased by 91 percent over the same period, from $1,329 in 1974 to $2,542 in 1981 (U.S. Department of Commerce 1984). In 1981, the most recent year for which data are available, new capital expenditures in apparel were $650 million in the apparel industry versus $1.7 billion in the textile industry and $65 billion in all nondurable manufacturing (Nehmer and Love 1985: 235).

Employment and Wages and Job Loss

The apparel industry's pattern of investment is evident in its employment structure (see Tables 4–2 and 4–3). The industry is labor intensive; production workers account for over 85 percent of all employees. The workers in apparel are also consistently older, composed of more women and minority workers, and less educated than workers in manufacturing as a whole. Women account for over 80 percent of the work force in apparel, while minority workers account for approximately 19 percent (Nehmer and Love 1985: 235). As significant—especially in terms of potential mobility—is the relative lack of education among apparel workers. In 1975, the most recent year for which data on education are available, the apparel industry was the largest employer of people with less than a ninth-grade education: of the industry's 1,186,000 employees, approximately 400,000 had not completed the ninth grade (Arpan et al. 1982: 10–11).

Table 4–1. Concentration Ratios in the Apparel Industry, 1984.

SIC	Segment[a]	Total No. of Establishments	Total Employment (in thousands)	No. of Est. with more than 20 Employees	Percent of Industry Shipments by 4 Largest Companies
2311	MB suits and coats	737	69.5	270	21
2321	MB shirts and nightwear	928	92.3	249	17
2327	MB separate trousers	514	53.3	179	25
2328	MB work clothing	656	94.4	81	49
2331	WM blouses and shirts	1415	81.4	463	12
2335	WM dresses	6953	149.5	4480	8
2337	WM suits and coats	1672	71.5	605	15
2341	WC underwear	698	71.2	219	22
2361	Children's dresses and blouses	519	32.2	145	15

Source: U.S. Department of Commerce (1984).

[a]MB = men's and boys'.

WM = women's and misses.

WC = women's and children's.

Table 4–2. Production Employment, Average Weekly Hours, and Hourly Earnings of Production Workers in Apparel, 1970–1984.

Year	Employment	Average Weekly Hours	Hourly Earnings
1970	1,196.2	35.3	$2.39
1971	1,177.0	35.6	2.49
1972	1,208.0	36.0	2.60
1973	1,249.7	35.9	2.76
1974	1,174.9	35.2	2.97
1975	1,066.6	35.2	3.17
1976	1,134.3	35.8	3.40
1977	1,129.4	35.6	3.62
1978	1,144.6	35.6	3.94
1979	1,116.8	35.3	4.23
1980	1,079.4	35.4	4.56
1981	1,059.5	35.7	4.97
1982	981.2	34.7	5.20
1983	984.3	36.2	5.37
1984	1,016.5	36.4	5.53

Source: International Ladies' Garment Workers' Union Research Department (1985).

Low-wage jobs are the norm in apparel, where a worker's average annual wages are below the poverty line for a family of four.[2] Hourly wages in the industry fell from 73 percent of the average manufacturing wage in 1968 to 61 percent in 1982. Over the same period, apparel workers' real hourly wages declined by 16 percent.

Industry employment has plummeted by 700,000 jobs since 1960 (Barmash 1987: 25), with 180,000 of those lost between 1973 and July 1987 (Starobin 1987). Compounding the social problem of job loss is the fact that it does not occur smoothly or incrementally through, for example, attrition or layoffs. Instead, it frequently occurs discontinuously as entire plants close and companies go bankrupt, eliminating all jobs at once. And unlike the case of plant closures in the Sunbelt, where new plant openings have more than counterbalanced closings, the 3,200 apparel-industry firms that have closed in the United States in the last decade have not been replaced by the entry of new firms (de la Torre et al. 1984: 23). Evidence of this disruption is clear

Table 4-3.   Apparel Employment by Industry Segment, 1986 (in thousands).

SIC	Segment[a]	Total Employment	Production Employment	Average Hourly Earnings
2311	MB suits and coats	72.1	62.0	$5.95
2321	Men's shirts	89.4	70.7	5.33
2327	MB trousers	55.8	44.9	5.27
2328	MB work clothing	93.5	83.2	5.34
	Total	310.8	260.8	—
2331	WM blouses	83.1	68.7	$4.72
2335	WM dresses	114.0[b]	93.2	5.55
2337	Women's suits and coats	53.2	46.8	5.41
	Total	250.3	208.7	—
2361	Child's dresses/blouses	31.0	26.1	$5.16
2363	Child's coats and suits	5.1	4.7	5.27
	Total	36.1	30.8	—

Source: U.S. Department of Commerce (1987).
[a]MB = men's and boys'; WM = women's and misses.
[b]Estimated 1985 data.

from the trade balance in apparel, which has deteriorated sharply in the 1980s, plunging from −$4.7 billion in 1980 to −$17.6 billion in 1986 (see Table 4–4).

The Structure of Demand

While imports were surging into the domestic market, the industry was also shaken by a radical shift in the level and composition of demand for apparel. The shift from traditional suits and dresses to casual wear imposed diverse, and often conflicting, demands on the industry. The increase in market segmentation that accompanied the more relaxed rules about "appropriate" dress made manufacturing flexibility, quick distribution, and a wide product range sources of competitive advantage, all factors that favored the specialized, small firms that dominate

Table 4-4. U.S. Imports, Exports, and Trade Balance in Apparel, 1967–1986 ($ millions).

Year	Imports	Exports	Balance
1967	595.2	118.6	−476.6
1968	786.0	130.8	−655.2
1969	1,012.8	163.8	−849.0
1970	1,152.8	154.5	−998.3
1971	1,401.5	164.1	−1,237.4
1972	1,718.3	198.0	−1,520.3
1973	1,955.5	229.3	−1,726.2
1974	2,095.4	332.7	−1,762.7
1975	2,318.1	340.6	−1,977.5
1976	3,256.5	434.2	−2,822.3
1977	3,649.7	524.1	−3,125.6
1978	4,833.3	551.0	−4,282.3
1979	5,015.0	772.1	−4,242.9
1980	5,702.8	1,000.6	−4,702.2
1981	6,756.1	1,032.1	−5,724.0
1982	7,386.1	774.9	−6,611.2
1983	8,649.3	663.7	−7,985.6
1984	12,029.0	637.9	−11,391.1
1985	16,056.0	755.0	−15,301.0
1986	18,554.0	899.0	−17,655.0

Source: Unpublished U.S. Department of Commerce data.

the domestic industry. The explosion of demand for denims and corduroys and the increasing demand for natural fabrics, however, militated against niche strategies for national apparel industries as a whole simply because the fastest growing market segments were in garments that required less construction time and therefore lower labor input per unit.

Changes in synthetic fiber technology and relative material prices also had a significant effect on the competitive conditions of the industry. The popularity of man-made fibers during the 1960s gave the United States a brief period of comparative advantage, since the production of synthetic fibers and fabrics was centered there and provided its apparel makers with a ready supply of fashionable and competitive inputs. Man-made fibers captured over 50 percent of the world's consumption of textile fibers by 1979, with synthetic fibers accounting for over three-quarters of this total. Apparel manufacturers benefited considerably as the high level of innovation in processing and production in the fiber and textile complex drove down prices throughout the 1960s and 1970s. By the 1970s, however, this advantage faded as synthetic fiber technology spread to fast-growing markets in low-wage countries.

The shift toward synthetic fabrics also had a perverse effect on competitiveness. Lower material costs, which emphasized the role of other factors in the total cost structure, accentuated the significance of labor cost differentials, thus shifting the terms of competition to the advantage of low-wage producers.

INTERNATIONAL TRADE IN APPAREL

In 1958 almost every garment sold in the United States was made in the United States, and total imports were less than $300 million. Twenty-five years later, one of every four garments sold in the United States was made somewhere else, and imports had increased to an equivalent wholesale value of $13.5 billion, or 25 percent of the total wholesale value of all apparel sold in the country (American Apparel Manufacturers Association 1984: 2). Table 4–5 details the loss in market share of domestic apparel producers from 1973 to 1983, a period of substantial growth in apparel imports. The fact that real consumption was growing during this period only makes the market share data more disturbing. Unlike the apparel market in Western Europe, real apparel

Table 4–5. Market Share of U.S. Apparel Production of Domestic Apparel Consumption (percentages).

	1973		1983	
	Units	Dollars	Units	Dollars
All tailored clothing[a]	77	85	60	70
Undergarments and nightwear[b]	96	98	90	92
Total	80	88	67	75

Source: American Apparel Manufacturers Association (1984: 2).

[a]Tailored clothing included coats, dresses, jackets, skirts, knit and woven shirts and blouses, sweaters, play clothes, trousers, jeans, slacks, and shorts.

[b]Undergarments and nightwear includes hosiery, robes and dressing gowns, and other apparel.

consumption in the United States grew at the healthy pace of 4.1 percent annually between 1970 and 1985 (Council of Economic Advisors 1987). This increase, however, did not benefit the domestic industry. Imports captured domestic growth along with a growing share of the entire domestic market for apparel.

After 1980 the value of apparel imports skyrocketed, growing at approximately 15 percent annually. Two factors encouraged import penetration: the appreciation of the dollar and the lackluster export performance of domestic apparel manufacturers. While the strength of the dollar explains some of the import surge from Western European producers during this period, it does not explain the surge from Asian producers. The value of the currency of the developing countries in Asia, especially Hong Kong, South Korea, and Taiwan—three of the Big Four (China is the fourth) apparel exporters into the U.S. market—is tied to the value of the dollar. A weighted index of the values of Asian currency constructed by the Federal Reserve Bank of Atlanta in 1986 (Rosensweig 1986) indicates that on a trade-weighted basis, the dollar depreciated only slightly against the Asian currencies after 1985. Thus even as the dollar depreciated against the yen and Western European currencies, over relatively long periods of time the terms of trade between the dollar and the currencies of the largest Far Eastern apparel producers did not change substantially. In the short run, the Asian countries tended to peg their currencies' value to the dollar's value, while over the longer term some devalued their own currencies against an already depreciating dollar.

The surge in imports was not counterbalanced by an export drive by domestic producers. To some extent this reflects the conservatism and provincialism of the domestic industry. Its history of family firms and small town ties makes it ill prepared to compete in foreign markets. Yet exporting has never been a primary focus of competition because the United States is the world's largest market for apparel. First of all, the trade data clearly indicate the presence of underlying differences in trade behavior among developed and developing countries. Not surprisingly, as Table 4–6 documents, the developed nations engage in intraindustry trade, which is the trade outcome of specialization in production, while the developing nations export into industrial markets with little exchange, clearly an import-substitution strategy. So while it is true that Western Europe did and does offer some marketing opportunities for domestic producers, generally the developing countries have not. Until very recently, apparel has been exclusively an export

Table 4–6.   Clothing Exports by Main Areas, 1980
(in billions of dollars).

	Destination		
Origin	Developed Countries	Developing Countries	Eastern Bloc
Developed	$15.7	$2.1	$0.4
Developing	13.8	2.8	0.5
Eastern Bloc	2.0	0.7	2.3

Source: General Agreement on Tariffs and Trade (1984: Table 2.11).

industry in the industrializing and less developed countries. Low per capita income and the absence of Western habits of consumption yielded few market opportunities there.

In competing for the European market, domestic manufacturers have been limited by their lesser fashion sense than that of European producers. Once again, this difference reflects less an inherent inability to compete than the substantial differences between U.S. and European market structures. It appears that the average European consumer is much more fashion sensitive than the average U.S. consumer. In Europe the apparel market is substantially segmented by class, while in the United States all classes tend to favor the same styles (Sable 1982). As a result, U.S. apparel producers are unused to manufacturing for highly fashion sensitive markets and disadvantaged in exporting into them.

ESTIMATING EMPLOYMENT LOSS DUE TO TRADE

In the postwar period, apparel imports have continually increased and apparel employment in all industrialized countries has steadily declined. These two facts are clear. The dispute centers on the connection between these two phenomena. The growth in imports may be linked to the decline in employment in apparel through (1) accounting studies that partition job loss into the proportion of employment change attributable to changes in demand, increases in productivity, and changes in the level of imports; (2) counterfactual analysis that asks what employment would have been in the absence of imports; (3) input-output analyses that trace direct and indirect job loss; and (4) estimates of apparel employment in other countries.

Accounting models are conventionally used to disaggregate changes in employment between two points in time into changes in domestic demand, exports, imports, and productivity growth. Accounting studies on the employment-displacing effect of trade in apparel during the 1960s and 1970s concluded that changes in productivity per employee were considerably more important in reducing employment in the industry than were the effects of trade. Charles Frank of the Brookings Institution studied the effects of trade on employment in nineteen industries and found that during the period 1963–1971, apparel was one of only four job-losing sectors in the United States. According to Frank, imports accounted for only 0.8 percent of the decline in employment in each year, although exports were so sluggish that they had no positive effect on employment. During this period, domestic demand for clothing, which increased at only half the rate of growth of total demand for all manufactured output, was a stronger determinant of domestic employment than trade. Overall, Frank found that 55,000 jobs were lost in the apparel industry as a result of increased import penetration; for all manufacturers, the total loss was 354,000 (see Table 4–7). This led Frank (1977: 37) to conclude that "job losses due to trade are insignificant compared to those due to increased productivity or fluctuations in aggregate demand." Domestic demand swamped the effect of foreign trade as a determinant of employment levels, a finding that is consistent with the relatively small trade deficit in apparel until the end of the period.

Frank's calculations, which were made at a highly aggregated level, may well have concealed intraindustry employment differences. The apparel industry comprises a large number of products, and it is not at all clear that every segment was losing international competitiveness in comparison with developing country producers. The results of a study by Anne Krueger (1979) reveal that at the four-digit SIC level, there was, in fact, wide variation in performance across industry segments. In men's and boys' shirts and work clothing, for example, employment expanded. In the work clothing and children's clothing segments, strong domestic demand growth substantially counterbalanced the negative affect of productivity and imports (see Table 4–8).

Other studies based on roughly the same method support the general conclusion that productivity growth appears to have had a negative effect on employment that was nearly three times greater than the effect of net import penetration (de la Torre et al. 1984). When applied to Western Europe, for example, the accounting method yields fundamentally the same results as it does for the United States. For 1962–1975, a study by Frank Wolter of the Institut fur Weltwirtschaft at the University

Table 4-7. Sources of Growth of Employment In Selected Import-competing Industries, United States, 1963–1971 (percent per annum).

	Growth Rate			Contributions to Growth of Employment				
SIC Industry Class	Total Employment[a] (1)	Production Man-hours[b] (2)	Productivity per Employee (3)	Productivity per Man-hour (4)	Domestic Demand (5)	Exports (6)	Imports (7)	Trade[c] (8)
22. Textiles	−7.5	−7.7	−9.5	−9.7	2.2	0.1	−0.2	−0.1
23. Apparel	−3.6	−4.8	−6.2	−7.4	3.4	0.0	−0.8	−0.8

Source: Frank (1977: 29).

[a]Alegbraic sum of columns 3, 5, 6 and 7; numbers have been rounded.

[b]Algebraic sum of columns 4, 5, 6 and 7; numbers have been rounded.

[c]Algebraic sum of columns 6 and 7; numbers have been rounded.

Table 4-8. Sources of Labor Displacement in the U.S. Apparel Industry, 1970–1976.

SIC[a]	Segment[b]	Demand Growth	Labor Productivity	Imports	Employment
2311	MB suits and coats	−0.85%	−1.73%	−1.21%	−3.79%
2321	MB shirts	5.06	−2.55	−2.38	0.15
2327	MB pants	0.35	−2.76	0.65	−1.76
2328	MB work clothing	6.32	−1.47	−1.45	3.41
2341	WC underwear	0.23	−3.05	−0.03	−2.84
2342	Corsets and allied garments	−0.30	−7.20	−1.33	−8.84
2369	Children's clothing	8.30	−5.08	−4.37	−1.15

Source: International Labor Organization (1980b).

[a]Standard Industrial Classification.

[b]MB = men's and boys'. WC = women's and children's.

of Kiel shows that displacement due to productivity growth amounts to 463,400 jobs in textiles and 160,000 in clothing, while the corresponding effect of growth in imports was apparent in a job displacement of 141,800 and 144,600, respectively, of which only 24,200 (17 percent) and 45,900 (32 percent) were caused by imports from developing countries (Keesing and Wolf 1980: 36–37). De la Torre's (1984) study of job changes between 1970 and 1980 for eight countries, including the United States and Japan, conforms with other studies of this type: on average, productivity increases in the eight countries had a negative effect on employment that was nearly three times greater than the effect of increases in net trade penetration.

Four points tend to mitigate the view, inherent in the accounting model approach, that trade has had only an insignificant effect on employment. First, it is unlikely that import penetration and productivity growth are independent occurrences. Because the notion of independence among imports, exports, domestic demand, and productivity improvements is built into accounting models, these models tend to yield fairly credible employment numbers and fairly incredible explanations of job loss. Accounting models miss the several ways in which imports spark productivity improvements. To begin with, as imports expand, the weakest firms will go bankrupt first, leading to an immediate jump in productivity. Then, import pressure will most likely accelerate the search for methods of dealing with the industry's main weakness, its labor intensity. Second, accounting models do not consider the job losses that occur upstream in textile and fiber production. Third, the exceptionally slow growth of retail and wholesale prices of apparel in the United States over the last two decades suggests that the pressure of imports may have eroded profit margins by forcing competitive price-cutting (Council of Economic Advisors 1987).[3] Finally, these studies were conducted before the import surge of the 1980s. A similar event in Western Europe in the 1970s saw an enormous amount of job loss and community disruption, the same effects that are now occurring in the United States as imports continue to grow.

Another way of linking imports and job loss is to look at employment per unit of domestic output and then ask what employment would have been in the absence of imports. Using counterfactual analysis, a World Bank study (Balassa 1979) estimated job loss by assuming that all OECD countries used American labor input coefficients to produce their exports and replace imports in their trade with developing countries. This led to the result that the combined trade balance with these countries in 1976 would have implied a net loss of 230,700 jobs in apparel and textiles together in all OECD countries, including 115,600 in the United States and 95,900 in the EC countries (Balassa 1979).

Keesing and Wolf addressed the same problem. Their study began with a set of much more complicated assumptions but reached essentially the same conclusion as the World Bank study. For apparel, their model indicates that if there had been no trade with developing countries, there would have been about 125,000 additional jobs in the American apparel industry in 1978, compared with the estimated 1978 employment level of 1.24 million, an increase of 10 percent (Keesing and Wolf 1980: 115).

At the heart of counterfactual analysis is the assumption of the stability of unit labor requirements, a questionable assumption given productivity improvements in the industry. Analyses that assume constant labor coefficients tend, over time, to overestimate job loss due to trade. While accounting models miss the short-run labor displacing effects of trade, counterfactual analyses miss the longer run productivity effect that reduces unit labor requirements.

Input-output (I-O) analysis deals with interindustry transactions generated by the demand for final products. An I-O model permits one to understand the structural interdependencies that exist across the economy. Using this method an analyst can show the total expansion (or contraction) in output (or employment) in all industries as a result of the change in output in the final processing sector (Bendavid 1974: chap. 7; Miernyk 1965: chap. 3). I-O analysis traces the direct and indirect effects of a change in final demand. The direct effect is the labor in the industry needed to produce the industry's own output, while the indirect effect is the labor in all other industries needed to produce the final processing sector's output.

A 1981 I-O model by Economic Consulting Services analyzed the fiber, textile, and apparel industries as an interrelated production complex, a set of industries that are linked together by a large volume of interindustry sales and purchases. According to this model, $30.5 billion in final demand for apparel in the domestic economy created 463,009 jobs outside of the complex (in other manufacturing sectors, finance, services, and distribution) and 1,449,245 jobs in sectors closely tied to apparel (mainly fiber and textile production) (Economic Consulting Services 1981). Thus for every additional $1 million in final demand for apparel, the economy generated approximately 450 jobs within the complex and 150 jobs in other manufacturing and service sectors. By inference, imports in 1984 of − $11,391.1 million had an employment price of approximately 500,000 jobs in apparel and textiles and 170,000 jobs in other manufacturing and service sectors.

Keesing and Wolf (1983) estimated the indirect job loss in textiles that was caused by apparel imports. From their analysis it appears that, omitting shipments within the apparel sector, purchases from the textiles industries were equivalent to 29 percent of the value of the apparel sold. Using I-O counterfactually, Keesing and Wolf argue that if apparel imports from developing countries had not taken place, the net employment-creation effect might have been a 3–4 percent increase in textile employment, or 29,000 additional jobs. The implication of their analysis (1980: 115–116) is that one job is lost indirectly in textiles for every four or five jobs lost directly in apparel. To portray comprehensively the true employment effect of imports, of course, the indirect employment effect must be summed over all sectors in the economy. This suggests that the loss of apparel production from domestic locations threatens jobs in other parts of the economy that are indirectly linked to domestic apparel manufacture. The important strategic point is that jobs lost in apparel because of bankruptcies or offshore production may not have the same employment effect as jobs lost because of, for instance, intensive automation. In the first instance, both direct employment and indirect employment would be lost. In the second instance, automation, which would undoubtedly displace thousands of apparel workers, would at the same time preserve linked jobs by keeping the production of apparel, and therefore the demand for ancillary goods and services, in the United States.

I-O analysis has also been used to construct "job opportunities" models. This analytic strategy is based on estimating the number of domestic jobs that would have been required to produce the same dollar value of imports. Using a 367-sector I-O model, Aho and Orr (1981) estimated that between 1964 and 1975 trade reduced employment opportunities in apparel by 103,000, a decline of 87,000 job opportunities in apparel and 16,000 in supplier industries. Moreover, the industries most adversely affected by trade employed "more women and minorities and their work forces were less skilled than industries that benefited most from trade. In addition, workers in the adversely affected industries had lower earnings and were more likely to have a family income below the poverty level than those in trade enhanced industries" (Aho and Orr 1981: 34).

Using a seventy-nine-sector I-O model, the U.S. International Trade Commission (1986b) estimated the labor content of merchandise trade for the years between 1978 and 1984. In this analysis the labor content of U.S. imports (that is, the labor required to produce all intermediate inputs in the traded good) is assumed to be the labor inputs that would be required to make the same dollar amount of the domestic substitute. Labor content thus estimates the change in domestic labor demand, or the change in job opportunities, associated with imports. Over the period, the ITC study estimated that trade reduced job opportunities in the apparel industry by 225,800 work-years.

While apparel was consistently one of the industries with the largest total labor content of imports over the last two decades, the job opportunity studies probably understate the loss of job opportunities in apparel. If imports are priced much lower than domestic output,[4] then estimates of the domestic labor requirements needed to produce an equivalent dollar amount of imports will significantly understate the labor content of imports. The International Ladies' Garment Workers' Union research department has developed a technique to convert import prices of apparel into prices for comparable output produced in the United States (International Ladies' Garment Workers' Union 1985).[5] Based on this adjustment, the labor content of imports would be approximately double the one presented by the ITC (U.S. International Trade Commission 1986b: 118).

A final way to measure the employment lost in the United States is to look at the employment gained in developing countries that have substantial apparel industries. Obviously, this is a crude indicator, but it does illustrate the magnitudes involved and the shifting geography of apparel employment. The International Labour Organization (1980b: 27) comments that:

> While employment has been declining in the industrialized countries, it has taken a sharp leap upwards in certain countries where the manufacture of clothing for export has increased in recent years. In Singapore, the number of workers employed in the clothing industry more than doubled between 1970 and 1978, rising from 12,698 to 32,792 workers. Employment indices in the industry were 185.3 for Hong Kong (1970 = 100) and 153.3 for the Republic of Korea in 1976.

Obviously, the most significant limitation in using this type of data is that productivity differences affect the rate at which workers in developing countries can directly replace apparel workers in developed countries. And because estimates of comparative productivity differ enormously, it is difficult to use this indirect method to estimate the domestic employment effect of imports. On the one hand, the International Labour Organization (1980b) reports that production per worker in various less developed countries varied from 80 percent of the European rate in Hong Kong or Morocco to more than 100 percent of the U.S. rate in Mexico and South Korea. On the other hand, the AAMA, the industry's trade group, argues that "while U.S. wage rates are often five times [or twelve times] the rates paid in LDC's, U.S. productivity is normally 35% to 100% greater" (American Apparel Manufacturers Association 1984: 30).

While one might justifiably be skeptical of trade association data, the unreliability of productivity estimates, whatever the source, make any assessment difficult. The U.S. Bureau of Labor Statistics considers its own productivity figures on the domestic apparel industry so unreliable that it does not publish them. Because of the internationalization of production there is always a great risk of double counting output. In the United States the partial assembly of garments offshore means that some output is probably double counted, first as an import under USTU 807 and USTU 807A, and then again as domestic output (Brand 1987).[6] Even style changes can change productivity measures; short skirts, for instance, have shorter seams than long ones, and thus reduce sewing time per garment. Similarly, untailored and loosely structured clothing also require less labor per garment (Mankoff 1987). The organization of the labor process, the structure of the payment system, the nature of the labor force (for example, the use of children's labor), and the degree of coercion exercised in the workplace all affect productivity measures. Cross-national comparisons founder on each of these issues. In regard to productivity estimates, skepticism is justified.

In summary, analysts generally agree that trade has reduced domestic employment in the apparel industry. If one assumes—somewhat artificially—that trade and productivity growth are unrelated, then the effect of trade on employment has been less important than productivity growth as a cause of job loss. With those conservative assumptions, imports reduced employment by 1 to 2 percent annually from the mid-1960s through the mid-1970s. Conclusions based on I-O analysis define a much broader range of employment effects, ranging from a low estimate of 100,000 to a high of 500,000 from the mid-1970s to the mid-1980s, a period of intense import penetration.

The Costs of Job Loss

After assessing the magnitude of job loss that is attributable to trade, the question becomes what happens to those who lose their jobs? The Canadian Department of Industry, Trade and Commerce's Labour Force Tracking Project (1980) studied this issue by looking at the initial duration of a spell of unemployment of displaced workers. Clothing and textile workers represented 47 percent of the sample of 9,626 workers who were displaced. Among the clothing workers, 25 percent left the labor force following separation from their jobs. Initial periods of unemployment for laid-off apparel workers were longer for women than for men, and the mean period of initial unemployment was twenty-one weeks for male workers and thirty-one weeks for female workers.

The U.S. data on wage change, while not broken down by industry, indicated that 53 percent of the men and 60 percent of the women earned less after the first job change than they had before it (Corson et al. 1979). Table 4–9 reports the U.S. Department of Labor estimates of the value of net earnings losses over three years resulting from job loss in the apparel industry. The estimates distinguish between those workers who were permanently separated from their jobs and those who were recalled from a layoff. This report implies that income loss, after taking government assistance into account, was relatively small, amounting to $5,600 over three years. It is important to recognize, however, that this estimate applied a 3 percent real discount rate to apparel workers' earnings.

Table 4–9. Mean Discounted Present Value of Earnings Losses of U.S. Apparel Workers.

	Never Recalled by Employer	Recalled by Employer	Total
Earnings losses	10,800	2,100	4,400
Benefits			
Unemployment insurance	2,900	800	1,400
Trade adjustment assistance	2,300	900	1,300
Net Loss	5,600	400	1,800

Source: Corson et al. (1979).

Trade and the Unions

Particularly in the last decade, international trade in apparel has eroded the domestic employment base. The affect of trade on the apparel unions is less clear. The erosion of union membership predates the industry's import problems. Between 1973 and 1985 membership in the International Ladies' Garment Workers' Union (ILGWU)—the prime organizers of workers in the women's and children's apparel industry—fell by 51.2 percent, twice as quickly as total apparel employment. Moreover, the rate of unionization in the women's and children's apparel segment of the industry dropped by almost 20 percent, far outstripping the contraction in the national slump in unionization (Silvia 1987: 17). It is important to recognize, though, that the membership base of the Amalgamated Clothing and Textile Workers Union (ACTWU) and the ILGWU began to shrink largely in response to the shifting geography of industry employment.[7] It is also important to note that, while not altering this basic trend toward less organization of the apparel work force, imports have contributed to the declining strength of the unions.

One attempt to model the factors influencing ILGWU membership concluded that imports alone account for a statistically significant share of the decline in membership (Kahn 1986). Kahn specified two models to explain the decline in membership in the ILGWU. The first specification of the model was essentially a political model. It posited that the change in ILGWU membership was a function of the change in consumer prices, changes in unemployment rates in manufacturing, and the strength of the Democratic Party in the U.S. House of Representatives. The alternative model was an explicitly economic one. It explained change in membership as a function of imports as a proportion of industry value-added, the substitutability of capital for labor, and the ratio of labor costs to total costs. For those who imagine that unions have a lasting and effective connection with the Democratic Party, it may be surprising to learn that the political model had very little explanatory power. The economic specification, on the other hand, was quite convincing. Indeed, Kahn concluded that "if *only* imports are included in the regression, 25 percent of the variance in the change in union membership is explained" (Kahn 1986: 283).

Imports damaged the unions by intensifying competition between domestic union and nonunion firms. Accelerated competition for shrinking domestic markets took several forms, all of which undermined unionization rates and the unions' efforts to organize new shops. Nonunion shops were able, for example, to cut the piece rate and reduce production costs, while union firms could not because they were bound by collective bargaining agreements that fixed the rate for the life of the contract. Higher cost union firms, less able than their nonunion competitors to cut production costs quickly, were the first to go out of business. And in a domestic political climate hostile to unions, employers that adopted militant union-busting approaches threw up an almost impenetrable wall to union organizing efforts (Starobin 1986). Overall, the surge of imports into the domestic market added one more factor to an already unfavorable set of circumstances confronting the apparel unions.

MANAGED TRADE IN APPAREL

National policy has sought to control the growth of textile and apparel imports for the last two hundred years. Beginning with the Tariff Act of 1816, which justified protection on the basis of protecting an infant industry from import-created market disruption, negotiated trade in fibers, textiles, and clothing has been standard practice. And since the Tariff Act of 1930, tariffs on textiles and apparel have remained higher than those on other manufactured goods. The tariff wall surrounding these sectors arose from the economic and political importance of textiles and apparel in the United States and the industries' greater import sensitivity as compared with more capital-intensive industries. Yet high tariffs, estimated to be 20 percent on average (OECD 1983), have failed to stave off domestic job loss and declining market share.

In 1961 and 1962 two multilateral agreements were negotiated: the Short-Term Agreement (STA) and its successor, the Long-Term Agreement (LTA). The LTA remained in effect for five years and was renegotiated to extend through 1973. While the LTA was in effect, imports of cotton textiles products grew rapidly, from 310 million pounds in 1962 to 564 million pounds in 1973. U.S. production during the same period fell from 4.2 to 3.7 billion pounds, and the overall import penetration level reached 15 percent by 1972 (Nehmer and Love 1985).

The most recent attempt to deal with growing imports, although not with the proliferation of producers and products, is the Multifiber Agreement (MFA). The MFA has been in effect since 1974, and covers textiles and apparel made of cotton, wool, manmade fibers, and, since August 1, 1986, other vegetable fibers such as linen, ramie, and silk blends. At that time the MFA was extended, for a third time, for five years through July 1991. The MFA's purpose is to allow signatories to negotiate bilateral agreements between themselves and other countries to regulate trade in textiles and apparel. The twenty-five bilateral agreements currently in force impose some restraints on American imports.

In addition to bilateral limits, the MFA authorizes unilateral action against imports that disrupt or threaten to disrupt the domestic market. Article 3 specifies that the minimum restraint level may be set only at the level of actual imports or exports during the calendar year ending two months prior to the request for consultation. Moreover, in almost all cases import surges must have occurred *before* consultations take place. Thus, the MFA will not (and most likely, cannot) limit imports. Rather, it tries to manage the growth of trade in textiles and apparel. It provides for a minimum annual growth rate of 6 percent for the specific products covered by bilateral agreements. The U.S. market, however, has been growing well below this minimum for some years. This indicates that imports captured a rising share of the domestic market, even when they stayed within the MFA growth limits. The import problem had two additional dimensions, neither of which was explicitly acknowledged by the existing trade regime: the number of supplying countries was increasing, and the number and value of products were growing.

The structure of the MFA presented foreign producers whose imports approached the bilateral limits with incentives to circumvent the limits or, more threateningly, to move out of controlled into uncontrolled product categories, which frequently contained higher value and more fashion-sensitive products. The People's Republic of China exemplifies the first incentive. When China approached its quota on wool sweaters, its producers hired subcontractors in Hong Kong, a country that had not yet filled its wool sweater quota, to assemble pieces of wool sweaters that were knit at home. Although the United States filed a complaint, it was heard by the enforcement body established by the MFA only after the sweaters were imported.

The second incentive is more threatening to U.S. producers and workers in the long run. It results from the use of quotas instead of tariffs as the implementation mechanism in the MFA. Quotas measure import penetration by quantity—poundage or thousands of dozens of articles of clothing. By not controlling the value of imports, as a tariff would, the MFA implicitly encourages producers to move into higher value products per unit of controlled quantity. The changing composition of imports under the MFA regime is consistent with this interpretation. Between 1962 and 1978 the value of apparel imports increased by 121 percent, from sixty-three cents to $1.72 per square yard equivalent (SYE). The increase in the wholesale price index for the same period was only 105 percent (Arpan et al. 1982: 64). This trend accelerated under the MFA: between 1970 and 1977 the SYE value of apparel increased by 114 percent, while the wholesale price index increased by only 76 percent (Arpan et al. 1982: 64). Factoring in the exchange rate effect shows that some of the escalation in the price per SYE may have resulted from import prices increasing relative to domestic prices, especially at the end of the period. Nevertheless, it is clear that the major reason for the increased value per unit of quantity is that, since the early 1970s, foreign suppliers have shifted from textiles toward higher value apparel. Indeed, ". . . apparel accounted for 41 percent of the total 1970 poundage of U.S. cotton, wool and man-made products covered under bilateral agreements fiber imports and 42 percent in 1974. This ratio then rose to approximately 62 percent by 1982" (Nehmer and Love 1985: 245).

Of course, the domestic textile industry is not free of import disruptions. On the contrary, the reduction of market share for domestic apparel producers directly reduces demand for domestic fiber and yarn. As Nehmer and Love (1985: 246) point out, "the decline of U.S. textile production, as measured by U.S. textile mill consumption of fibers, from 11.1 billion pounds in 1974 to 10.1 billion pounds in 1982, roughly matches the rise of total textile apparel imports from 0.9 billion pounds to 1.7 billion pounds during the same period."

The MFA, then, has not substantially slowed import penetration or market disruption in apparel. From 1982 to 1985 imports of MFA-regulated products increased by 62 percent. Unregulated products also proliferated. Foreign producers began to use new fiber blends that were unregulated (linen, ramie, and silk, for instance) or fabrics that blend regulated fibers (cotton and wool, for example) with unregulated fibers to keep the proportion of regulated fiber in the garments below the MFA limit. Garments that are 49 percent cotton, for example, are exempt from the MFA, while garments that are 50 percent cotton are subject to regulation. While the most recent round of MFA negotiations brought some unregulated blends under the purview of the MFA, the general problem continues and the incentive to shift production into unregulated categories persists.

The effectiveness of the MFA hinges on how governments negotiate and enforce their rights and obligations under bilateral agreements. A significant quantity of U.S. imports is subject to restraints imposed by bilateral agreements. In 1982, for example, 72 percent of all American textile and apparel imports were covered by bilateral agreements (Nehmer and Love 1985: 243). Yet these controls regulate only the most import-sensitive products, a relatively small number of product lines (Nehmer and Love 1985: 261).

CORPORATE STRATEGIES

Despite the pervasiveness of managed trade, the future of the domestic apparel industry hinges on two decisions: the political one about protection and the economic one about automation. One outcome is clear for labor: employment will continue to decline. Indeed the crucial employment question concerns the thousands of related jobs that exist because there is apparel production in the United States. For the industry as a whole, three outcomes are possible: continuing protection, continuing erosion of apparel and its linked employment because of the quiet abandonment of apparel manufacturing by domestic firms, or a substantial breakthrough in automation that will reduce direct employment in apparel but sustain related employment in the United States.

Continuing Protection

The high rate of job loss in the apparel industry during a period of intense protection leads to the simple conclusion that the abolition of managed trade would result in an enormous loss of jobs in the United States—a conclusion that unifies free trade advocates and protectionists. Keesing and Wolf (1980: 154) of the Trade Policy Research Centre estimate that the job loss in the U.S. apparel industry under free trade would reach 570,000 jobs by 1990. And as I argued earlier, protection in the form of bilateral agreements does not guarantee employment stability; it only slows the rate of job loss. It is conceivable, of course, that a stronger and more effective system of trade management could be developed. For now, however, this is unlikely because of the Reagan administration's hostility toward congressional legislation that would limit the share of the market available to imports. But even in a more hospitable political climate, countervailing interests will counteract the effectiveness of protection, thus assuring the slow erosion of domestic employment and production in apparel. Support for free trade will come from a variety of sources. Retailers and importers will demand free trade in the interest of the higher profits imports provide because of their higher retail markup (Parsons 1987a). Developing countries will oppose protection in the interest of securing desperately needed foreign exchange and of forwarding their economic development strategies. Export-oriented U.S. firms, principally the suppliers of military hardware and advanced technology, will support open markets in apparel as the necessary quid pro quo for access to foreign markets. And finally, the strategic interests of the United States will militate against wholly effective protection (Gilpin 1987): the importance of China to U.S. economic and military interests is one example of the conflict between the protection of a domestic industry and the perceived international interests of the United States.

The Continuing Erosion of Employment

A more likley scenario is the continuation of some manner of rather leaky protection, accompanied by a series of corporate decisions by domestic apparel firms that will result in the erosion of domestic employment in apparel and, as important, the loss of jobs in other sectors that exist because apparel is produced in the United States. The decisions U.S. firms are now making fall into two related categories: (1) whether to compete on the basis of cost by moving production abroad, through either subcontracting or using wholly or partially owned Item 807 plants or (2) whether to abandon competition as apparel manufacturers in favor of competing as designers, distributors, and merchandisers of apparel, much of which is made outside the United States.

Off-shoring Production. Needless to say, domestic firms that choose to engage in price competition with low-wage producers must seek out low-cost, high-productivity locations. Table 4–10 shows the nominal labor cost differential among LDC producers as compared with the United States—a differential that ranges from 5 percent of U.S. wages in China to 32 percent in Hong Kong. As argued above, one should be skeptical of productivity estimates. Here it is sufficient to note that all analysts agree that the wage gap persists even when adjustments are made. Company data cited by de la Torre et al. (see Table 4–11) show

Table 4–10. Apparel Industry Wage Rates in Selected Countries.

	1975			1982		
	Hourly Wage	Wage and Fringe	Index	Hourly Wage	Wage and Fringe	Index
United States	3.20	4.00	100	5.20	6.50	100
Far East						
Hong Kong	0.80	0.55	24	1.80	2.05	32
Taiwan	0.50	0.60	15	1.50	1.75	27
Korea	0.35	0.45	11	1.00	1.25	19
Singapore	0.45	0.65	16	0.90	1.35	21
Philippines	0.20	0.25	6	0.40	0.50	8
China	0.12	0.15	4	0.20	0.30	5
Latin America						
Jamaica	—	—	—	0.75	0.95	15
Costa Rica	0.30	0.40	10	0.60	0.80	12
Haiti	0.15	0.20	5	0.30	0.40	6
Other countries						
Portugal	0.95	1.20	30	1.20	1.50	23
Egypt	0.20	0.35	9	0.40	0.55	8

Source: U.S. Department of Labor.

Table 4–11. Effective Labor Costs in the Apparel Industry, 1978.

	Wage and Benefits ($/hr.)	Productivity Rating (U.S. = 100)	Effective Labor Costs	
			($/hr)	(U.S. = 100)
United States	4.50	100	4.50	100
West Germany	5.50	95	5.79	129
Japan	3.75	70	5.36	119
Hong Kong	1.10	90	1.22	27
Taiwan	0.77	80	0.96	21
Singapore	0.80	70	1.14	25
South Korea	0.60	80	0.75	17
Dominican Republic	0.60	60	1.00	22

Source: de la Torre et al. (1984: 71).

productivity-adjusted wage differences in the range of 20 to 25 percent of U.S. wages. The competitive problem this wage gap presents becomes clear upon examining the effect of nominal labor costs on total production costs. Table 4–12 breaks down the cost components as a proportion of the total cost of production by alternative production locations. According to this table, the "best" U.S. production methods could compete with offshore production. "Best," however, is difficult to define since both variable costs (material and labor) and fixed costs (overhead and so on) decline. Indeed, it appears that the anticipated cost savings come from shifting some share of production costs onto workers in the form of lower wages and onto material suppliers in the form of lower prices. Nonetheless, when compared to typical U.S. production costs, offshoring offers a cost advantage of 4.7 to 7.2 percent. Table 4–13 details production costs for two kinds of men's sports shirts manufactured in different locations. Asian production sites yielded a landed cost advantage of 6 to 29 percent, depending on the product.

Public policy reinforces the economies of offshore production. Item 807 of the Tariff Schedule of the United States provides an incentive for domestic firms to produce offshore. Under Item 807 imported goods that are assembled in foreign countries from U.S.-manufactured

Table 4–12. Cost Comparison of Men's Woven Polyester/Cotton Dress Shirts.

Cost Component	Production Location			
	U.S. Typical (%)	U.S. Best (%)	807 Caribbean	Far East
Material	48.6	46.3	48.4	39.3
Labor (cut, sew, finish, excesses, indirect labor, and fringes)	40.3	35.0	18.5	12.1
Factory overhead, other costs, and contractor margins (duty, freight, insurance, brokerage fees, profit)	11.1	10.2	8.1	3.3
	—	—	20.3	35.4
Total	100.0	91.4	95.3	92.8

Source: American Apparel Manufacturers Association (1984).

Table 4–13. Price Estimates for Fancy Sport Shirts, 1983.

Woven, 65% Polyester/35% Cotton, Yard-dyed, Long Sleeve, Two Pockets	Made in Own Plant	U.S. Contractor	807 Contractor	Korean Contractor	Sri Lankan Contractor	Taiwanese Contractor
Fabric	na	2.38	—	1.94	2.07	1.88
Labor and overhead	na	5.46	—	1.62	1.77	2.21
Total F.O.B.	6.92	7.84	—	3.56	3.84	4.09
Duty: 271/2% + $.19/lb.			0.00	1.06	1.12	1.19
Other importing costs			0.00	0.32	0.49	0.42
Total importing costs			0.00	1.38	1.61	1.61
Landed $ cost per unit	6.92	7.84	6.27	4.34	5.45	5.70
% of own price	100	113	91	71	79	82
100% Cotton, Yard-dyed, Long Sleeve, Two Pockets						
Fabric	3.00	3.00	na	2.58	2.52	1.96
Labor and overhead	3.25	5.24	na	1.83	1.93	1.00
Total F.O.B.	6.25	8.24	na	4.41	4.45	2.96
Duty: 21%				0.93	0.93	0.62
Other importing costs				0.41	0.49	0.15
Total importing costs				1.34	1.42	0.78
Landed $ cost per unit	6.25	8.24	6.59	5.75	5.87	3.74
% of own price	100	132	105	92	94	50

Source: American Apparel Manufacturers Association (1984: Table V-5).

na = not available.

components are subject to duty only on the value of the imported product less the value of the U.S.-fabricated components. Only the value that is added to the U.S. components is dutiable when the product is reimported into the United States (U.S. International Trade Commission 1986a: 1–1). Under Item 807, U.S. apparel firms can export fabric for sewing, hemming, stitching, or any other operation that does not change the form of the exported component.

Imports of most textiles and apparel under Item 807 are subject to quantitative restraints under the MFA. Duty-free treatment and quotas have both been liberalized, however, under the Caribbean Basin Economic Recovery Act, commonly referred to as the Caribbean Basin Initiative (CBI), implemented January 1, 1984. When the CBI program was originally announced, President Reagan had stated his intention to provide more liberal quota treatment for CBI textile and apparel imports. On February 20, 1986, he announced a new "special access program" to liberalize quota treatment on imports on apparel and made-up textiles such as bed linens. The program is designed to provide CBI countries with greater access to the U.S. market for their products entered under Item 807 that have been assembled with fabric that has been produced and cut in the United States. The twenty-two CBI countries have been invited to conclude bilateral agreements with the United States that will permit guaranteed levels of access for their qualifying apparel and textile products. These levels will be separate from the quotas applicable to textile and apparel products not assembled completely with textiles made and cut in the United States.

The use of Item 807 increased steadily during the 1960s and reached a plateau of 8 to 10 percent of total U.S. apparel imports in the late 1970s as the growth Item 807 imports fell below the rate of growth for all imports (International Labour Organization 1980b: 15) (see Table 4–14). Between 1982 and 1985 imports of textiles, apparel, and footwear under Item 807 increased by 80 percent, to $1.17 billion, although in the aggregate, Item 807 continued to represent a small proportion of total imports. Nonetheless, Item 807 is significant in terms of employment, accounting for 95 percent of the labor content of production that is exported and reimported. This is because sewing operations, the most labor-intensive part of apparel production, are sent abroad (Starobin 1986).

Between 1982 and 1985 one-half of the growth of Item 807 apparel imports was generated by the two largest suppliers, Mexico and the Dominican Republic. Imports from Mexico rose by 82 percent and those

Table 4–14. U.S. Imports of Apparel under Item 807: Market Value in Foreign Countries ($ millions).

Period	Total Imports	Item 807.00 Value	807 Imports as Percent of Total Imports
1965	578.2	1.7	0.3
1966	628.1	6.4	1.0
1967	687.5	12.2	1.8
1968	863.0	24.0	2.8
1969	1,079.1	40.5	3.8
1970	1,247.7	50.4	4.0
1971	1,502.5	69.3	4.6
1972	1,859.4	95.0	5.1
1973	2,118.5	141.0	6.7
1974	2,313.6	238.3	10.3
1975	2,630.6	253.3	9.6
1976	3,635.6	292.5	7.9
1977	4,338.4	327.9	7.6
1978	5,353.5	418.9	7.8
1979	5,469.4	476.7	8.7
1980	6,007.9	524.0	8.7
1981	7,361.3	596.3	8.1
1982	8,092.4	564.1	7.0
1983	9,547.6	638.4	6.7
1984	13,322.1	794.6	6.0
1985	14,840.4	964.3	6.5

Source: International Ladies' Garment Workers' Union (1985) and U.S. International Trade Commission (1984).

from the Dominican Republic increased by 78 percent during that period. These two countries, along with Haiti and Costa Rica, accounted for two-thirds of Item 807 imports of apparel in 1985 (see Table 4–15).[8] Even before the inception of the CBI program, the largest share of Item 807 imports came from countries in Central and South America and the Caribbean (General Agreement on Tariffs and Trade 1984: 104).

Despite the rise in Item 807 imports, they continue to represent a minor element of total imports (see Table 4–14). After peaking at 10 percent in 1974, the share of Item 807 imports declined 4 percent by 1984. And CBI, which affected the composition of Item 807 supplier

Table 4–15. Item 807 Imports of Cotton, Wool, and Man-made Fiber Textiles by Area, 1983–1986 ($ millions).

Area	1983	1984	1985	1986
CBI countries[a]	0[b]	427	551	672
Mexico	0[b]	254	280	319
Europe	0[b]	16	17	20
Hong Kong	na	31	30	23
Taiwan	na	7	8	11
Korea	na	7	14	11
All others	0	37	50	48
Total	0	779	950	1,104

Source: U.S. International Trade Commission (1986a).

[a]Dominican Republic, Costa Rica, Haiti, Honduras, Belize, Guatemala, and Barbados.

[b]Less than $500.

na = not available.

countries, did not affect the share of imports under the Tariff Schedule Item. In addition, with a few exceptions, Item 807 imports account for only a small percentage of total imports across most product categories (see Table 4–16). Body-supporting garments, trousers, and shirts and blouses accounted for two-thirds of total Item 807 imports in 1985 (U.S. International Trade Commission 1986a).

Domestic manufacturers of brassieres depend upon Item 807, using factories and workers in low-wage countries (principally the Philippines, Mexico, the Dominican Republic, and Costa Rica) to assemble and, sometimes, package brassieres for retail sale. The importance of Item 807 for this industry segment has led to a round of direct foreign investment in 807 plants. In the Philippines, one of the largest 807 suppliers in this product line, the factories were developed under U.S. financing and control (U.S. International Trade Commission 1986a: 4–6). In dramatic contrast to all other apparel segments, Item 807 imports of body-supporting garments account for 70 to 80 percent of total imports. In no other industry segment do Item 807 imports constitute such a large share of total imports.

In contrast, the use of Item 807 by manufacturers of trousers, slacks, and shorts has increased twice as fast as total trouser imports between 1982 and 1985, and, because trousers contain more fabric than most apparel articles, the duty-free value of Item 807 imports increased by

Table 4-16. Ratio of 807 Imports to Total Imports for Selected Articles, 1982–1985.

Article	1982	1983	1984	1985
Body-supporting garments	83.0	79.7	74.3	77.2
Trousers, slacks, and shorts	7.3	7.3	9.2	10.8
Shirts and blouses	4.5	4.2	4.3	4.5
All apparel	7.0	6.7	6.0	6.5

Source: U.S. International Trade Commission (1986a).

173 percent over the same period. Yet Item 807 imports accounted for only 10.8 percent of total trouser imports in 1985. The most notable change in this category was in the source of Item 807 imports. Because of the special treatment accorded Item 807 imports assembled from U.S.-made and cut textiles, all but a small part of this increase in trouser imports under Item 807 came from the CBI countries.

Item 807 imports of shirts and blouses also surged, rising 190 percent between 1982 and 1985. But since total imports rose at the same pace, the Item 807 share of total imports remained stable. And unlike trousers, the duty-free value of shirts and blouses was only about 50 percent of the total value, compared to approximately 66 percent of all other apparel items. This difference arose from the minor use of U.S.-fabricated components in Item 807 shipments from Hong Kong, Taiwan, and South Korea, which together accounted for 25 percent of the Item 807 imports in 1985. "The shirts entered under Item 807 from the 'Big Three,' which accounted for less than 2 percent of their total shirt shipments of almost $2.3 billion in 1985, reportedly are manufactured from foreign-made and -cut materials, except for certain U.S.-produced findings such as buttons" (U.S. International Trade Commission 1986a: 4–7).

To date, firms' experiences with Item 807 have been mixed, which probably explains its limited growth. For example, Casualwear, Inc., a small women's wear producer, invested in a joint venture in Haiti in the mid-1960s. After one year it found that extremely low wages ($1 per day) could not compensate for low productivity and high turnover. The cost per Haitian unit produced and shipped to the United States was 90 percent of its American cost. Soon afterward Casualwear moved to a twin plant that straddled the Mexican-U.S. border. By sewing and assembling 20 to 30 percent of its output in Mexico, Casualwear was able to lower its average costs while maintaining better marketing services than a foreign exporter inexperienced and uncomfortable with foreign production (Parsons 1987b). At the same time, some large apparel companies, many of which produce standard commodity products like men's dress shirts, underwear, and brassieres, have mastered the use of 807 plants. Manhattan Industries, Philips-Van Heusen, Warnaco, and Kellwood (all among the fifteen largest U.S. apparel firms) import 30 percent of their total requirements from offshore assembly or subcontracting abroad—they do not own the facility in either case, but simply supply the cut fabric and provide some technical assistance (de la Torre 1978: 95). Overall, however, it is unlikely that Item 807 will ever represent a substantial share of imports.

Abandoning Manufacturing. Subcontracting production is another strategy available to domestic firms. In reality, extensive subcontracting means that domestic apparel firms move out of the manufacturing sector and become design, marketing, and distribution companies. In women's outerwear this trend is clear. Between 1977 and 1982, women's outerwear manufacturers declined by 35 percent, while jobbers and contractors increased by 52 and 26 percent respectively (U.S. Congress 1987: 62).[9]

The corporate strategy, of which subcontracting is the manufacturing aspect, involves competing on the basis of product differentiation rather than price. Liz Claiborne, the world's largest women's apparel company, with estimated sales of nearly $220 million in 1983, is an excellent example of the merchandising strategy. The company does not manufacture any of its merchandise: it contracts out 100 percent of its designs and then markets them to the country's top department and specialty stores. By sourcing designs that comply with its fabric and quality specifications, the company does not tie up its own capital and can market its goods at competitive prices, while offering a highly diverse line. Liz Claiborne utilizes over seventy suppliers in the United States and abroad. Approximately 68 percent of the company's products are manufactured outside the United States, mainly in Hong Kong, Korea, and Taiwan (First Manhattan Co. 1983).

The combination of product identification and low-cost production locations has worked well for other apparel firms as well. One of the most dramatic stories is Puritan Fashions' agreement to launch a line of jeans under the signature of Calvin Klein with massive advertising support. Likewise, Palm Beach, an old and staid men's suit company, began to emphasize innovation and designer products in the early 1970s. Among its early successes was acquiring the Evan Picone name for a line that targeted white-collar working women. The company's sales doubled to $230 million from 1973 to 1978, its earnings increased six-fold, and its return on equity of 25 percent was three times the industry average (de la Torre et al. 1978: 92).

For diversified firms that possess a strong brand name, a merchandising strategy is an attractive competitive strategy. The risk that a firm runs with a nonmanufacturing strategy is that it will be placed in a competitive squeeze. On one side, pressure will come from domestic retailers who are both able and willing to hire designers, to act as their own jobbers and subcontractors, and even to market clothing under store-cum-designer labels. On the other side are foreign subcontractors who can enter the design and marketing end of the business. Even more threatening is the abundant supply of easy-to-copy styles. Indeed, the very overnight success of new entrants into the apparel merchandising business—the Liz Claibornes, Esprits, and Jordaches—indicates the volatility of the market and the ease with which brand names are overthrown.

To overcome this risk and to reap the advantages of producing close to the market, there are signs that domestic firms are using undocumented female labor to construct a domestic putting out system, thus reaping the "advantage" of cheap labor while maintaining proximity to the market. In metropolitan areas with large pools of undocumented immigrant labor—Los Angeles, New York, Chicago, and San Francisco—the employment of workers at subminimum wages and without minimal protections like Social Security, unemployment insurance, and workmen's compensation is a burgeoning part of the industry. It is difficult to estimate the magnitude of this practice. The Federal Reserve Bank of Dallas (Hill and Pearce 1987) estimates that 10.5 percent of all "illegal alien employees" are employed in the apparel industry and that 39 percent of the apparel industry's work force is composed of undocumented workers, making the apparel industry one of the largest participants in what could be called the "underground labor market." In addition to the small apparel establishments there is also a growing number of homeworkers. In Chicago, for example, ten or so major dress and sportswear manufacturers subcontract to seamstresses who work at home. While this practice exists in a statistical void insofar as government employment data are concerned, estimates of homeworkers range from several hundred to several thousand in Chicago alone. In San Francisco, where apparel production employment is very small according to the government data, one can hear the whir of sewing machines throughout Chinatown and watch non-English speaking Asian women entering and leaving buildings carrying the paraphenalia of their trade. For the women workers in the new putting out system wages approach Third World levels. One woman who works at home reported that she received "50 cents a shirt [and that] it takes a half hour to do a shirt" (Goozner 1987: 5).

The putting out system offers domestic apparel manufacturers a solution to a competitive dilemma: quick turnaround is becoming a crucial basis for competition, but, because of the labor intensity of production, labor rates remain an inescapable part of price competition. So producers must now compete on the basis of price and style: the first requires low-wage labor; the second, proximity to the market.

Automating Production

Firms that remain apparel manufacturers and also want to capture the competitive advantage of producing close to the market must face the wage disparity issue head-on. Automating production is the most obvious strategic choice, but it is a double-edged strategy that would overcome the competitive problem of labor-intensive production but also guarantee the elimination of domestic production employment in the industry. It would, however, keep production located in the United States and therefore continue to generate demand for linked goods and services and maintain labor demand in those linked sectors (Cohen and Zysman 1987).

Technical innovation in apparel is following two tracks. On one track is what one industry executive called the search for "a mechanical Puerto Rican," an offensive remark that captures in a phrase the Taylorist approach to organizing the industry's labor process. In cooler terms, the automation of apparel must reduce labor intensity while maintaining a firm's ability to shift its product mix rapidly; the machinery must be flexible. On the other track is a still inchoate effort to establish Quick Response (QR) production. In broad outline, a QR strategy calls for a shorter manufacturing cycle, lower inventories, more frequent reorders, and a faster flow of information between retailers, manufacturers, and suppliers.

The objective here is not to analyze the possibilities and limitations of the automation of production in apparel in detail.[10] It is necessary to note, however, that the traditional industrialized production of apparel is a multistage activity (preassembly, assembly, and finishing) in which material handling constitutes 40 to 60 percent of total costs and 80 percent of the total manufacturing time (General Agreement on Tariffs and Trade 1984: 51). Aside from the automatic sewing machine, an epochal innovation that made industrialized sewing feasible, innovation has not come quickly. Indeed, the most significant innovations have affected the pre-sewing stage (the grading, marking, and cutting of fabric). Computerized grading systems, which automatically cut patterns of various sizes; automatic fabric spreaders; computerized marking machines; and several types of innovative fabric cutters have restructured pre-assembly operations in ways almost unimaginable ten years ago. Yet the result of these innovations has been double-edged. They affect a stage of the production process that accounts for less than 5 percent of total labor costs, yet at the same time, they affect the most highly skilled members of the industry's work force. These innovations have little effect on the wage gap problem, and reduce labor requirements for the industry's most skilled production workers.

Sewing and fabric handling remain the major barriers to automation and the source of the industry's labor intensity. And while labor costs do differ among producers, based on the complexity of the garment, sewing constitutes 90 percent of total labor costs (General Agreement on Tariffs and Trade 1984: 51). Automating sewing is the critical issue. Since the late 1960s a stream of incremental innovations has rationalized the sewing process, reduced the skill requirements of operators, increased sewing speeds, and enhanced the uniformity of sewing operations. But all of these innovations taken together—including the advent of numerically controlled sewing machines—has not altered the central place of sewing machine operators in the industry's occupational structure, which remained essentially unchanged between 1977 and 1983 (see Table 4–17).

CONCLUSION

Neither internationally managed trade in apparel nor a range of production and merchandising strategies is likely to halt the erosion of the domestic employment base in the apparel industry. A trade deficit of almost $18 billion in 1986 and the loss of 700,000 jobs since 1960 summarize the industry's plight: low-wage nation competitors continue

Table 4–17. Percentage Distribution of Occupational Employment in the Apparel Industry, 1977, 1980, and 1983.

	1977	1980	1983
Total Employment	1.3 mil	1.3 mil	1.1 mil
Managers and officers	3.41%	3.6%	3.11%
Professional and technical	1.12	1.40	1.53
Service	1.27	1.20	1.16
Production	83.61	83.21	83.92
Pressers, hand	3.52	3.53	1.28
Pressers, machine	1.77	1.73	2.68
Nonworking supervisor	2.17	1.96	2.70
Inspector	2.65	2.23	
Sewing machine operator, garment	47.82	47.09	49.83
All-around tailor	.25	.17	na
Patterncutter	.11	.13	.95[b]
Patternmaker	.31	.30	na
Spreader	1.09	1.02	na
Marker	.38	.35	na
Folder	1.24	1.36	na
Clerical	8.73	9.14	8.60
Shop clericals[a]	3.93	4.05	3.34
Sales	1.39	1.45	1.67

Source: U.S. Department of Labor (1980, 1982, 1985) and unpublished U.S. Bureau of Labor Statistics data.

[a]Includes production clerks and coordinators, shipping packers, shipping and receiving clerks, shade-ticket markers, and all other plant clericals.

[b]Includes patterncutters and patternmakers.

na = could not be determined because of occupational reclassification.

to capture an expanding share of the domestic market, and domestic employment continues to contract. This is a severe, and growing public policy problem because the workers who have been and will continue to be displaced are uneducated, minority women—many of them undocumented workers—who are likely to experience long spells of unemployment and have difficulty moving into growing economic sectors. And neither macroeconomic adjustment of the exchange rate nor international management through the Multifiber Arrangement appears capable of turning the situation around.

Formal economic accounts of the affect of trade on domestic employment find that in the early 1960s through the early 1970s, changes in aggregate demand and productivity growth were more important determinants of the contraction of employment than imports were. These studies are in keeping with the relatively small trade deficit over this period. Yet the persuasiveness of these studies falls short; they assume the independence of events that were surely interdependent—the growth of productivity and the growth of imports. The I-O studies are more convincing. Quite importantly, I-O includes both the direct and indirect employment effects. Moreover, I-O models note that the decline in domestic labor demand reduced "job opportunities" for disadvantaged workers even in the 1960s and early 1970s. From the 1970s to the present, the apparel industry has experienced one of the most severe contractions in job opportunities of any domestic manufacturing sector, a deficit of 220,000 to 500,000 work-years.

Presently, no strategy has been developed that will solve the industry's competitive problems. A level of protection that would reserve the domestic market for the domestic industry—either through congressional legislation or through tightening the enforcement of the MFA—seems unlikely. The use of partial offshore production by domestic producers, while successful for some industry segments, represents a small and relatively stable share of total imports. Even automation is a long shot. Larger firms are subcontracting direct manufacturing functions, while focusing on design, acquisition of materials, and distribution. As a result, production employment is growing in subcontracting establishments and in the domestic underground labor market of sweatshops and homework as it shrinks in traditional manufacturing establishments. Optimism is unwarranted. International trade in apparel has pushed the employment outlook for female, minority, poor, badly educated, and non-English speaking workers from bad to worse.

NOTES

1. For an excellent history of managed trade in apparel see Aggarwal (1985).
2. To some extent, the erosion of earnings is a direct result of the location decisions of apparel firms. In the post–World War II period, U.S. apparel manufacturers, seeking low-wage nonunion labor, shifted production from the Northeast to the Southeast and then to the West and Southwest. Wage differentials were significant. For example, a trained

cutter—one of the most skilled jobs in the industry—earned between $4.36 and $5.33 an hour in 1977 in any northern state. The same worker in a southeastern or a south central state earned between $3.71 and $4.63 an hour—that is, 80 to 85 percent of the equivalent northern wage. Differences in the rate of unionization tell the same story. In 1977, the apparel industry was 90 percent unionized in the North, 33 percent in the South, and 44 percent in the West. As a consequence of the regional shift, apparel employment in the North dropped by 80 percent immediately after World War II. Even over the last decade, the difference in rates of job loss among regions is staggering, down 30 percent in the North compared with 8 percent in the South and West.

3. The consumer price index for apparel rose from 1967 = 100 to December 1986 = 210.9, compared to the index for all items, which rose from 1967 = 100 to December 1986 = 331.1. The producer price index for industrial commodities showed the same trend. Textile products and apparel rose from 1967 = 100 to December 1986 = 211.0. The index for total industrial commodities rose from 1967 = 100 to December 1986 = 309.3.

4. This claim usually applies to goods before wholesale and retail markups. Presumably, goods of the same quality sell at the same retail price.

5. The ILGWU no longer uses this method to estimate import penetration. Instead of calculating conversion factors for the value of imports, the ILGWU (1987) now calculates total consumer demand for apparel in wholesale value terms. Imports are then equal to domestic demand net of the value of shipments of domestically produced apparel.

6. Economists at the U.S. Bureau of Labor Statistics are attempting to construct a productivity measure that will overcome some of these problems. At this point, however, they are uncertain about the measure's reliability and do not know whether it will produce publishable data. In any event, the measure will only apply to men's and boys' suits and coats; the ubiquity of sweatshops and homework in the women's wear segments makes it unlikely that the Bureau will be able to develop reliable productivity measures for them (Brand 1987).

7. See note 2.

8. Some of the steepest growth in imports was from South Korea, the fifth largest supplier of Item 807 shipments, from which imports rose 386 percent during 1982–1985. Unlike all other suppliers, whose shipments consisted primarily, if not almost exclusively, of apparel, however, Korea's shipments were mostly of footwear.

9. Manufacturers perform all operations pertaining to the production of garments. Jobbers control design, acquire material, and arrange for sale but perform no manufacturing functions. Contractors receive cut materials and assemble them into finished garments.

10.   For an analysis of the automation of apparel production see Parsons (1987a and 1987b) and Hoffman (1985).

REFERENCES

Aggarwal, Vinod K. 1985. *Liberal Protectionism: The International Politics of Organized Textile Trade.* Berkeley: University of California Press.

Aho, C. Michael, and James A. Orr. 1981. "Trade-sensitive Employment: Who Are the Affected Workers?" *Monthly Labor Review* 104, no. 2 (February): 29–35.

American Apparel Manufacturers Association (AAMA). 1984. *Apparel Manufacturing Strategies.* Arlington, Va.: AAMA.

Arpan, Jeffrey, et al. 1982. *The U.S. Apparel Industry: International Challenge, Domestic Response.* Atlanta: College of Business Administration, Georgia State University.

Balassa, Bela. 1979. "The Changing International Division of Labor in Manufactured Goods." World Bank Staff Working Paper No. 329. Washington, D.C.: The World Bank, May.

Barmash, Isadore. 1987. "Garment Industry in a New Squeeze." *New York Times.* September 25.

Bendavid, Avrom. 1974. *Regional Economic Analysis for Practitioners.* New York: Praeger Publishers.

Brand, Horst. 1987. Supervisory economist at U.S. Bureau of Labor Statistics, Office of Productivity and Technology. Telephone interview with the author. September 11.

Canadian Department of Industry, Trade and Commerce. 1980. *A Report on the Labour Force Tracking Project: Costs of Labour Adjustment Study.* Ottawa: Department of Industry, Trade and Commerce.

Cohen, Stephen S. and John Zysman. 1987. *Manufacturing Matters: The Myth of the Post-Industrial Economy.* New York: Basic Books.

Corson, Walter, Walter Nicholson, David Richardson, and Andrea Vayda. 1979. *Survey of Trade Assistance Recipients.* Washington, D.C.: Department of Labor.

Council of Economic Advisers. 1987. *Economic Report of the President.* Washington, D.C.: U.S. Government Printing Office, January.

de la Torre, José, Michael Jay Jedel, Jeffrey S. Arpan, E. William Orgam, and Brian Toyne. 1978. *Corporate Responses to Import Competition in the U.S. Apparel Industry.* Atlanta: College of Business Administration, Georgia State University.

———. 1984. *Clothing Industry Adjustment in Developed Countries.* London: Trade Policy Research Centre.

Economic Consulting Services. 1981. "The Dependency of the United States Economy on the Fiber/Textile/Apparel Industrial Complex." Mimeograph. November 12.

First Manhattan Co. 1983. *Liz Claiborne Basic Report.* September.

Frank, Charles. 1977. *Foreign Trade and Domestic Aid.* Washington, D.C.: Brookings Institution.

General Agreement on Tariffs and Trade. 1984. *Textiles and Clothing in the World Economy.* Geneva: GATT, May 4.

Gilpin, Robert. 1987. *The Political Economy of International Relations.* Princeton, N.J.: Princeton University Press.

Goozner, Merrill. 1987. "Home Sewing Thrives amid Controversy." *Chicago Tribune.* September 13, sec. 7, p. 1.

Hoffman, Kurt. 1985. "Clothing, Chips and Competitive Advantage: The Impact of Microelectronics in the Garment Industry." *World Development*, 13, no. 3.

International Labour Organization. 1980a. *Contract Labour in the Clothing Industry.* Second Tripartite Meeting for the Clothing Industry. Geneva: International Labour Organization.

————. 1980b. *The Employment Effects in the Clothing Industry of Changes in International Trade.* Geneva: International Labour Organization.

International Ladies' Garment Workers' Union Research Department. 1985. "Estimation of Apparel (Knit and Woven) Imports: Methodological Note." Mimeograph. New York: ILGWU, January 18.

————. 1987. "Import Penetration in the Apparel Industry: A Technical Study." Prepared for the Fiber, Fabric and Apparel Coalition for Trade. Mimeograph. New York: ILGWU, September.

Kahn, Shulamit. 1986. "Trends in Union Membership in the Postwar Period: The Case of the ILGWU." Industrial Relations Research Association Series. *Proceedings of the Thirty-eighth Annual Meeting.* December 28–30, 1985. New York.

Keesing, Donald B., and Martin Wolf. 1980. *Textile Quotas against Developing Countries.* Thames Essay No. 23. London: Trade Policy Research Centre.

Krueger, Anne. 1979. *LDC Manufacturing Production and Implications for OECD Comparative Advantage.* Cited in International Labour Organization, *The Employment Effects in the Clothing Industry of Changes in International Trade.* Geneva: International Labour Organization, 1980.

Mankoff, Walter. 1987. Assistant Research Director, International Ladies' Garment Workers' Union. Telephone interview with author, September 21.

Miernyk, William H. 1965. *The Elements of Input-Output Analysis.* New York: Random House.

Nehmer, Stanley, and Mark W. Love. 1985. "Textiles and Apparel: A Negotiated Approach to International Competition." In Bruce R. Scott and George C. Scott, eds. *U.S. Competitiveness in the World Economy.* Boston, Mass.: Harvard Business School Press.

Organization for Economic Cooperation and Development (OECD). 1983. *Textile and Clothing Industries: Structural Problems and Policies in OECD Countries*. Paris: OECD.

Parsons, Carol A. 1987a. "Flexible Production Technology and Industrial Restructuring: Case Studies of the Metalworking, Semiconductor and Apparel Industries." Unpublished Ph.D. dissertation, University of California, Berkeley.

––––––. 1987b. "Technological Innovation and the Changing Labor Process in a Traditional Industry." Paper presented at the 1987 Annual Meeting of the American Political Science Association, Chicago, Ill., September 3–6.

Rosensweig, Jeffrey A. 1986. "The Atlanta Fed Dollar Index and Its Sub-Indexes." Federal Reserve Bank of Atlanta Working Paper 86-7, August.

Sable, Charles. 1982. *Work and Politics: The Division of Labor in Industry*. Cambridge, Mass.: Cambridge University Press.

Silvia, Stephen J. 1987. "Unions, Industrial Relations Systems and Crisis: The Impact of Sectoral Decline on West German and American Apparel Unions." Paper presented at the 1987 Annual Meeting of the American Political Science Association, Chicago, Ill., September 3–6.

Starobin, Herman. 1987. Chief Economist, ILGWU. Telephone interview with the author, December 21.

U.S. Bureau of the Census. *County Business Patterns*. Various issues.

U.S. Congress. Office of Technology Assessment. 1987. *The U.S. Textile and Apparel Industry: A Revolution in Progress—Special Report*. OTA-TET-332. Washington, D.C.: U.S. Government Printing Office, April.

U.S. Department of Commerce. 1984. *U.S. Industrial Outlook, 1984*. Washington, D.C.: U.S. Government Printing Office.

––––––. 1987. *U.S. Industrial Outlook, 1987*. Washington, D.C.: U.S. Government Printing Office.

U.S. Department of Labor. Bureau of Labor Statistics. 1980. *Occupational Employment in Manufacturing Industries, 1977*. Bulletin 2057. Washington, D.C.: U.S. Government Printing Office, March.

––––––. 1982. *Occupational Employment in Manufacturing Industries*. Bulletin 2133. Washington, D.C.: U.S. Government Printing Office, September.

––––––. 1985. *Occupational Employment in Manufacturing Industries*. Bulletin 2248. Washington, D.C.: U.S. Government Printing Office, December.

U.S. International Trade Commission. 1984. *Imports Under Items 806.30 and 807.00 of the TSUS, 1979–1982*. Publication 1467. Washington, D.C.: ITC, January.

U.S. International Trade Commission. 1986a. *Imports Under Items 806.30 and 807.00 of the Tariff Schedules of the United States, 1982–85.* Report on Investigation No. 332–237, Under Section 332(b) of the Tariff Act of 1930. Publication 1920. Washington, D.C.: ITC, December.

———. 1986b. *U.S. Trade-Related Employment: 1978–84.* Publication 1855. Washington, D.C.: ITC, May.

5 TRADE AND EMPLOYMENT IN AUTOMOBILES
The Short-Run Success and Long-Run Failure of Protectionist Measures

Robert E. Scott

The U.S. auto industry has struggled for the past fifteen years. The oil price shocks of the 1970s led to increased demand for small, efficient cars, which domestic firms were unable to sell at their usual rate of profit. They have found it difficult to counter the competitive success and rapid market share growth of Japanese small car makers. Environmental and safety regulations have significantly increased the cost of building and operating cars sold in the United States. Thus in the 1970s and 1980s, the U.S. auto industry has experienced steadily rising imports, declining industry employment, and periodic profit crises.

Despite these problems, the domestic industry remains strong, although it no longer dominates the U.S. market. U.S. manufacturers face little competition in large car markets, except for the most expensive luxury vehicles. They possess distribution and service networks and have established reputations that will make it difficult for newcomers to penetrate large car markets. Furthermore, U.S. automakers are earning substantial profits and have the financial and technological ability to adapt rapidly to changed market conditions, as is shown by the recent introduction of several successful new cars.

I thank the Berkeley Roundtable on International Economy (BRIE) and the Hudson Institute's Herman Kahn fellowship program for research support.

While the outlook for U.S.-based producers may be favorable, the prospects for domestic employment opportunities are less sanguine. The literature that is reviewed in this chapter shows that the growth of automotive imports over the past fifteen years has significantly eroded job opportunities. In the future, U.S. firms must respond to the competitive threat posed by Asian-based producers—who have developed the ability to build equivalent (or better) small cars at a lower cost than U.S. firms—if they are to avoid further loss of market share and profits. While all of the ways in which domestic firms can adapt will reduce total labor demand in this sector, employment losses can be minimized by increasing the competitiveness of domestic assemblers and parts-supplying industries. Offshoring of parts production, direct foreign investment by Japanese assemblers, and direct importing of cars by U.S. firms will all result in greater employment losses in the U.S. auto industry than would occur if production were retained in more efficient domestic firms.

In response to the rapid growth of imports and the loss of domestic jobs in this industry, the United States opted for trade protection in the early 1980s. The Japanese government agreed to a series of VRAs, which limited their auto exports to the United States, and the U.S. government imposed a substantial tariff increase on Japanese small pickups. The literature shows that while these policies did reverse the industry's profit slump in the early 1980s, they were also very costly for consumers. In addition, this chapter suggests that trade protection did not substantially improve the long-run competitiveness of U.S. auto producers; it also helped other foreign producers to increase their penetration of the U.S. market. An effective trade policy would have taken into account the effects of the oligopoly structure of the industry, the role of its trade union, and the special characteristics of production technology in this sector.

Trade protection for the auto industry should be designed to improve the competitiveness of domestic producers in order to help maintain employment levels in this sector. The industry must resist the temptation to earn excessive profits through unnecessary price increases if it is to become competitive. Domestic firms seem unwilling or unable to competitively price on their own when given trade protection. U.S. automakers used the VRAs to raise prices, especially for larger models (where there was less competition), and to keep prices high for small cars. Thus a public agreement between the industry and the government, with price restraint standards and enforceable penalties for noncompliance, appears necessary.

An effective agreement would also include labor representatives in the bargaining process and would incorporate incentives to raise productivity levels and improve the quality of domestic products. The key to improving productivity and quality levels is to bring labor and management together to work out strategies for reorganizing production, eliminating arbitrary job definitions, and incorporating new technologies in the most effective ways possible. Organization is the critical component of this process. Many studies have shown that the Japanese productivity advantage is the result of new or better ways of arranging production, rather than deeper capital investment or more sophisticated production technology. Historical prohibitions on labor participation in production management have limited the rate at which new forms of organization have been adopted in the U.S. auto industry.

The VRAs did not include mechanisms to encourage price or profit restraint on the part of the domestic producers or to bring together the participants in the industry in cooperative efforts to improve competitiveness. An effective trade policy would have required commitments from each stakeholder in the industry; each would have been required to make sacrifices for the common good of the industry. Auto workers might accept a cut in their real wages if they knew that the industry was also going to reduce profits and that salaried workers and management were also going to accept wage reductions. They might agree to further cuts in the numbers of job categories if there were a joint plan for reducing employment through attrition or if workers were enticed to leave because more effective job training programs were ordered. Incentives for productivity improvement would rise if significant profit-sharing included production workers, not just management employees. With the rise in imports that occurred in 1985 and 1986, as the VRAs were relaxed and the newly industrializing country producers entered the market, the pressure for renewed import protection for the auto industry increased. The lessons that were learned from trade protection in the early 1980s should not be ignored in future policy debates.

An analysis of the effects of trade on motor vehicle employment begins with a review of the industry's structure. The first section of this chapter describes the prevailing patterns of employment and output and also examines the factors that have influenced the competitive status of domestic auto producers, including manufacturing cost differences, exchange rate fluctuations, and shifting patterns of demand. Accounting-type studies, which measure the labor content of trade and consider its importance relative to other factors, are then reviewed. The chapter goes on to consider the effects of recent trade protection measures. The literature on the VRAs ignores the long-run effects of the dramatic increase in the prices of domestic small cars in 1980 and the other indicators of declining domestic competitiveness, and thus underestimates the number of job opportunities saved by trade restraints. In response, new estimates of the effects of the protectionist measures are developed. The chapter concludes with a discussion of future trends in auto industry trade and employment patterns.

THE STRUCTURE OF THE U.S. MOTOR VEHICLE INDUSTRY

Direct employment in motor vehicles assembly and parts production reached an all-time peak in 1978 of 1,123,000 persons,[1] 5.5 percent of total manufacturing employment (Bureau of Labor Statistics 1985a). Approximately two indirect job opportunities are created for each person employed in the motor vehicle industry (Bureau of Labor Statistics 1985b). Thus more than 3 million people were directly and indirectly employed in U.S. production of new vehicles in 1978. Direct employment in the industry fell to fewer than 800,000 persons in 1982; it then recovered to 982,000 in 1985. A steep, secular decline in employment began in the late 1970s. Total direct employment grew by about 1.5 percent between 1973 and 1978, but declined by about 12 percent between 1978 and 1985 (all cyclical peaks).

The industry is heavily unionized and workers are comparatively well paid. In 1983 production worker average hourly earnings were $12.12, 37 percent above the average manufacturing wage in that year (Bureau of Labor Statistics 1985a). If benefits are included in the calculation, the disparity is even larger. Total compensation per hour was $19.02 in the motor vehicle industry, about 55 percent higher than the manufacturing average (Crandall 1984).

Hourly earnings in the auto industry were rising between 1970 and 1977, both in real terms and relative to the manufacturing average. Between 1977 and 1984 real earnings were quite stable, averaging about $11.75 per hour (in real 1982 dollars). Average real earnings in the manufacturing sector were also stationary over this period; the ratio of auto to manufacturing wages was essentially constant throughout the 1977–1984 period.

Some authors (for example, Kreinin 1984) tend to focus exclusively on high-production worker wages as the cause of the auto industry's competitive problems. However, analysis of the MCD (discussed below) suggests that a number of factors contribute to the domestic industry's problems, including white-collar labor costs, productivity levels, materials costs, and quality problems. In 1979, when Japan's car sales were in their most rapid growth period, the average Japanese small car list price was $750 higher than that of domestic small cars. Costs (and wages) were not the only factor in the success of Japanese imports.

Vehicle production has historically been concentrated in the Great Lakes region of the United States, with a few assembly plants located on the East and West coasts. However, most of the West Coast plants have closed and a few plants have opened in the South in recent years. Even within these regions, production is concentrated within just a few states. Half of all U.S. employment in vehicle assembly in 1984 was located in the state of Michigan. Seventy percent of employment in this sector was located in just four states (Michigan, Missouri, Ohio, and Wisconsin).[2] As the fortunes of the domestic auto industry have declined, these states have been particularly hard hit.

Employment in domestic vehicle production depends on overall levels of auto demand, the shares of domestic producers in U.S. and world markets (and, recently, on the amount of U.S. production by foreign-owned firms), and trends in the structure of the production process. The nature of auto demand in the United States and some of the underlying determinants of market shares and firm behavior will be reviewed in the remainder of this section.

Shifting Patterns of Vehicle Demand and Rising Imports

The U.S. motor vehicle market is the largest in the world. Despite the effects of the energy and environmental crises, the U.S. auto market was stable or growing in the 1970s and 1980s. The future pattern of demand for autos, a critical determinant of output and employment in the domestic industry, has been the subject of several recent studies.[3] The consensus view is that, on average, the number of vehicles sold in the United States will exhibit a constant or rising trend in the future. This chapter addresses both car and truck production because small trucks (the bulk of all trucks sold) are close substitutes for cars, use many common parts, and are produced by the same industry, referred to here as the auto industry. The number of new vehicles (cars and trucks) sold appears to have leveled off in recent years, averaging 13.4 million units per year over the 1974–1978 business cycle and only 12.9 million over the 1979–1986 cycle.[4] However, the industry encountered a set of unique problems in this period. Altshuler et al. (1984) suggest that, on average, the number of vehicles sold will exhibit a constant or increasing trend in the future.

Although the average size of the domestic market for new vehicles has shown no significant trend over the past fifteen years, domestic producers have been losing market share in the 1970s and 1980s for several reasons. First, the energy price shocks of 1973 and 1978 increased the demand for small, fuel-efficient vehicles. Between 1970 and 1973 the small car share of the number of autos sold in the United States averaged 30.8 percent.[5] From 1974 to 1976, following the first oil crisis, the small car share rose to an average of 43.5 percent. From 1976 to 1978, the years preceding the second round of OPEC oil price increases, the average small car share remained roughly constant at 43.9 percent. Higher gasoline prices then sent the small car share up to 55.8 percent over the 1979–1981 period. With the decline in gasoline prices in the early 1980s, the share of small cars declined to about 50 percent.

The Japanese share of the U.S. auto market, shown in Figure 5–1, increased with each jump in gasoline prices. Between 1970 and 1973 Japanese auto imports (all small cars) averaged 6.1 percent of the total U.S. market. After the 1973 oil embargo, their share rose to 9.3 percent between 1974 and 1976. Their share growth continued between 1976 and 1978, when they averaged 12.5 percent of the market. The growth in Japanese imports then accelerated after the second oil price hike to average 20.0 percent between 1979 and 1981. After 1980 Japanese vehicle exports to the United States were limited by U.S. trade restraints. Thus the growth of Japanese imports is at least partially explained by the shift in demand patterns to small cars. However, import share data also suggest that several other factors were at work.

First, note that the market share of Japanese firms increased substantially during the 1976–1978 period, when there was no appreciable growth in the overall share of small car sales. Furthermore, Figure 5–1 shows that during this period, the dollar lost more than one-third of its value against the yen, raising the delivered cost of Japanese imports. It is also informative to compare Japanese import performance during the two large upswings in small car demand, after the oil price shocks of the 1970s. After 1973 the small car share grew by 12.7 percentage points. Japanese imports captured about one-quarter of this share growth. After 1978 the small car share grew by 11.9 percentage points.

Figure 5-1. Exchange Rate Levels and the Japanese Share of the U.S. Auto Market.

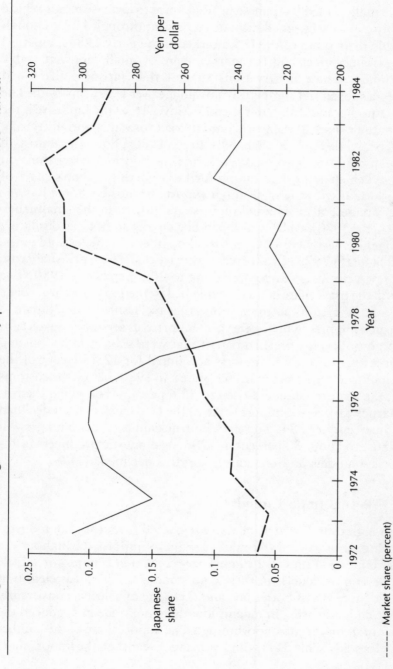

----- Market share (percent)
——— Exchange rate (annual average)

Source: U.S. International Trade Commission (1985c); *International Financial Statistics.*

Japanese imports captured about two-thirds of the share growth in this period. Finally, in 1980 Japanese firms planned to increase motor vehicle assembly capacity by an additional 20 percent through 1983, enough to double their share of the U.S. market in the early 1980s, a period when gasoline prices and the market share of small cars were stable or declining. These observations suggest that Japanese firms had achieved a substantial competitive advantage over U.S. firms by the late 1970s. Another indication of the competitiveness of the Japanese is the fact that their share of the world auto market rose substantially during the 1970s (while the U.S. share fell). In the 1980s, however, almost all European countries also imposed formal or informal restrictions on Japanese vehicle imports, limiting further growth in Japan's share of the world market, at least through exports from their home base.

The Japanese also achieved rapid share growth in the small truck market in the 1970s, which was expanding rapidly at the time, displacing additional domestic labor. Of the total number of vehicles sold in the United States in 1972, 19.4 percent were trucks. The truck share rose to 26.8 percent in 1978, before falling to 20.0 percent in 1980. The decline in the truck share is largely explained by the 1979 shift in gasoline prices and by a 1980 customs ruling that reclassified most Japanese small truck imports (which were then imported as separate chassis cabs and cargo bodies) as finished trucks that were subject to an existing 25 percent tariff. In 1972 imports accounted for 12.7 percent of the number of trucks sold in the United States. In 1980, before the customs ruling, the import share had risen to 33.6 percent. Following the ruling on truck tariffs, the import share of the U.S. truck market declined to 25.8 percent in 1984. The share of trucks in total demand grew in the 1980s, to about 30 percent in 1986, as domestic producers introduced new models and real gasoline prices declined.

Recent Import Trends

Even though overall vehicle demand remained firm, the U.S. industry was losing employment and market share to imports throughout the 1970s. Tables 5–1 and 5–2 summarize recent trends in motor vehicle trade. Several tendencies in these data stand out. First, it is clear that net trade (in terms of both units and the value of sales) is consistently negative and increasing in magnitude; therefore trade has reduced the number of domestic job opportunities. The import share of the number of vehicles sold (Table 5–1) is higher in every year than the import share

Table 5–1. U.S. Motor Vehicle Trade: Quantities Exchanged and Share of Apparent Domestic Consumption, 1970–1984 (in thousands of units).

Year	Domestic Consumption Quantity	German Imports Quantity	Share	Japanese Imports Quantity	Share	All Sources of Imports Quantity	Share	Net Trade (X–M) Quantity	Share
1970	10,003	675	6.75%	408	4.08%	2,179	21.78%	–1,795	–17.94%
1971	12,941	771	5.96	788	6.09	2,826	21.84	–2,338	–18.07
1972	13,518	677	5.01	857	6.34	2,818	20.85	–2,282	–16.88
1973	14,704	677	4.60	785	5.34	2,763	18.79	–2,102	–14.30
1974	12,183	620	5.09	1,034	8.49	2,975	24.42	–2,163	–17.75
1975	10,447	370	3.54	837	8.01	2,370	22.69	–1,504	–14.40
1976	13,586	350	2.58	1,385	10.19	3,024	22.26	–2,144	–15.78
1977	15,020	423	2.82	1,571	10.46	3,319	22.10	–2,412	–16.06
1978	15,718	416	2.65	1,931	12.29	3,768	23.97	–2,882	–18.34
1979	14,135	496	3.51	2,014	14.25	3,683	26.06	–2,711	–19.18
1980	11,130	339	3.05	2,475	22.24	3,863	34.71	–3,096	–27.82
1981	10,865	234	2.15	2,368	21.79	3,589	33.03	–2,910	–26.78
1982	10,072	259	2.57	2,157	21.42	3,623	35.97	–3,143	–31.21
1983	12,420	240	1.93	2,301	18.53	3,945	31.76	–3,293	–26.51
1984	14,544	335	2.30	2,515	17.29	4,586	31.53	–3,846	–26.44

Sources: U.S. Department of Commerce (1986); U.S. International Trade Commission (1985c).

Table 5-2. U.S. Motor Vehicle Trade: The Value of Sales and Shares of Apparent Domestic Consumption, 1972–1984 (in billions of 1982 dollars[a]).

Year	Domestic Consumption Value	German Imports Value	German Imports Share	Japanese Imports Value	Japanese Imports Share	All Sources of Imports Value	All Sources of Imports Share	Net Trade (X–M) Value	Net Trade (X–M) Share
1972	101,951	3,043	3.0%	2,912	2.9%	14,308	14.0%	−10,574	−10.4%
1973	110,786	3,642	3.3	3,067	2.8	15,370	13.9	−10,723	−9.7
1974	91,115	3,465	3.8	3,996	4.4	16,681	18.3	−10,841	−11.9
1975	83,600	2,545	3.0	3,496	4.2	14,857	17.8	−7,658	−9.2
1976	109,515	2,537	2.3	5,550	5.1	18,265	16.7	−11,223	−10.2
1977	126,737	3,311	2.6	6,793	5.4	20,495	16.2	−13,284	−10.5
1978	134,515	3,852	2.9	9,688	7.2	24,467	18.2	−17,172	−12.8
1979	121,279	4,060	3.3	10,064	8.3	23,307	19.2	−15,182	−12.5
1980	92,327	3,834	4.2	11,737	12.7	23,776	25.8	−17,253	−18.7
1981	94,629	2,790	2.9	12,057	12.7	23,159	24.5	−17,114	−18.1
1982	90,153	3,173	3.5	11,107	12.3	24,664	27.4	−20,107	−22.3
1983	114,246	3,303	2.9	12,063	10.6	27,462	24.0	−22,110	−19.4
1984	119,383	4,219	3.5	13,632	11.4	33,261	27.9	−27,408	−23.0

[a]Nominal trade values (U.S. International Trade Commission 1985c) were converted to constant 1982 dollars using GNP-implicit price deflators for the United States (Council of Economic Advisors, 1986). The GNP deflator was chosen over the motor vehicle industry price indices because the industry indices are adjusted for changes in the quality of cars sold, which eliminates the price effects of such features as safety devices and pollution controls. Changes in the real value of output, and hence employment, are best determined by using an unbiased price index such as the GNP deflator. The value of sales by domestic producers was estimated by summing the value of product shipments from SIC 3711 (motor vehicles and car bodies) and SIC 3713 and 3716 (truck and bus bodies). SIC 3715 (truck trailers) was omitted because heavy trucks are not included in the trade data series used above.

Sources: U.S. Department of Commerce (1986); U.S. International Trade Commission (1985c).

of the value of sales (Table 5–2) because the average import was cheaper than the average domestic vehicle. U.S. producers perform better in the larger, more expensive model lines. However, over this period, import prices appear to be catching up with domestic models. The number of vehicles imported from all sources grew by 67 percent between 1972 and 1980, while the import share of the value of the domestic market increased by 84 percent.

Important country-specific differences in import patterns are apparent in Tables 5–1 and 5–2 and in Figure 5–2. Imports from Japan grew consistently over the 1970–1980 period in both unit and sales-value terms. Japanese sales in the United States exhibit less cyclical variability than does overall domestic consumption. The average real unit value (actual wholesale values divided by the implicit price deflator for the U.S. GNP, Table 5–2) of Japanese imports rose 27.6 percent over the 1972–1980 period, versus 11.3 percent for all vehicles sold in the United States. These data suggest that Japanese assemblers were moving into more expensive product lines in the U.S. market. This process was accelerated by the trade restraints that were imposed in the 1980s on Japanese vehicle exports to the United States. Between 1980 and 1984 average unit value rose 14 percent (in real terms) for Japanese imports.

German exports of cheap small cars to the United States (principally Volkswagens) were displaced by Japanese models in the 1970s. German firms successfully maneuvered the transition to higher valued export cars in this period. The number of German vehicles that were sold in the U.S. market declined steadily throughout the 1970s and 1980s. However, the German share of the value of U.S. sales was roughly constant (Table 5–2). Thus average real unit values for German imports rose by 150 percent over 1972–1980 and another 11.5 percent between 1980 and 1984.

U.S.-Canadian vehicle trade involves a much larger amount of intraindustry product shipment than does U.S.-German or U.S.-Japanese trade. In 1984, 94 percent of all U.S. auto exports (in value terms) were sold to Canada. The U.S. and Canadian motor vehicle markets are almost completely integrated, with production in both countries dominated by the major U.S.-based firms.[6] However, the United States ran a trade deficit with Canada on finished vehicles over the entire 1970–1984 period (Figure 5–1). This was partially offset by a positive trade balance on motor vehicle parts, but on the whole, the U.S. trade balance on all motor vehicle products has generally been negative and has been growing on average in the last ten years. Since 1976 the Canadian dollar

Figure 5–2.   U.S.-Canadian Motor Vehicle Trade Balance.

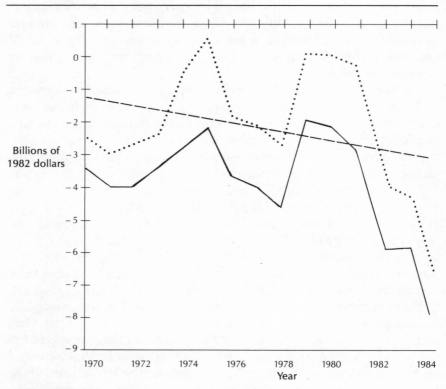

Billions of 1982 dollars

Year

___ Finished vehicles
.... Total auto products
---- Trend of total auto products

Source: U.S. International Trade Commission, (1985c).

has been steadily depreciating against the U.S. dollar, losing about one-third of its value, thus lowering relative production costs in Canada for U.S.-based firms. U.S. firms are responding to the lower value of the Canadian dollar by moving a greater share of North American production to Canadian plants.

The Japanese Cost Advantage

There is wide agreement in the literature that U.S.-based firms cannot produce small cars of comparable quality levels as cheaply as Japanese assemblers can. Toder (1978) estimated that the Japanese were almost cost competitive with United States producers in 1973 (for high-volume production) and had a cost advantage for volumes of under 300,000 units per year of any particular subcompact car. By 1979 the Japanese producers appeared to have gained a $1,500–2,000 per unit cost advantage in small cars. By 1979 the quality of small cars that were sold by Japanese firms was higher than that of domestic small cars that were sold in the U.S. market. The prices of U.S. small cars were lower, on average, than Japanese small cars (Feenstra 1985a, 1985b), and yet domestic manufacturers were losing market share because of the price/quality gap.

Cole and Yakushiji (1984) and Flynn (1982) review all of the published estimates of the size of the MCD in the 1979–1980 period. Their analysis covers ten estimates of the total *manufacturing cost* differential that report MCDs ranging from $1,304 to $2,489. Given an additional cost of $400 for tariff and transportation costs, the average *landed cost* advantage for Japanese producers for a standard subcompact was $1,468 for the ten studies reviewed by Cole and Yakushiji. A recent set of revised estimates of the MCD is presented in Table 5–3.

There have been extensive debates in the literature about the types of estimates that are shown in Table 5–3. The remainder of this section will analyze the components of the MCD, discuss the technical problems associated with its measurement, and the current state of the MCD.

Labor Costs. The labor cost factor in Table 5–3 has received the most attention. Labor costs are usually divided into two categories: differences in wage rates and differences in labor productivity. Flynn (1983) examined four of the above MCD estimates and found that the proportion of the labor cost difference that was attributed to wage rates ranged from 26 percent to 60 percent, while the proportion attributed to labor productivity ranged from 18 percent to 74 percent.[7] Flynn noted that if wages are higher in the United States, then the costs of lower U.S. labor productivity are greater than they would be if wages were the same in both the United States and Japan (and vice versa). He suggests that labor costs be split into three components—wage costs, productivity costs, and joint effects (wage differences multiplied by productivity differences)—thus explaining part of the variation in estimates of the components of the labor cost gap.[8] Flynn revised the labor cost breakdowns for the four MCD studies and derived new estimates of the components of the labor cost gap. These averaged 37 percent labor productivity, 36

Table 5-3.   Estimates of U.S. and Japanese
Manufacturing Costs for a Standard
Subcompact, 1979-1980.[a]

Cost Component	Japanese Cost	U.S. Cost	Cost Difference
Labor costs[b]	$ 878.33	$2,310.91	$1,432.58
Materials	2,143.67	2,969.88	826.21
Selling and advertising	556.00	427.25	(128.75)
Capital	516.00	283.97	(232.03)
Total manufacturing cost	4,094.00	5,992.01	1,898.01
Tariff and transportation[c]	400.00	0	(400.00)
Total landed cost	4,494.00	5,992.01	1,498.01

[a]These estimates are based on a study by Abernathy, Harbour and Henn (1981), which originally estimated a landed cost differential of $1,650. Flynn's revision corrected for a problem by which adjustments were made for differences in model mix and level of vertical integration of U.S. and Japanese firms. Costs are expressed in U.S. dollars, assuming 210-15 yen per dollar.

[b]Includes the effects of both wage rate and labor productivity differences.

[c]Includes only transportation to port of entry. U.S. delivery costs are excluded.

Source: Flynn (1982).

percent wage rates, and 27 percent joint effects, although there is still a wide disparity in these estimates among the individual studies.

Flynn's analysis suggests that labor productivity and wage rates are equally important determinants of the labor cost differential. Flynn (1984) also notes that the disparity between U.S. and Japanese white-collar wages is greater than the wage difference for production workers, and, as a result, about half of the difference in compensation costs in 1980 could be attributed to white-collar wages, while only one-third of U.S. motor vehicle workers held white-collar jobs. This illustrates the importance of separately considering blue- and white-collar labor costs.

Production Worker Wages. Real hourly earnings of U.S. production workers were constant between 1977 and 1984. This section will compare *nominal* wage rates in the United States and Japan, at various exchange rates, to evaluate relative wage levels in the two countries. Changes in the yen/dollar exchange rate and the use of profit sharing in the Japanese compensation system complicate comparisons of relative wages in the two countries. The BLS estimated that in 1983 total hourly compensation (including fringe benefits) of U.S. auto workers was

$19.02 per hour, while their Japanese counterparts earned $7.91 (Crandall 1984). However, the average value of the dollar in 1983 was about 240 yen. By April 1987 the dollar had fallen to 145 yen. At that rate, the comparative hourly costs would have been $19.02 (United States) and $13.09 (Japan) in 1983. By 1987 hourly costs had risen to roughly $23 in the United States and $16.50 in Japan.[9]

The BLS apparently does not include profit sharing in its calculation of hourly compensation costs. Flynn (1984) provides a detailed breakdown for one Japanese producer who had a total hourly compensation of cost $10.80 in 1983 (at 240 yen per dollar). Profit sharing represented $2.57, and other direct and indirect payments equaled $8.23. The latter figure is nearly identical to the BLS total compensation estimate for that year ($7.91). The addition of profit sharing (at 145 yen per dollar) yields a complete estimate of comparative hourly compensation rates of roughly $23 in the United States and $21 in Japan in 1987. Thus the shift in exchange rates has apparently eliminated most of the production worker wage gap.

White-Collar Labor Costs. The ratio of the wages of salaried employees to production workers is much higher in U.S. firms than in Japanese firms. As a result, the fall in the value of the dollar between 1985 and 1987 did not eliminate the white-collar wage gap. In 1980, assuming 240 yen per dollar, white-collar compensation costs were $28.28 per hour in the United States and $12 per hour, including profit sharing, in Japan (Flynn 1984). At 145 yen per dollar, the Japanese white-collar cost was $19.86. Salaried employees represent about one-third of the labor that goes into an auto. In 1987 there was still a significant wage gap between U.S. and Japanese firms at the white-collar level.

Other Cost Factors. The Japanese advantage in the cost of materials reflects both productivity and wage differences (Cole and Yakushiji 1984). The U.S. advantage in selling costs probably reflects scale economies in advertising.[10] Capital cost differences are at least partially explained by differences in rates of return in 1978–1980 (a period of declining profits in the U.S. industry). The use of capital costs for a normal business year in the United States would probably increase estimated capital costs for domestic producers, and the estimated MCD.

Reliability of the MCD Estimates. There are at least three fundamental problems with the kinds of estimates that are shown in Table 5–3. The first is the way in which exchange rate fluctuations affect relative production costs. In recent years the yen/dollar rate has varied widely from the 210–215 level used in Table 5–3, as shown in Figure 5–1. If it is assumed that all of the Japanese production and delivery costs listed in Table 5–3 are paid in yen and that productivity and domestic currency costs remained at their 1980 levels, then estimated landed costs would be equal at an exchange rate of 159 yen per dollar. The fact that the dollar was as low as 145 yen by April 1987 would suggest that exchange rate movements had eliminated the MCD. However, it appears that all Japanese production costs are not paid for in yen; the Japanese obtain an increasing share of parts and materials from Taiwan and other countries whose currencies move with the dollar.[11] Thus the MCD has probably been reduced but not eliminated by recent exchange rate movements.

A second general problem is that the data base that was used for most of the studies of the MCD is quite limited and has not been publicly evaluated. All of the analyses that were reviewed by Cole and Yakushiji are based on either private, firm-specific data or a proprietary data set developed by Harbour.

A third general problem with the literature on the MCD is that it ignores dynamic trends in production costs. Dynamic factors could increase or decrease the estimated MCD. Growth in the average age of Japanese auto workers could lead to rapid relative wage growth because there are strong seniority premia built into the Japanese wage structure. Productivity growth in the U.S. auto industry may have exceeded that in Japan in the past six or seven years. However, Japanese producers may have gone further in sourcing components from low-wage NICs producers.

Manufacturing Costs in 1987. Despite the 1985–1987 fall in the value of the dollar, U.S. producers continue to claim an efficiency disadvantage, and they are pursuing various options designed to improve their competitiveness, including the adoption of new technologies, changes in the organization of production, changes in supplier relationships, and new quality control methods. *Japanese producers still possess a significant cost advantage.* The wage gap has been reduced, but there is little evidence of sufficient productivity growth in the United States to close the gap in the number of hours that it takes to build a typical small car. Japanese producers have diminished the effect of the dollar's fall by switching to suppliers in other countries with lower costs.

Recently, new producers in Korea and Yugoslavia have entered the U.S. market and have had very substantial rates of sales growth. Very little public information is available about the relative costs of production in these countries. However, the prices of their cars are below those of U.S. producers. Domestic firms are now being squeezed on the one hand by Japanese firms that are turning out high-quality products very efficiently and on the other hand by new producers that are making very low-cost, low-quality cars for the bottom of the U.S. market.

TRADE PATTERNS, EMPLOYMENT, AND COMPETITIVENESS

The domestic motor vehicle industry has been challenged by growing competitive problems in a number of market segments. Rising imports have significantly reduced employment opportunities. Several large recessions and price increases for new equipment that is needed to comply with government regulations have also reduced demand for cars and trucks. Rising unemployment and declining profits in the 1970s and 1980s led to a debate about the industry's difficulties (which is reviewed here). Two primary, interrelated issues are discussed. The first is the number of job opportunities that were eliminated in the United States by rising vehicle imports. The second is the relative importance of the effects of trade and the effects of macroeconomic factors on job opportunities. These issues have been addressed in several accounting-type studies.

In 1980 and 1981 the U.S. government responded to the auto industry's problems by imposing a large tariff on most Japanese truck imports (through an administrative measure) and by negotiating the VRAs with the Japanese government, which put a ceiling on auto exports to the United States. These agreements were extended several times and remained in effect in 1987. There is an extensive debate about the effects of the VRAs on employment in and the competitiveness of the domestic auto industry in the 1980s. This discussion revolves around estimates of what domestic output and employment in the 1980s would have been without the VRAs. This literature is then critiqued, and new estimates of the impacts of the VRAs on the U.S. auto industry are presented.

The Effects of Trade on Employment

The U.S. trade deficit in motor vehicles was growing throughout the 1970s and early 1980s, as shown in Table 5–1. At that time there were fewer jobs available than there would have been if vehicle trade had been in balance. One input-output study suggests that between 1970 and 1980, there was an 11 percent decline in the number of domestic job opportunities (about 88,700 work-years) because of the increase in net imports in this industry (Lawrence 1984). The USITC found that if trade had been in balance in 1980, there would have been an additional 170,000 job opportunities in the motor vehicle industry, a 21 percent increase over actual employment levels in that year (USITC 1986).[12] Despite the effects of trade protection, the labor content of trade in the motor vehicle industry rose to 301,000 work-years in 1985.

Input-Output Studies. There are three measures of employment from trade that have been estimated by using input-output techniques. The first is the *direct* effect, which is the number of job opportunities that would have been preserved in the motor vehicle industries if imports had equaled exports in this sector (hereinafter referred to as balanced trade). The second measure is the employment effect of motor vehicle trade in industries that supply parts and materials used to make cars, such as steel and tires (the *indirect* effect). The third measure is estimated by counting up the indirect effects of trade in other industries on output and employment in autos (for example, the effects of a fall in grain exports on the number of trucks sold to grain farmers). Each type of indirect effect has been estimated in at least one of the studies reviewed below. However, since vehicle production is such an important source of demand for the products of other industries, this section will focus on the direct effect and on the indirect effect of trade on employment in parts and materials supplier industries.

The Lawrence (1984) and U.S. International Trade Commission (1986) estimates discussed above include both direct and indirect effects of trade on *vehicle industry* employment. The USITC also evaluated the direct employment content of trade for the years 1978 through 1985. They estimate that 115,000 job opportunities (11.4 percent of industry employment) would have been created in 1978 if there had been balanced trade in vehicles. By 1980 this figure had risen to 125,000 work-years, despite the fact that the value of total domestic auto consumption fell by almost one-third between 1978 and 1980. By 1985 the employment effect of vehicle trade had risen to 219,000 work-years, despite the effects of trade restraints. This is explained, in part, by a shift to higher valued Japanese auto imports that occurred under the VRAs.

An unpublished study from the BLS can be used to estimate the indirect effects of trade on job opportunities in supplier industries. For each work-year of labor content that is embodied in the products of the motor vehicle industry, two additional work-years of employment are required in supplier industries.[13] In 1978, in addition to the 115,000 work-years of direct labor, 232,000 work-years were embodied in the intermediate products that were displaced by net vehicle imports. Thus the total (direct and indirect or supplier industry employment effects) labor content of vehicle trade in 1978 equaled 347,000 work-years, or 39 percent of the labor content of all U.S. trade in 1978. This illustrates the major role played by motor vehicles in the U.S. trade deficit. By 1985 the total labor content of U.S. vehicle imports had risen to 661,000 work-years, but the labor content of U.S. trade grew more rapidly, so the vehicle industry share fell to 24 percent.

Domestic Problems Versus Foreign Trade. One of the most widely quoted input-output studies of the effects of trade on employment is by Lawrence (1984). His work casts doubt on the view that trade is deindustrializing the U.S. economy. He used an accounting framework to allocate changes in value-added and employment in fifty-two manufacturing industries to changes in foreign trade and changes in patterns of domestic demand. Lawrence contends that structural change in employment and output patterns in the United States has been driven by changes in the patterns of domestic demand and that growth in imports played a secondary role in that process. His conclusions are controversial.

Lawrence estimated the direct and indirect effects of trade on employment in vehicle production. He found that over the 1970s, the auto industry was the only sector in which "the employment decline was due to trade and that without trade, employment would have grown" (Lawrence 1984: 60). Between 1970 and 1980 (years that have similar levels of capacity utilization) Lawrence found that total employment in motor vehicles and equipment fell by 1.3 percent, the sum of a 9.9 percent increase due to domestic demand and a 11.1 percent decline due to the change in foreign trade (88,700 work-years).

Despite these results, Lawrence still claims that "even in automobiles, problems stem from domestic sources" (Lawrence 1984: 60). He supports this claim by noting the large decline in U.S. vehicle output between 1973 and 1980. Nineteen seventy-three was a peak output year in autos, and in 1980 the industry was in the midst of a major recession. Lawrence found that between 1973 and 1980, employment fell by 19.2 percent, the sum of a 12.8 percent decrease due to domestic demand and a 6.4 percent decrease due to the change in foreign trade (about 62,500 work-years).

Lawrence's analysis of the 1973–1980 period is analytically flawed. By comparing the level of net trade in a boom year (1973) with that in an extremely depressed year (1980), he overstates the importance of domestic demand in the industry's difficulties and underestimates the effects of trade on employment because the value of imports would have been much larger if 1980 had been a cyclical peak. The debates about the effects of trade on employment are concerned with long-term   ·   secular trends. When analyzing secular trends, it is best to compare cyclical peaks or average import levels over complete business cycles.

A constant share analysis is one way to correct for cyclical effects in order to compare two years that have different levels of capacity utilization.[14] If the import share of the value of motor vehicle sales had remained constant between 1973 and 1980, then the employment content of trade would have been 87,400 work-years lower than it actually was (versus Lawrence's estimate of 62,500).[15] The constant share approach suggests that trade was responsible for a 9 percent decrease in demand for labor between 1973 and 1980, while domestic demand was responsible for a 10.2 percent decrease (compared with Lawrence's estimates of 6.4 percent and 12.8 percent, respectively). Thus, even over this recessionary period, trade appears to be about as important as domestic demand in explaining the decline in domestic auto industry employment.

Problems Common to Input-Output Studies. The input-output studies that were reviewed in this section suffer from the general flaws in accounting-type models that were pointed out by Martin and Evans (1981), Grossman (1982), and Dickens (Chapter 2). First, increased foreign competition can lead domestic producers to adopt new, labor-displacing technologies, making it difficult to distinguish between the employment effects of trade and those of productivity growth. Second, the input-output approach also assumes that imported products are perfect substitutes for domestically produced goods and that the "labor content of U.S. imports of a good are estimated to be the labor inputs that would be required to make the same dollar amount of the domestic substitute" (U.S. International Trade Commission 1986). However, domestic substitutes for imported cars would be more costly (per unit) because more labor is required to produce domestic small cars and wages and the other components of auto production costs are higher in the United States than they are in Japan. As a result, fewer cars would be sold in a protected domestic market (because prices would be higher), but more labor would be required to build each car. The input-output approach can overstate or understate the employment effects of trade, depending on the elasticity of market demand and the relative costs of domestic and foreign production.[16]

Although the assumption that imports could be replaced with domestic substitutes of similar cost is not valid, there is another useful interpretation of the labor content estimates that are derived from the input-output approach. To the extent that the import problem in autos is a result of less efficient production technology in the domestic industry (rather than factor cost problems), these estimates can be interpreted as the employment cost of the technology gap between U.S. firms and foreign competitors. This appears to be an appropriate description of the situation in the 1970s, when significant growth in the share of small cars took place. Japanese producers had concentrated on efficient production of small cars for their home market, while U.S. producers lagged behind in small car production technology. Despite the problems discussed here input-output type measures provide the only complete estimates available of the employment content of trade in this period.

Exchange Rate Effects. A number of studies, discussed in previous chapters, have suggested that the competitive problems of U.S. manufacturing industries in the early 1980s are simply the result of the rise in the dollar. The auto industry's competitive problems began in the 1970s, before the dollar's appreciation began, which suggests that exchange rates are not the only factor in this industry's predicament. However, it is still useful to review the effects of exchange rates on this sector. One recent study has evaluated the effects of movements in the real exchange rates on employment and output in U.S. manufacturing industries in the 1970s and 1980s (Branson and Love 1986). Although this study does not directly estimate the effects of trade on employment, it does provide information about the relative trade sensitivity of employment in the motor vehicle industry.

Between 1977 and 1980, the period of rapid import growth, the value of the dollar was falling. Branson and Love's results indicate that exchange rate effects tended to *increase* employment during this period (despite the fact that overall employment in this industry was declining). Between 1980 and the first quarter of 1985, the value of the dollar (as measured in Branson and Love's study) increased by 54.6 percent. Branson and Love's study suggests that employment fell by 25.7 percent in the motor vehicle industry and by 9 percent in the manufacturing sector as a whole because of exchange rate effects. However, actual employment in the auto industry rose by 11.5 percent over this period. The tendency of exchange rates to depress employment in this period was outweighed by increases in aggregate demand, by the fall in the real price of energy, and by trade restrictions; all of these tended to increase overall employment in the auto industry.

Two conclusions about trade and the auto industry emerge from analysis of Branson and Love's results. First, changes in the value of the dollar were not responsible for the dramatic rise in imports that took place over the 1977–1980 period. Second, the auto industry is much more sensitive to exchange rate effects than the average manufacturing industry is, which reinforces the argument that relative manufacturing costs play a large role in the competitive problems of the domestic auto industry.

Three conclusions emerge from this review of the effects of trade on employment:

1. There would have been 115,000 more direct job opportunities in the vehicle industry in 1978 if trade had been balanced, and 125,000 more in 1980 (an 8.7 percent increase in two years).
2. Vehicle trade has a much larger effect on labor demand in supplier industries than in the industry itself. In 1978 the total (direct and indirect) labor content of vehicle trade was 347,000 work-years, or 39 percent of the labor content of all U.S. trade in that year. By 1985 the total reached 661,000 work-years, despite the effects of trade protection.
3. In the 1970s trade appears to have been the most important factor in the decline of auto sector employment. Lawrence finds that between 1970 and 1980, the growth in net imports had a labor content that was equal to 11.1 percent of industry employment in 1970. Constant share analysis suggests that even when comparing the boom year of 1973 with the 1980 recession, trade and domestic demand contributed almost equally to the decrease in employment. Changes in the value of the dollar did not play an important role in the industry's decline in this period.

The Effects of Trade Protection: 1980–1984

Between 1977 and 1980 the Japanese share of the number of cars that were sold in the U.S. auto market nearly doubled, rising from 11.9 percent to 22.4 percent. In 1980 Japanese firms planned to increase motor vehicle assembly capacity by an additional 20 percent through 1983 (U.S. Department of Transportation 1981: 62), enough to double their share of the U.S. market again in the early 1980s. From 1978 to 1980 the growing recession reduced the total number of autos that were sold in the United States by 23 percent. In the same period the number of Japanese imports that were sold rose by 28 percent, leading to a 30 percent decline in domestic production. Two hundred thirty-eight thousand auto industry workers were on temporary or indefinite layoff in December 1980 (U.S. Department of Transportation 1982). The threat of further extensive job loss in the auto industry led to congressional hearings on a series of protectionist measures (such as local content legislation) and resulted in an agreement between the U.S. and Japanese governments to "voluntarily" restrain the number of Japanese autos exported to the United States.[17] Protection of the domestic truck market was also increased substantially in 1980 through an administrative measure that increased the tariff on Japanese truck imports from 4 percent to 25 percent.[18]

From the U.S. perspective there were at least two reasons for supporting the Japanese export quotas. First, there was the potential for further job loss. Second, there was a widely expressed desire to give the industry some "breathing space" to allow it to eliminate or reduce the MCD and to catch up to Japanese innovations in auto production technology. By 1980 Japanese producers had lower wages, higher rates of labor productivity, and lower parts costs than their U.S. competitors. If the U.S. automakers were to become competitive in small cars, they would have to respond to problems in each of these areas.

Preserving employment and improving competitiveness would appear on the surface to be conflicting goals. However, they are in fact closely linked for several reasons. Unless the competitiveness of the domestic industry is improved, there will be very large losses in domestic market share in the future. Thus the choice for domestic workers is not whether to maintain current employment levels or accept productivity improvements that reduce the labor content of autos. The choice is between making those productivity improvements and losing a much larger share of employment to imported products. This argument is reinforced by the fact that two workers are displaced in supplier industries for each worker that is displaced in the auto industry. Thus it is in the interest of both the union and management to improve productivity and product quality in the domestic auto industry.

This section will examine the trends and determinants of employment by and the competitiveness of U.S. automakers over the period of the VRAs. The effects of the breathing space were apparently negated from the outset by the failure of the U.S. government to develop policies that were appropriate for the problems and the structure of this particular industry. The domestic motor vehicle industry is highly concentrated, and most of the work force is represented by a powerful labor union, the UAW. Given the structure of the industry and its labor market, a quid pro quo that would restrain the growth of wages and prices in exchange for protection could have helped the industry to use the VRA period to increase its competitiveness. There would be at least three essential ingredients in such an agreement. The first would provide incentives for, or require, the firms in the industry to limit prices and profits. The second would involve new cooperative labor-management efforts to reorganize production to increase productivity and product quality through continued capital investments, the use of new technology, and new patterns of job responsibilities. The third would involve commitments to restrain wage growth and address the high cost of white-collar labor in the industry. Union participation in reorganization plans would be an essential part of any quid pro quo agreement.

Without an external restraint, firms in such a highly concentrated industry would be unable to resist the opportunity to raise prices and profits under import protection, leading workers to demand their fair share of the pie in the form of wage increases.[19] An effort was apparently made to reach an agreement between the industry and the UAW, which would be enforced by the government. At least some members of both the industry and the union expressed the need for a three-way pact, but the government refused to participate, opting instead to negotiate the VRA with the Japanese government and "let the market" handle the adjustment process.[20] We will show that the administration's failure to take advantage of this opportunity led to dramatic price increases and may have damaged the long-run competitiveness of the domestic industry.

The Effects of the VRAs on Quality, Output, and Employment Patterns.
An assessment of the employment effects of the VRAs depends on an

assessment of the potential market share of Japanese imports in 1984 without the restrictions. A number of recent reports from academic economists and government agencies that have addressed this issue are analyzed below. The MCD is the most important factor in the debate about the potential share of Japanese imports in U.S. auto sales. The Japanese advantage was concentrated in the small car market segment (compact and subcompact vehicle classes) when the VRAs went into effect. As shown earlier, the small car share (in terms of the number of units sold) of the U.S. auto market rose steadily, from 30.8 percent in the 1970–1973 period to a peak of 55.8 percent in 1979–1981, as a result of the rapid growth of energy prices in the 1970s. The decline of gas prices in the early 1980s reduced the small car share to about 50 percent.

Quality Upgrading and the VRAs. In 1980, 87.7 percent of Japanese imports (in terms of the number of units sold) were concentrated in the small car class (66.6 percent in subcompacts and 20.9 percent in compacts).[21] Luxury small cars and sports cars, the remaining segment, represented 12.3 percent of Japanese exports in 1980. By 1984, under the effects of the VRAs, the share of compacts had risen to 33.4 percent and the luxury/sports car share had risen to 18.2 percent of Japanese exports to the United States. These trends illustrate one result of the VRAs, the shift to higher priced models.

Robert Feenstra (1985a, 1985b) has studied the price and quality change effects of the VRAs. The basic intuition behind Feenstra's work is straightforward. Faced with a numerical quota on the number of cars that can be sold in the U.S. market, a Japanese producer will maximize profits by selling cars that have the highest per-unit profit, which are generally the more expensive cars. Feenstra has carefully broken down the effects of the quota into pure price change and the effects of quality upgrading. He finds that "nearly all of the rise in [suggested retail] import prices can be explained by the upgrading of individual models" (Feenstra 1985a: 56). He found that for a sample of Japanese cars, average unit value rose by 29.4 percent between 1981 and 1985, while the average quality level rose by 21.7 percent.[22] For a sample of U.S.-made small cars, average prices rose by only 14.6 percent and quality by only 9.1 percent over the same period (Feenstra 1985a). The VRAs caused Japanese producers to build more expensive, more "heavily loaded" cars for the U.S. market.

Tariffs Versus Quotas. The shift to higher valued exports is one reason why a tariff on Japanese imports would have been a more effective policy measure than a quota. A tariff would not have created the incentive for Japanese producers to move into more highly valued models, as Feenstra (1985b) shows in an analysis of the truck tariff increase. In his truck sample, the quality of Japanese exports increased by only 11.5 percent between 1981 and 1985, and most of that growth occurred in 1985 in response to new model offerings in the United States. There are at least two reasons why a tariff might have been preferable to a quota in the automobile case. First, the quota gave the Japanese production experience in larger, more profitable models. It also created incentives that led them to sell technology to Korean producers to help them penetrate the low-priced end of the U.S. auto market. These acts gave foreign producers learning curve experience that may have permanently improved their competitiveness in these market segments. Second, the quota transferred substantial profits to Japanese producers that would have been retained in the United States under a tariff.

Perspectives on Output Effects of the VRAs. The actual market shares of Japanese producers and of all imports from 1979 to 1984 are shown in Tables 5–1 and 5–2. A number of recent reports address the question of the potential Japanese market share in the absence of the VRAs. Three of the most widely quoted studies will now be discussed in order to establish the general methodological approach in the literature. A new, alternative approach is then developed. The principal problem with the published literature is that it fails to adequately model the dynamic supply-side behavior of Japanese and U.S. producers and thus underestimates the effects of the VRAs on output and employment.

Crandall (1984) simply asserts, with no justification, that "[i]t is difficult to see how the [VRAs] could have shifted more than 8 percentage points of the market from Japanese imports to U.S. cars by 1983." The USITC (1985a) fitted a logarithmic time trend to the Japanese share of the U.S. auto market for 1967–1980. Although this estimation "predicted share values that were lower than actual values [in the late 1970s]," it was used to project market shares of Japanese producers for the period 1981–1984. The USITC estimated that Japanese producers would have gained a 28.4 percent share of the U.S. market in 1984 without the VRAs.

A logarithmic time trend underestimates the effect of the VRAs on Japanese market share because it does not reflect the capacity expansion plans and dynamic market growth strategies of the Japanese firms. Crandall's estimate and the USITC's time trend analysis of Japanese market shares fail to account for the dramatic increase in the Japanese market share that occurred between 1979 and 1980 (Table 5–1), when the Japanese share of total vehicle sales in the United States jumped eight percentage points in a single year to a total of 22.4 percent of the U.S. vehicle market. A risk-averse member of the UAW might reasonably have wondered if the Japanese were going to gain four to five percentage points a year for the next several years. By 1980 Japanese producers had built an effective marketing network, they had a quality product that met the needs of half of the U.S. auto market, and they had developed a substantial cost advantage. The U.S. industry's chance of stopping the increase in Japan's market share was probably quite small, or at least it was perceived to be so.

The USITC, as did other authors, also overlooked the signs of a substantial decline in the competitiveness of the U.S. auto industry in the late 1970s. The studies that were reviewed previously suggest that Japanese producers had developed a substantial competitive advantage in small cars by 1980, one that would grow with the value of the dollar in the early 1980s. The pricing policies of the U.S. automakers only served to make matters worse. This problem is illustrated by Feenstra's (1985a) analysis of the effects of the VRAs on employment, quality, and prices in the U.S. auto market. Between 1980 and 1981 Feenstra found that the prices of Japanese autos rose by about 8.4 percent. Two-thirds of this amount (5.3 percent) is attributed to quality change and one-third (3.1 percent) to pure price change. He maintains that the effects of the quotas on U.S. output and employment can be estimated by evaluating the effect of the 3.1 percent of pure price change on production and revenues of U.S. producers using a range of estimates of the elasticity of demand for imported autos.[23] He finds that, depending on the elasticity used, the employment content of excluded Japanese autos ranged between 5,600 and 22,300 workers in 1981.

The critical flaw in Feenstra's analysis is that he ignored the fact (revealed in his own data) that the real prices of U.S. small cars rose by 11.1 percent in 1980 and 6 percent in 1981 and that without the VRA effect on Japanese prices, there would have been very large shifts in market share to Japanese cars in the long run from these domestic price increases. It is estimated that the cross-price elasticity of demand between U.S. cars and Japanese imports (in the long run) is estimated to lie somewhere between 2 and 5 (Toder 1978). Thus a 15 percent increase in the relative price of U.S. small cars (if maintained) would sift 30 percent to 75 percent of demand to Japanese producers in the long run. The domestic market was not in equilibrium in 1981, when the VRAs were enacted. Toder's elasticity estimates suggest that the employment effects could have been orders of magnitude larger than Feenstra's estimates by the mid-1980s.

A New Approach. Evaluation of the effect of the VRAs on U.S. output and employment rests on an assessment of the ultimate potential for Japanese penetration of the U.S. auto market in the absence of the VRAs. Clearly, Japanese producers had a competitive advantage in small cars when the VRAs were introduced. The issue is: Could the Japanese have captured the entire small car market? Some buyers were obviously willing to purchase more expensive (or inferior) U.S.-made small cars. The MCD analysis (presented earlier) suggests that even the 40 percent devaluation of the dollar that occurred in the 1985–1987 period was insufficient to eliminate the MCD and that growth in Japanese market share would have occurred even without the increase in the value of the dollar that occurred in the early 1980s.

Instead of speculating about potential Japanese import price cuts in the absence of the VRAs, this section estimates the potential market share of the Japanese in the absence of trade restraints by directly evaluating their potential market share in the size classes in which they compete with U.S. producers. Japanese producers apparently dominate the subcompact market, which has held steady at about 30 percent of the total number of autos sold in the United States in recent years (U.S. International Trade Commission 1985a).[24] In the absence of trade restraints, it seems reasonable to assume that they would probably have captured essentially all of this demand in the early to mid-1980s, if not under their own labels, then through direct imports by U.S. car producers.

Compacts and small luxury and sports cars made up another 20 percent of the number of autos sold in the United States in the early 1980s. Under the VRAs, Japanese producers have been able to increase their share of the compact car market. According to Feenstra's research, during this time they were substantially *increasing* the prices of their exports in this market sector (despite the rise in the dollar, which should have lowered their U.S. costs and made it possible for them to lower their prices and further increase their share of this segment, if they chose to). Because domestic producers are more competitive in this market segment, it is unlikely that the Japanese could capture all of this market, but 50 percent of the segment is a reasonable estimate of their market potential in compacts and luxury/sports cars during the VRA period.

Combining these estimates of Japanese market potential in each market segment yields an estimated Japanese market potential of 40 percent of the total number of autos sold in the United States, based on 1984 market segment shares. This estimate is an upper bound on the potential market share of Japanese auto imports in the short run, although their ultimate market share could be higher if demand shifts in the direction of smaller cars again in the future or if the Japanese move successfully into the production of larger autos. If they had achieved this level of market penetration, effectively ending market domination by the U.S. big three, a decline in the value of the dollar would be unlikely to drive down the import share until the dollar fell low enough to give a substantial cost advantage to U.S. producers (probably well below the 145 yen per dollar rate).

At this point it seems reasonable to ask whether Japanese producers could have managed to produce, deliver, and sell enough cars to attain a 40 percent market share in the short span of four years (1980–1984). There are at least two facts that indicate that they could indeed have captured this much of the U.S. auto market. First, the Japanese had in place capacity expansion plans in 1980 that would allow them to produce enough vehicles to double their share of the U.S. market by 1983 (from 22.2 percent to 44.4 percent). Europe is the only other major export market in which those cars could have been sold. However, by 1980 most European countries had strict controls on Japanese auto imports. Second, note that in the 1978–1980 period, Japanese exports increased their share of the U.S. vehicle market by five percentage points per year. These facts suggest that it was feasible for the Japanese share of the U.S. market to rise from 22.4 percent to 40 percent between 1980 and 1984.

A slightly more conservative estimate of the Japanese market share without the VRAs would assume no growth in their share of the compact, luxury, and sports car markets, based on the theory that their move into these markets, from subcompacts, was entirely the result of the VRAs (following Feenstra's quality argument) and that they only achieved a 75 percent share of the subcompact market. In 1980 about 37 percent of the compact, luxury, and sports cars that were sold in the United States were made in Japan. If 75 percent of the subcompacts and 37 percent of the compact, luxury, and sports cars that were sold in the United States in 1984 had been made in Japan, then the Japanese share of the U.S. market would have been about 30 percent. Thirty percent to 40 percent of the U.S. market thus appears to be a reasonable estimate of the potential range of the Japanese share of the U.S. market in 1984 if the VRAs had not been put in place.

The 30 percent to 40 percent market share estimate is much larger than the estimates of Crandall, Feenstra, and the USITC, which are shown along with other recent estimates of the output and jobs saved by the VRAs in Table 5–4. In 1984, 1,948,714 Japanese autos were exported to the United States, which represented 18.4 percent of total U.S. auto sales, down from 22.4 percent in 1980, before the VRAs went into effect (USITC 1985c). If the Japanese share of the U.S. auto market had risen to 40 percent in 1984, then roughly 2.3 million units of actual 1984 U.S. auto output would have been displaced (21.3 percent of U.S. motor vehicle production in 1984).[25] The labor content of this amount of output would be roughly 146,800 work-years of direct, auto industry employment (with the 30 percent market share assumption, the labor content would be 110,000 work-years).[26] If the Japanese share of the U.S. market had reached 40 percent, an additional 297,000 work-years of indirect labor in supplier industries would also have been lost; this factor is not considered in any of the analyses shown in Table 5–4.

Table 5–4. Employment Content of Imports Displaced by the VRAs.

Source	Time Frame	Loss in Domestic Output (thousands of units)	Labor Content of Imports Displaced
Tarr and Morkre (1984)[a]	1980–1981	121	4,598
Feenstra (1985)[b]	1980–1981	53 to 212	5,600 to 22,300
Crandall (1984)[c]	1981–1983	712	26,200
USITC (1985)[d]	1981–1984	618	44,100
Commerce Department (1985)[e]	1981–1985	720 to 1,128	32,000 to 62,000
This chapter	1980–1984	1,725 to 2,300	100,200 to 137,900[f]

[a]Tarr and Morkre (1984).

[b]Feenstra (1985a).

[c]Crandall (1984).

[d]U.S. International Trade Commission (1985c).

[e]U.S. Department of Commerce (1985).

[f]Employment estimate includes the effects of foreign direct investment (discussed below).

The Truck Market. As mentioned at the beginning of this section, the Japanese hold a significant share of the U.S. truck market and were affected by a substantial tariff increase in 1980. The Japanese share of this market reached a peak of 21.7 percent of the truck market in 1980, rising rapidly from an 8.7 percent share in 1978 (U.S. International Trade Commission 1985c). With the tariff in effect, the Japanese share of the truck market fell to 14.3 percent in 1984. Assuming, conservatively, that 21.7 percent is an upper bound on Japanese truck share, at least 296,000 additional Japanese trucks could have been sold in the United States in 1984, if the tariff had not been in effect. This figure represents an additional 2.8 percent of total U.S. motor vehicle production in 1984, with a direct labor content of approximately 19,100 work-years.[27]

In sum, the analysis in this section suggests that the direct labor content of all Japanese vehicles that might have been imported in an unprotected market in the early 1980s was between 129,200 and 165,900 work-years. As explained above, this does not necessarily imply that this many jobs would have been eliminated in 1984, or that they would all disappear in the long run.

It is important to note that foreign direct investments by Japanese producers in U.S. assembly plants has increased auto industry employment in the United States. These investments might not have been made without trade protection, so the jobs that were generated should be deducted from the above labor content estimates to obtain a complete picture of the employment effects of trade restraints. Direct employment in the two Japanese-owned plants that were in operation in the United States in 1984 (Honda in Ohio and Nissan in Tennessee) was about 4,900 workers, assuming full capacity output (United Auto Workers Research Department 1987).[28] Approximately 5,000 workers were probably employed in related parts plants in the United States, yielding a total direct employment effect of about 9,900 jobs. Thus the net employment savings from trade protection in the early 1980s probably ranged between 119,300 and 156,000 direct work-years.

Crandall's labor content estimate (26,200 jobs saved in 1983) and the USITC's estimate (44,100 jobs saved in 1984) appear to be too low to be credible. The other labor content estimates that were cited in Table 5–4 also appear quite low in comparison with the estimates generated here. They all suffer from similar methodological defects, ignoring the long-run effects of the rise in the relative price of domestic small cars that took place before the VRAs were established, assuming that Japanese auto prices would have remained constant had the VRAs not taken effect (even with the rise in the value of the dollar), and assuming that the import price elasticity was relatively low in this period.

The Effects of Trade Restraints on the Competitiveness of the U.S. Auto Industry. During the period of the VRAs, there have been significant increases in prices, profits, and wages in the domestic auto industry. There has also been rapid growth in the offshoring of parts production, with important consequences for domestic employment and productivity. This section briefly analyzes the developments in each of these areas.

The Effects of the VRAs on the Prices of Domestic and Foreign Autos. The economic literature contains many studies of the price effects of trade restraints for both domestic and Japanese autos. The USITC (1985a) examined list prices for a selection of subcompact, intermediate, and full-sized domestic models and for small and luxury Japanese cars. U.S. full-sized sedans and Nissan and Toyota imports (fully equipped) had list price increases ranging from 21 percent to 33 percent between April 1981 and February 1985. The suggested retail prices of fully equipped domestic subcompacts rose by only 5 percent to 7 percent over the same period. These data suggest that U.S. producers exercised some restraint in subcompact pricing. However, Feenstra (1985a) points out that domestically produced small cars had substantial real price increases just before the VRAs went into effect (11 percent and 6 percent, respectively, for the 1979–80 and 1980–81 model years) and were able to maintain these price levels during the period of the quotas, as shown in Figure 5–3. Figure 5–3 also shows that the real price of Japanese imports *fell* by 4 percent between 1979 and 1980, further widening the gap between domestic and Japanese cars.

Figure 5–3 also shows that the average prices of Japanese cars were higher than those for U.S. cars throughout this period. This reflects the fact that the average quality level of U.S. cars was far below that of the Japanese competitors (Feenstra 1985a, 1985b). The quality gap widened during the VRAs. According to Feenstra,[29] between 1980 and 1984 the average quality of U.S. cars rose by about 10 percent, while that of Japanese cars rose by about 27 percent. The rate of growth in Japanese auto prices is confirmed by a study of actual transaction prices (including dealer markups, which grew rapidly during 1983 and 1984 in some regions) that was done by the BEA, which found that between 1981 and 1985, actual prices that were paid for Japanese cars rose by 27.5 percent (U.S. International Trade Commission 1985c). Transaction price data for U.S. models were not reported.

Figure 5–3.   Average List Prices of Small Cars (in constant 1982 dollars).

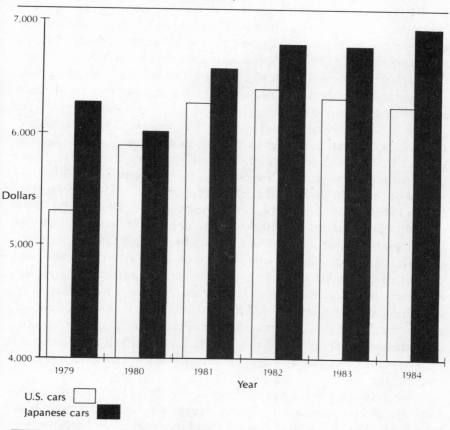

Sources: Feenstra (1985a, 1985b).

The trade data in Tables 5–1 and 5–2 allow calculation of average unit value data for imports over the 1981–1984 period. According to the Tariff Schedule of the United States (TSUS) trade statistics, the real (wholesale) unit value of Japanese imports to the United States rose by 6.4 percent between 1981 and 1984. In comparison, the real unit value of German imports rose by 5.6 percent. Given the fact that there was substantial appreciation in the real value of the dollar against both the yen and the German mark in this period, several inferences are suggested. First, Japanese producers appear to have substantially increased the yen price of their exports over the period of the VRAs, although they already had a substantial cost advantage over domestic producers (and, presumably, were earning a high rate of profit before the VRAs went into effect). Second, similar conclusions can be made about the mark prices and profits of German producers, suggesting that adjustment to excess profits is a slow process in the auto industry. Finally, it appears that domestic auto producers chose to use the VRAs to maintain high prices for small cars and to substantially increase the prices of larger cars rather than hold down prices and attempt to increase market share.[30]

The Effect of the VRAs on Profits. The USITC (1985a) collected profit data from all six domestic producers of automobiles (including the four U.S.-based producers, Volkswagen-America, and Honda). These firms suffered four years of losses from 1979 through 1982; they bottomed out in 1980, when all six lost $4.7 billion on U.S. operations. In 1983 the industry recovery led to profits of $5.3 billion, and 1984 profits were estimated at $10.4 billion. The USITC believes that the industry's profit turnaround was caused by increases in output since the industry has significant scale economies. That report also mentions the role of cost reductions, such as the elimination of excess capacity. However, the role of the domestic price increases that were allowed by the VRAs was not mentioned. The price increases that were discussed above significantly added to average revenue because most U.S. production was concentrated in the intermediate and full-sized range of the market. These price increases would probably not have been as large without the VRAs.

If the industry, the UAW, and the government had reached an agreement on quid pro quos for the VRAs, then prices and profits could have been held down. Some would argue that higher prices and profits were necessary so that the industry could afford to make productivity improving investments. However, under the VRAs, with the dramatic increase in profits, the level of capital expenditures in the industry has declined since 1981, even in nominal terms. In 1981 capital investment peaked at $7.7 billion; it had fallen to $5.1 billion by 1983 (U.S. International Trade Commission 1985a). A fundamental argument in favor of price/profit restraints as part of a quid pro quo package is that high prices are part of the industry's problem of falling market shares.

The Effect of the VRAs on Wages. As discussed earlier, the wages of auto workers were constant during the VRAs, in both real terms and relative to the average manufacturing wage. The MCD analysis suggests that after the effects of the dollar's devaluation are taken into account, the wages of white-collar workers are a more important contributor to the MCD than are production worker wages. Real wage reductions by either group could be one way in which the competitiveness of the domestic industry could be improved. However, there are a number of other productivity improving measures that could achieve the same result (for example, reorganization of the structure of work, use of new technologies, quality control programs). It is unlikely that production workers would be willing to take significant wage reductions unless white-collar workers and the companies also participated in wage and profit restraints. None of these would be possible without a mechanism designed to bring the stakeholders in the process together to negotiate solutions to the industry's problems.

Moving Parts Production Offshore. Manufacturers have tried to cut costs in the 1980s by moving some parts production processes to offshore locations. The United States had a surplus in motor vehicle parts trade in every year between 1964 and 1982.[31] The United States had trade deficits in parts trade of $944 million in 1983 and $2,552 million in 1984. The pattern of these deficits suggests that the behavior of exchange rates might explain recent trade problems in auto parts. However, anecdotal evidence suggests that a number of manufacturers have established parts plants in LDCs and entered into long-term supply contracts with Japanese firms.[32] These data suggest that temporary exchange rate changes may result in permanent changes in the output of and employment in the domestic parts industry. Parts production has employed almost as many workers as motor vehicle assembly in recent years.

New Technology and Changing Employment Patterns. The auto industry has increasingly attempted to respond to the MCD through increased use of automated production equipment. As a result, there has been a significant increase in the proportion of skilled maintenance workers in the auto assembly industry. According to information from the UAW, the ratio of production workers to skilled trades fell from 8:1 to 5:1 from 1945 to 1978. Since 1978 the pace of this change has accelerated, the ratio now stands at 4:1, implying that the share of skilled trades people that are employed in the assembly sector has increased by 25 percent in 6 years.[33] Thus there was and will continue to be a substantial need for the training of maintenance workers in this industry. The overall number of such workers will depend, however, on how successful the industry is in closing the MCD gap. There are two closely related questions here. First, can the industry eliminate the production cost advantage of Japanese auto makers through the intensive use of sophisticated, computerized production machinery that eliminates production labor? Second, while this race is taking place, will auto makers in both countries be passed up by low-wage producers who are attempting to gain entry into the lowest cost subcompact market? Both of these issues are considered in the next section of this chapter.

FUTURE EMPLOYMENT TRENDS IN THE DOMESTIC AUTO INDUSTRY

There are three distinct competitive strategies that are being considered by the major auto producers today. Their mix will influence domestic auto employment, the pattern of skills that are demanded, plant locations, unionization, and the character of the labor adjustment process. The three alternatives are: offshoring of component and final assembly to low-wage locations, capital investment and joint ventures to catch up with the Japanese production system, and, finally, some forms of trade protection to aid domestic producers or workers. All three strategies have been used in the United States in the recent past.

U.S.-based auto makers are offshoring production and simultaneously attempting to catch up with Japanese production technology. There is ample evidence that U.S. companies are purchasing an increasing share of components (and complete small cars) from foreign suppliers, with attendant job losses in the United States. At the same time, they are developing new and renovated production facilities in the United States, such as GM's Buick City complex and the GM/Toyota New United Motors plant, that consciously attempt to implement the principles of the Japanese system of production management. The evidence suggests that this bimodal competitive strategy is partly the result of the failures of the VRA policy and the rapid growth in the value of the dollar that occurred between 1980 and 1985. It is not clear which of these strategies will emerge as the most effective competitive weapon. It is most likely that a mixed approach will continue to be applied for a number of years.

Japanese auto producers have recently decided to build a number of auto plants in the United States, partly in response to political pressure for protection of domestic jobs. As production in these facilities rises, some new job opportunities will be created. Cost-effective production in these plants will also "vitiate the familiar arguments among managers and workers in existing facilities that success of foreign auto makers is based on cultural and site-specific factors"[34] and will lead to increased experience with the Japanese system of organizing production.

In 1987 Japanese firms had plans to assemble 1,830,000 cars and trucks per year by 1990 in seven U.S. plants. Four of these plants were in operation in 1987.[35] It is estimated that each of these plants will result in the direct and indirect employment of 6,700 workers (including supplier industries). Thus those plants will generate about 47,000 jobs by 1990 (about half of them in the auto industry and the rest in supplier firms). However, the UAW points out that the typical U.S. auto plant generates about 25,000 jobs, with the difference explained by the fact that most of the parts that are used in the Japanese assembly plants are imported. Thus the seven plants will displace about 175,000 U.S. jobs, for a net loss of 128,000 jobs by 1990.

Ultimate labor displacement in the 1985–2000 time frame will depend on the ability of the domestic industry to respond to the competitive challenge of the Asian-based producers and on the types of trade policies that are developed (or not developed) for this industry. The potential Japanese and Korean market share potential probably exceeds 40 percent of the domestic auto market. This is because the Japanese have gained experience in building compact and luxury cars under the VRA and could potentially capture most of this market and because they, along with their Korean partners, have the potential to dominate the subcompact market. In the compact and luxury segments, perceived quality is probably as important (if not more so) than price competitiveness. Japanese producers appear to have a solid advantage over U.S.-based firms in their reputation for quality. Ford and, to a certain extent, Chrysler seem to have made substantial progress in improving the quality of their products. GM's ability to achieve higher quality will be a critical determinant of whether or not the domestic-based industry as a whole will be able to meet the quality challenge in the small car market.

The parts-purchasing behavior of foreign-owned assembly plants in the United States is another important determinant of future domestic employment opportunities. If the fall in the value of the dollar and, possibly, new trade policies encourage the Japanese to buy a larger share of their parts and supplies in the United States, then some of the 128,000 work-years of employment that is projected to be displaced by foreign direct investment can be retained in the United States.

The final issue that affects the employment content of trade in the 1985–2000 time period is the future of subcompact production in the

United States. Two questions will determine the outcome. First, can great strides be made in raising productivity levels in domestic production through new technology programs such as the GM Saturn project? Second, will exchange rate policies be used to reduce the growing U.S. trade deficit with the Asian NICs, raising effective wages in these countries by devaluing the dollar against their currencies? These currencies moved with the dollar as it fell in the 1985–1987 period, so there was no change in their comparative production costs.

Ultimately, Asian-based producers could capture 45 percent to 50 percent of the U.S. auto market in the 1990s, as compared to their 1984 share of 17.3 percent. If market demand stays in the range of 14.5 million units per year, as in 1984, an additional 4 to 4.8 million units of domestic production could be displaced by imports in the 1990s under these assumptions. This increase in imports could displace 260,000 to 310,000 additional work-years of direct employment demand (at 1984 employment/output levels). The actual market shares of the Asian-based producers, and hence domestic employment levels, will be determined by the industry's ability to close the cost and quality gaps in the 1985–2000 period, which will in turn be influenced by future trade policies.

CONCLUSIONS

The world motor vehicle industry is now in the midst of a fundamental transformation in the location and technology of the production process. This metamorphosis is being driven by the MCD between Japanese and U.S. producers and is incorporating important new production technologies as well as new locations of production. U.S. firms are developing new production technologies in an attempt to catch up with Japan's manufacturing advantages in small cars. However, these efforts are confronted by an additional challenge from new producers in Korea and other NICs who have achieved rapid growth in their auto exports to the United States in the 1985–1987 period. Ford and GM are responding to the competitive challenges by moving production of subcompacts to low-wage locations in Korea and Mexico.

The outcomes of this transformation hinge on the policies of the respective governments and the strategies of the firms involved in the struggle. Governments have intervened in each of the transformations that have affected the auto industry because of the size of the industry, its importance as a customer for suppliers of parts and materials, and the large number of high-wage jobs that it generates.

The U.S. auto industry employed 876,400 people in 1985. Total industry employment is likely to exhibit a declining secular trend in the future, as it has since 1978. If the industry increases its productivity and closes the MCD gap, then it could limit or reverse the growth of the market share of Asian-based producers. This strategy would involve the highest future employment levels (although these would still exhibit a declining trend over time). If the industry fails to catch up with the Japanese and continues to import small cars from Japan and the LDCs and if foreign direct investment continues to grow in the United States, then the rate of decline in industry employment will be larger. On balance, it appears that trade restrictions limited the employment content of trade in the short run. In the long run, the competitiveness of the domestic industry may have been injured by these trade policies, and the employment content of trade may be higher in the future than it would have been if these particular trade restrictions had not been enacted.

U.S. vehicle imports have grown very rapidly in the 1985–1987 period as the VRAs were relaxed and the NIC producers entered the market, leading to a new debate on the need for further trade protection. Trade policy for the auto industry should be designed to improve the competitiveness of domestic producers in order to help maintain employment levels in this sector. The industry must resist the temptation to earn excessive profits through unnecessary price increases if it is to become competitive. Domestic firms seem unwilling or unable to competitively price on their own when given trade protection. U.S. auto makers used the VRAs to raise prices, especially on larger models (where there was less competition), and to keep prices high for small cars. Thus a public agreement between the industry and the government, with price restraint standards and enforceable penalties for noncompliance, appears to be a necessary component of effective trade policies.

An effective agreement would also include labor representatives in the bargaining process and would incorporate incentives to raise productivity levels and improve the quality of domestic products. The key to improving productivity and quality levels is to bring labor and management together to work out strategies for reorganizing production, eliminating arbitrary job definitions, and incorporating new technologies in the most effective ways possible. Organization is the critical component of this process. Many studies have shown that the

Japanese productivity advantage is the result of new or better ways of arranging production, rather than deeper capital investment or more sophisticated production technology. Historical prohibitions on labor participation in production management have limited the rate at which new forms of organization have been adopted in the U.S. auto industry.

The VRAs did not include mechanisms to encourage price or profit restraint on the part of the domestic producers or to bring together the participants in the industry in cooperative efforts to improve competitiveness. An effective trade policy would have required commitments from each stakeholder in the industry. Each stakeholder would have been required to make sacrifices for the common good of the industry. Auto workers might accept a cut in their real wages if they knew that the industry was also going to reduce profits and that salaried workers and management were also going to accept wage reductions. They might agree to further cuts in the numbers of job categories if there were joint plans for reducing employment through attrition or for the establishment of more effective job-training programs that would entice workers to leave. Incentives for productivity improvement would rise if significant profit-sharing included production workers, and not just management employees. These types of changes were not encouraged by the VRAs. The lessons that were learned from trade protection in the early 1980s should not be ignored in future policy debates.

NOTES

1. This figure includes SIC categories 371, motor vehicles and parts, and 3465, automotive stampings. Note that the number of units produced in the United States also reached an historical high in 1978.
2. Seventy-four percent of auto stampings (SIC 3465) were produced in Michigan, Indiana, and Ohio. Sixty-two percent of parts production (SIC 3714) took place in Michigan, Ohio, New York, and Indiana (U.S. Department of Labor 1985c).
3. See, for example, Altshuler et al. (1984) and Cole and Yakushiji (1984).
4. Note that average sales over the 1979–1986 business cycle were diminished by the long, steep recession of the early 1980s. U.S. trade protection substantially increased the average prices in the early 1980s, thus reducing vehicle demand (relative to other goods). The U.S. International Trade Commission (1985a) estimated that the VRAs reduced total auto demand by about 3 percent in 1984.

5. Small car shares are approximations that sum the compact and subcompact shares of U.S. producers (*Automotive News* 1982, 1985) and the Japanese import share (U.S. International Trade Commission 1985c). This excludes imports of European small cars. However, the European share of the U.S. small car market is less than 1 percent.

6. The Auto Products Trade Act of 1965 eliminated tariffs subject to certain performance requirements in new motor vehicles and parts between the United States and Canada (U.S. International Trade Commission 1985b). This agreement applies to almost all trade in new vehicles between the two countries.

7. The studies reviewed by Cole and Yakushiji and by Flynn display a wide variation in assumptions about labor inputs, ranging from 38.6 to 99 hours per vehicle produced in Japan (mean estimate of 64.4 hours), and ranging from 59.9 to 144 hours per vehicle produced in the United States (mean estimate of 108.2 hours). These estimates are for labor used directly by major producers and are adjusted to correct for differences in model mix and levels of vertical integration. Wage rate estimates display a smaller variance, with mean estimated wages of $10.43 per hour in Japan and $19.47 per hour in the United States (Flynn 1982: 53).

8. Some studies assign joint effects to wages, and some to productivity, although they are a combined result of both factors.

9. Nineteen eighty-seven wages were estimated using 1980–1983 home currency growth rates. Japanese wage rates, measured in yen, grew slightly faster than those in the United States during this period, reflecting the strong seniority premia in the Japanese wage system.

10. See Kwoka (1984) for data on advertising costs per unit sold for different manufacturers.

11. See "Strong Yen Spurs Parts Imports from NICs, China" (1986: 11).

12. The job opportunity figures discussed here must be interpreted carefully. Strictly speaking, these figures reflect changes in the labor content of trade in the given years. If the trade deficit were eliminated (e.g., by import quotas), then domestic job opportunities would rise by these amounts only if domestic products were substituted for imports at the same price and in the same quantities, and if there were no simultaneous changes in other factors such as the level of aggregate demand.

13. The figures here are an approximation derived from the data in U.S. Department of Labor (1985b), which uses the 1977 input-output table and 1984 employment/output relationships to estimate direct and indirect employment required for each $1 million of sales to final users of motor vehicles. For each work-year of direct labor input, 2.02 work-years of indirect labor inputs were required, according to this input-output table. The ratio of direct to indirect employment (based on 1977

input-output coefficients) varies only if *relative* wage rates change over time. Between 1978 and 1984 average weekly earnings grew by 50.1 percent for all manufacturing jobs and by 51.3 percent for the motor vehicle industry. Thus the ratio calculated using 1984 employment/output relationships will closely approximate the ratio for 1978.

14. Lawrence uses a constant share analysis to evaluate the effects of trade over the 1978–1982 period. However, in 1982 the VRAs were already in effect, restraining Japanese auto exports to the United States, reducing the actual effects of trade in the 1978–1982 period.

15. The most important reason for the difference between the constant share and Lawrence estimates is that the constant share approach corrects for differences in aggregate demand by calculating the employment content of auto trade in 1980, if import market shares had remained at their 1973 levels (instead of using actual trade-related employment in 1973 for comparisons, as Lawrence does). The constant share approach thus uses a lower estimate of base year (1973) employment than does Lawrence, and the *change* in trade-related employment between 1973 and 1980 is therefore larger with the constant share approach. The estimate of the actual employment content of trade in 1980 is the same with both techniques.

16. There also appears to be a substantial potential problem with the trade data used by both Lawrence and the USITC, which are the results of a concordance made by the Bureau of Economic Analysis between the primary Tariff Schedule of the U.S. (TSUS) statistics and the Standard Industrial Classification (SIC) used to categorize industries for input-output modeling. The USITC estimated that the direct labor content of vehicle trade in 1980 was 125,000 work-years, or 15.9 percent of industry employment. Table 5–2 reports the value of motor vehicle imports taken directly from the TSUS statistics. These data show that in 1980 net trade equaled 23 percent of domestic shipments of motor vehicles. If this estimate is correct, input-output assumptions would suggest that the labor content of trade was also about 23 percent of 1980 employment. This large discrepancy suggests that further research is required on the data used in these types of studies.

17. Conditions in the auto industry in 1980 led to increasing pressure for protection from Japanese auto exports. In June 1980 the Ford Motor Co. and the UAW filed a joint petition for relief under Section 201 of the Trade Act of 1974. The USITC denied the petition in November 1980. In early 1981 legislation to restrict imports of Japanese cars was gaining support in Congress. On May 1, 1981, MITI announced a VRA that would reduce the number of auto exports to the United States to 1,832,500, 7 percent less than in 1980, for the Japanese fiscal year April 1, 1981. The VRA continued for two more years at a constant level of

exports and was extended for a fourth year at 2,015,000 units, a 10 percent increase (U.S. International Trade Commission 1985a). The VRA expired on April 1, 1985, but the Japanese government extended it for 1985–1986, at a level of 2.3 million units per year, 24.3 percent more than were allowed in 1984–1985 ("Rise in Car Exports Confirmed by Japan" 1985). The Export Restraint was renewed at the 2.3 million unit level in 1986–1987 (*New York Times* 1986).

18. Feenstra (1985b: 12–13) provides an interesting history of the small truck tariff:

> During the 1970s Japan exported an increasing number of compact trucks to the U.S., most as cab/chassis with some final assembly needed. In 1980 Congress asked the USITC to study the possible reclassification of Japanese imports, from "parts of trucks" as then applied to "complete or unfinished trucks." The former carried a tariff rate of 4%, whereas the latter had a duty of 25%. This unusually high rate was a result of the "chicken war" between the United States and Europe in 1962–63, when the U.S. retaliated against higher tariffs on poultry sales to West Germany. In 1980 the U.S. Customs Service announced that effective August 21 imported lightweight cab/chassis would be reclassified as complete trucks.

19. Firms and workers in any industry that is given trade protection could be expected to behave in a similar fashion in the short run. However, the motor vehicle industry has a history of above average rates of return on equity and a high degree of concentration (Kwoka 1984), and wages well above the manufacturing average, suggesting the existence of substantial barriers to entry. The temporary effects of trade policy on wages, prices, and profits could be expected to persist in an oligopoly with such market power.

20. Private interviews with senior auto executives by John Zysman and Laura Tyson, principal investigators with the Berkeley Roundtable on International Economy.

21. Market segment data in this paragraph from U.S. International Trade Commission 1985a.

22. (Feenstra 1985b: Table 2). Quality is defined by fundamental auto characteristics such as size, power, type of transmission, and the inclusion of power steering and air conditioning. Feenstra estimated the value of these attributes by using a hedonic price function model.

23. Feenstra claims that the portion of the price effect attributable to quality change will not result in any increased demand for autos, since these are real services that consumers are willing to pay for. Given the 3.1 percent residual price effect, and price elasticity estimates ranging from 2 to 5, he calculates the effects on revenue, production, and employment by using per unit revenue and employment coefficients from unspecified sources.

24.   All analysis of market shares in this section will be based on the numbers of units sold. Employment effects will then be calculated by adjusting for the difference in the labor content of small cars from average U.S. labor content levels.

25.   This figure does not include any adjustments for changes in the level of overall auto demand if the VRAs had been eliminated. Without the VRAs, average auto prices would have been lower in the United States, increasing overall auto demand. This would tend to offset some of the employment content effects suggested in the text. The USITC estimated that price increases due to the VRAs only reduced overall demand by 3 percent. However, price effects of the VRAs could be larger under the market share assumptions used here.

26.   Labor content was derived in a manner similar to the input-output analyses discussed earlier. Actual labor content per vehicle in 1984 was calculated from employment and output data. It was then assumed that small car production required 20 percent less labor per unit of output than the average vehicle, based on the results of the cost studies reviewed in section 1 (see Flynn 1982). Crandall (1984) and the U.S. International Trade Commission (1985a) use similar assumptions about the labor content of autos.

27.   Japanese imports consist primarily of small trucks and sell for prices similar to compact cars. Therefore it was then assumed that small truck production required similar amounts of labor inputs. Thus the technique used to estimate the labor content of small car trade was used to estimate the labor content of truck imports.

28.   Note that these plants were not fully operational in 1984, so these figures overstate the actual effect of foreign direct investment in 1984.

29.   Feenstra claims that most of the price increases can be accounted for by quality increases, as noted above. The unexplained rates of price increase (actual less quality increases) were 7.2 percent and 5.5 percent for Japanese and U.S. producers, respectively, over the 1981–1985 period in Feenstra's model.

30.   The ability of auto producers to raise large car prices was enhanced by at least three factors in 1983–1984. Higher prices on Japanese cars caused substitution out of foreign cars, which would have affected the demand for all domestic models. A decline in real gasoline prices led to some growth in the market share of larger cars. Finally, the economic recovery in 1983–1984 increased auto demand substantially, as shown in the sales figures in Tables 5–1 and 5–2.

31.   U.S. International Trade Commission (1985c). Truck cab and chassis data are excluded as these units are included in the analysis of finished truck imports.

32. See U.S. Department of Transportation (1982: 56–57) for a list of examples of long-term foreign parts sourcing agreements.
33. BRIE interview with Peter Unterweger, UAW Research Department, March, 1984.
34. Altshuler et al. (1984).
35. The data in this paragraph are from the United Auto Workers Research Department (1987).

REFERENCES

Altshuler, Alan, Martin Anderson, Daniel Jones, Daniel Roos, and James Womack. 1984. *The Future of the Automobile: The Report of MIT's International Automobile Program.* Cambridge, Mass.: MIT Press.

Automotive News. Various years. "Market Databook Issue," April.

Branson, William, and James Love. 1986. "Dollar Appreciation and Manufacturing Employment and Output" National Bureau of Economic Research Working Paper No. 1972, Cambridge, Mass., July.

Cole, Robert E., and Taizo Yakushiji. 1984. *The American and Japanese Industries in Transition: Report of the Joint U.S.-Japan Automotive Study.* Ann Arbor, Mich.: Center for Japanese Studies, University of Michigan.

Council of Economic Advisors. 1986. *Economic Report of the President.* Washington, D.C.: U.S. Government Printing Office, February.

Crandall, Robert W., 1984. "Import Quotas and the Automobile Industry: The Costs of Protectionism." *The Brookings Review* (Summer): 8–16.

Feenstra, Robert C. 1985a. "Automobile Prices and Protection: The U.S.–Japan Trade Restraint." *Journal of Policy Modeling* 7, no. 1: 49–68.

———. 1985b. "Quality Change under Trade Restraints: Theory and Evidence from Japanese Autos." Discussion Paper #298, Department of Economics. Columbia University, New York, August.

Flynn, Michael S. 1982. "Differentials in Vehicles' Landed Costs: Japanese Vehicles in the U.S. Marketplace." Working Paper Series No. 3, Center for Japanese Studies, University of Michigan, October 30.

———. 1983. "A Note on the Treatment of Labor Content as a Source of the Manufacturing Cost Differential." Working Paper Series No. 19, Center for Japanese Studies, University of Michigan, September 15.

———. 1984. "Estimating Comparative Compensation Costs and Their Contribution to the Manufacturing Cost Differences." Working Paper Series No. 21, Center for Japanese Studies, University of Michigan, January.

Grossman, Gene M. 1982. "The Employment and Wage Effects of Import Competition in the United States." National Bureau of Economic Research Working Paper No. 1041, Cambridge, Mass., December.

Kreinin, Mordechai E. 1984. "Wage Competitiveness in the U.S. Auto and Steel Industries." *Contemporary Policy Issues* No. 4 (January): 39–50.

Kwoka, John L., Jr. 1984. "Market Power and Market Change in the U.S. Automobile Industry." *Journal of Industrial Economics* 32, no. 4 (June): 509–22.

Lawrence, Robert Z. 1984. *Can America Compete?* Washington, D.C.: Brookings Institution.

Martin, J.P., and J. Evans. 1981. "Notes on Measuring the Employment Displacement Effects of Trade by the Accounting Procedure." *Oxford Economic Papers* 33, no. 1: 154–64.

New York Times, 1986. February 13.

"Rise in Car Exports Confirmed by Japan." 1985. *New York Times,* March 29.

"Strong Yen Spurs Parts Imports from NICs, China." 1986. *Japan Economic Journal,* October 11.

Toder, Eric J., with Nicholas Scott Cardell and Ellen Burton. 1978. *Trade Policy and the U.S. Automobile Industry.* New York: Praeger Publishers.

Tarr, David G., and Morris E. Morkre. 1984. *Aggregate Costs to the United States of Tariffs and Quotas on Imports: General Tariff Cuts and Removal of Quotas on Automobiles, Steel, Sugar, and Textiles.* Bureau of Economics Staff Report to the Federal Trade Commission. Washington, D.C.: FTC, December.

United Auto Workers Research Department. 1987. "U.S. Auto Jobs: The Problem is Bigger than Japanese Imports." January 12. Mimeo.

U.S. Department of Commerce. 1985. "Analysis of the Japanese Auto Export Restraint." Manuscript released by House Subcommittee on Oversight and Investigations.

———. 1986. *U.S. Industrial Outlook, 1986.* Washington, D.C.: U.S. Government Printing Office.

U.S. Department of Labor. Bureau of Labor Statistics. 1985. "B.L.S. Employment Requirements, Table (9EMPLOYE1984P)," Office of Economic Growth and Employment Projections, October 7. Mimeo.

U.S. Department of Transportation. 1981. *The U.S. Automobile Industry, 1980.* Report to the President from the Secretary of Transportation. DOT P-10 81 02. Washington, D.C.: Department of Transportation, March.

———. 1982. *The U.S. Automobile Industry, 1981.* Report to the President from the Secretary of Transportation. DOT-P-10 82 01. Washington, D.C.: Department of Transportation, May.

U.S. International Trade Commission. 1985a. *A Review of Recent Developments in the U.S. Automobile Industry Including an Assessment of the Japanese Voluntary Restraint Agreements.* USITC Publication 1648. Washington, D.C.: U.S. International Trade Commission, February.

————. 1985b. *The Internationalization of the Automobile Industry and Its Effects on the U.S. Automobile Industry.* USITC Publication 1712. Washington, D.C.: U.S. International Trade Commission, June.

————. 1985c. *The U.S. Automotive Industry: U.S. Factory Sales, Retail Sales, Imports, Exports, Apparent Retail Prices, and Trade Balances with Selected Countries for Motor Vehicles, 1964–84.* USITC Publication 1762. Washington, D.C.: U.S. International Trade Commission, October.

————. 1986. *U.S. Trade-Related Employment, 1978–84.* USITC Publication 1855. Washington, D.C.: U.S. International Trade Commission, May.

6 THE DOMESTIC EMPLOYMENT CONSEQUENCES OF INTERNATIONAL TRADE IN TELECOMMUNICATIONS EQUIPMENT

Jay S. Stowsky

When the phone rings nowadays, there is a good chance that the voice that is waiting on the wire has traveled in pulses of light over hair-like strands of ultrapure glass. Sound waves that once sent sparks of electricity cracking over copper wire now travel in digital bits, a coded series of ones and zeroes. The sound of the human voice is transmogrified into the language of the computer; yesterday's cumbersome assemblies of electromechanical switches are replaced by software-driven circuits that are etched into tiny silicon chips.

Throughout the 1960s and 1970s, new microelectronics-based communications technologies blurred the technical distinction between communications and computing. New technical possibilities created mounting pressures for a wider range of product choices from potential producers and corporate consumers of telecommunications equipment. On January 1, 1984, these pressures culminated in the breakup of AT&T's domestic monopoly. Since then, a multinational flood of electronics firms has rushed to serve the newly open market.

Telecommunications equipment is now expected to be one of the fastest growing traded sectors through the end of the century. Yet, while AT&T was bound to lose market share when its long-time monopoly status was finally fractured, U.S. firms have not been notably successful at filling in the cracks. Indeed, while U.S. exports have remained flat over the past several years, imports of telephone and telegraph equipment have skyrocketed.[1] Telephone and telegraph equipment imports doubled in 1983 alone, shifting the sector into deficit ($893 million) for the first time since 1974. By 1986 this sector was yielding a record annual trade deficit of $1.9 billion.

The effect of international monetary exchange rates on overall consumption of telephone and telegraph apparatus appears to have been negligible through 1983 due to the monopolistic structure or government ownership of the world's telecommunications industries. International trade accounted for only a small portion of consumption in major markets for most types of telecommunications equipment. The one exception is low-end customer premises equipment, such as cordless telephones and telephone handsets, where the changed U.S. regulatory climate has provided an opportunity for exchange rates to have an effect.

Nevertheless, even in this product segment, the effect of the dollar exchange rate has probably been minimal. Like many other consumer electronics products, these devices have been priced very low by foreign exporters in East Asia; when AT&T decided to move its residential phone set production from Shreveport, Louisiana, to Singapore in 1985, its domestic product was selling for $30 and higher compared to an average price of from $5 to $20 for phones coming in from East Asia. If transactions were conducted in the medium of the foreign currency, then exchange rate adjustments would surely have to be staggering to equate the foreign prices to U.S. prices. In any event, however, most of the transactions are dollar-denominated, rendering the effect of exchange rate fluctuations even less significant. Although imports of these items abated somewhat in 1986, most analysts traced this not to a decrease in the value of the dollar, but to oversaturation of the market for cheap phones plus a growing desire among U.S. consumers for a higher quality product.

The deteriorating competitive performance of U.S. suppliers of telecommunications equipment stems in large part from differences in government policy toward trade in this rapidly growing high-tech sector. Since the breakup of AT&T on January 1, 1984, thousands of companies, both foreign and domestic, have been free to compete without restriction in the U.S. market, an area that accounts for over 40 percent of global equipment consumption, the largest market in the world. But government protection and control have persisted in limiting the access of U.S. firms to foreign markets, just as domestic manufacturers are facing their greatest competition ever from abroad.

Despite the drama of the recent trade statistics, however, the direct effects of this deteriorating trade balance on domestic *employment* have probably been and are likely to continue to be marginal. This is due to the pervasive effects of technological innovation in both the products and production techniques of this increasingly microelectronics-based sector. In fact, even with anticipated increases in exports and overall output, the growing use of computerized manufacturing automation in production means that telecommunications equipment—though a major spur to economic productivity—will not constitute a major employment growth area in the future.

Moreover, to the extent that trade *does* affect jobs in this sector, the jobs that are most directly affected are not those of the well-paid, blue-collar, union members that are typically associated with the manufacture of past generations of electromechanical equipment. Rather, it is the thousands of circuit board assemblers and wafer fab technicians—mostly women, many nonwhite—and the scores of specialized, highly educated software designers and electrical engineers—mostly white, usually male—that will most likely feel the effects of increased international trade in telecommunications equipment. In the latter case, the relatively healthy, though slipping, market position of U.S. producers in certain high-value-added, software-intensive telecommunications products suggests the possibility of net job creation through trade. In the former case, lost market share at the more labor-intensive low end of the sector's product line raises the spectre of net job destruction. In either case, an overall deterioration in trade for all product segments portends a worsening employment picture in the sense that a smaller number of jobs will be created through trade or a larger number of jobs will be destroyed.

Almost certainly, the intensifying competitive pressures of international trade are quickening the pace of technological change in this sector. And particular trade pressure in labor-intensive product segments encourages U.S. producers to seek low-cost production locations offshore or to shift the domestic product mix toward higher end equipment that has increasingly automated production requirements. Thus trade must be counted as a significant *indirect* contributor to employment restructuring in the domestic industry. Still, it is the revolution in microelectronics that has transformed the products, production processes, and manufacturing strategies of telecommunications equipment firms—and that has been responsible, in the final analysis, for the breakup of AT&T's domestic monopoly.[2] That transformation echoes loudest in the declining level and changing composition of domestic employment in this sector.

Nevertheless, the transformation remains incomplete; the competitive outcome is undetermined. There are a variety of strategies for reorganizing production in response to the changed technological and competitive environment. The choice of particular production technologies which can be more or less labor-intensive, and the choice of particular locations for manufacturing and research facilities directly affect the use of labor in this sector. New manufacturing technologies permit *choices* about whether to automate and keep all or a part of the production process in the United States, whether to automate offshore, or whether to move offshore in order to gain access to growing foreign markets or to take advantage of cheap, though increasingly skilled, foreign labor.

Consequently, this chapter traces the domestic employment effects of trade in the telecommunications equipment sector by focusing on the strategic choices that firms are making in response to the new dynamics of competition in the industry. Examination of the manufacturing strategies of major telecommunications equipment producers in different product segments reveals that firms' technological and locational choices are powerfully influenced by the performance characteristics of the products themselves. Custom products require different levels of technical sophistication in the production process than do standard, commodity products and will thus generate employment for different skill categories of labor. To the extent that trade competition pressures firms that are located in the U.S. market to seek strategic advantage by producing at the high end of the industry product mix, the jobs that are created through trade will not be done by the same people whose jobs have been lost.

THE NEW DYNAMICS OF INTERNATIONAL COMPETITION AND TRADE

Microelectronics has transformed the products, production processes, and competitive strategies of U.S. producers of telecommunications equipment. Combined with the profound effects of divestiture and deregulation, the shift to digital technologies has created major new product markets, dissolving the competitive boundaries between traditional U.S. suppliers, such as AT&T and GTE. It has also introduced a formidable array of foreign and domestic entrants whose products used to be functionally distinct: IBM and Fujitsu in computers, Hughes and Martin-Marietta in aerospace, Hewlett-Packard and Sumitomo in electrical machinery and instrumentation, GE and Matsushita in consumer electronics.

Indeed, telecommunications equipment has only recently become a significantly traded product in international markets. For as long as the Bell System remained intact, AT&T was both the manufacturer and the market for most of the telecommunications equipment sold in the United States. In 1967, for example, imports accounted for only 0.8 percent of overall domestic consumption (U.S. International Trade Commission 1984: Table 4). Neither other domestic firms nor any foreign firms were able to penetrate the U.S. market in an important way until after 1968, when the FCC's *Carterfone* decision allowed the connection of non-Bell equipment to the publicly switched telecommunications network.

Slowly at first, then more forcefully as momentum built toward deregulation and divestiture, lower cost producers began to enter and fragment the Bell System's domestic equipment market. By 1974–75, the overall import/domestic consumption ratio had more than tripled since *Carterfone*, climbing to about 2.5 percent (U.S. International Trade Commission 1984: Table 4). Then, driven both by heightened pressure toward deregulation and the rising value of the dollar, the trickle of imports began to gather force like a flood tide. Imports increased by about 29 percent annually between 1972 and 1984. In fact, the compound annual rate of increase more than doubled in the early 1980s as compared to the decade of the 1970s jumping from about 22 percent between 1972 and 1980 to more than 45 percent between 1980 and 1984 (U.S. Department of Commerce 1986: Table 8).[3]

In 1979 the U.S. accounted for 31.6 percent of the import market for the telephone and telegraph equipment and parts that were supplied by the thirteen largest exporting nations; this figure grew to 44.6 percent in 1983 and surged to 53.1 percent in 1984 (U.S. Department of Commerce 1986: 30–34). Reflecting an inundation of cheap East Asian phones, U.S. telephone and telegraph equipment imports actually doubled in the single year that preceded the Bell System breakup (1983), swelling the import/new supply ratio to over 9 percent by the time divestiture officially commenced on January 1, 1984 (see Table 6–1).

Meanwhile, strict regulation of national telecommunications networks abroad continued to limit U.S. producers' commercial prospects on the export side. Exports represented less than 3 percent of the value of

Table 6–1.   Telephone and Telegraph Apparatus: Producers' Shipments, Exports, and Imports, 1980–1986 (in millions of dollars).

Year	Value of Shipments	Exports	Imports	Ratio of Imports to New Supply[a]	Ratio of Exports to Shipments
1980	$12,283	$557	$ 478	3.7	4.5
1981	13,268	653	564	4.1	4.9
1982	13,394	829	816	5.7	6.2
1983	13,527	790	1,683	9.1	5.8
1984	15,273	777	2,249	12.8	5.1
1985	17,178	832	2,378	12.2	4.8
1986	19,438	870	2,776	12.5	4.5

[a]New supply = producers' shipments plus imports.
Source: Compiled from official statistics of the U.S. Department of Commerce.

U.S. industry shipments until the mid-1970s, when the export/shipment ratio began to rise (U.S. International Trade Commission 1984: Table 4). That ratio peaked in 1982 at 6.2 percent ($829 million) before declining each year thereafter, largely due to the rising value of the dollar (see Table 6–1). U.S. exports increased in value by 11.8 percent annually between 1979 and 1984, compared to an overall average rate of 19.8 percent for the thirteen largest exporting nations. By 1984 the growth rate of U.S. exports was the fifth lowest among the thirteen, with the U.S. ranking third overall in world market share at 11.6 percent, compared to Sweden's 12.6 percent and Japan's 26 percent (U.S. Department of Commerce 1986: 30–43).

Beneath the industry-wide trends, however, lie significant differences in U.S. trade performance among individual subcategories of telecommunications equipment. Three basic types of equipment serve to make up a telecommunications network. *Terminal* equipment, such as a telephone handset, is equipment into which a communications signal can be introduced and from which a final signal can be received. *Transmission* equipment, such as coaxial cable or lightguide, microwave radio or communications satellites, carries the signal between terminals and switching centers. *Switching* equipment, located primarily in telephone companies' central offices, but sometimes, as in the case of PBXs, located on the customer's premises, routes calls between terminals and groups of terminals. Terminal and switching equipment that is located on the user's premises, or CPE, includes not only single line telephone sets and PBX equipment, but also modems, multiplexers, videoconferencing equipment, and facsimile machines. Over 2,000 companies sell CPE in the United States, with total sales nearing $14 billion in 1985 (U.S. Department of Commerce 1986: 30–32).

It is in low-end CPE that the U.S. trade performance has been particularly poor. As Table 6–2 indicates, most of the telecommunications trade deficit occurred in the category of "other telephone and telegraph apparatus, equipment, and components," which is dominated by products whose characteristics amplify the labor cost disadvantage of U.S.-based producers. While the export/shipment ratio in this segment stagnated, the import/consumption ratio climbed steadily, reaching 18.4 percent in 1985. This was in comparison to an import penetration figure of 12.2 percent that year for telephone and telegraph apparatus overall.

It should be emphasized, of course, that these import figures include products that were imported from the offshore manufacturing subsidiaries or contract production facilities of U.S. firms. Thus between 1978 and 1982, an average of 15.2 percent of the deficit was created by U.S. firms that took advantage of TSUS Items 806.30 and 807, which

Table 6–2. Additional Telephone and Telegraph Apparatus:[a] Producers' Shipments, Exports, and Imports, 1980–1985.

Year	Value of Shipments	Exports	Imports	Ratio of Imports to New Supply	Ratio of Exports to Shipments
1980	$6,892,651	$360,003	$ 231,813	3.3	5.2
1981	7,455,686	383,573	370,217	4.7	5.1
1982	6,979,856	440,606	443,702	6.0	6.3
1983	6,891,372	342,563	1,007,323	12.8	5.0
1984	8,147,949	369,927	1,387,641	14.6	4.5
1985	8,069,503	443,188	1,822,018	18.4	5.5

[a]Carrier line equipment, telephone sets, teleprinters, display terminals, modems, voice frequency equipment, telephone key systems, and other equipment, including telephone answering devices.

Source: Compiled from official statistics of the U.S. Department of Commerce.

encouraged the firms to move labor-intensive operations to low-wage countries in the Far East by enabling them to pay duty only on value added overseas. Nevertheless, the important trade story beginning in 1983 was the surge of imports built by non-U.S.-owned producers off-shore. In 1983 the share of imports accounted for by Item 806/807 fell dramatically to just 5.1 percent; it remained at 5.3 percent in 1984.

In part, the higher import figures for CPE reflect the earlier opening of the U.S. submarket to non-Bell System equipment.

Far East suppliers accounted for 75 percent of the U.S. import market for telephone and telegraph apparatus in 1984, most of it concentrated in low-end customer premises equipment; their import share of the U.S. market for telephones, for instance, was an unassailable 94 percent. Indeed, of all of the product segments reviewed here, the import penetration ratio was consistently the highest for standard telephone instruments, accounting for 40 percent of new supply in 1984 (see Table 6–3).

Japan was by far the largest source of U.S. imports of CPE, its share growing at an average annual rate of 45.7 percent between 1979 and 1983. Though smaller in absolute numbers than the Japanese imports of CPE, imports from other East Asian suppliers grew much faster. Imports from Hong Kong grew at an average annual rate of 157 percent between 1979 and 1983. Comparable rates were 139 percent for Taiwan and 99 percent for South Korea (U.S. International Trade Commission 1984).

As noted earlier, much of this growth can be traced to the explosion of imports of telephone handsets during 1983—one U.S. Commerce

Table 6–3. Telephone Instruments: Producers' Shipments, Exports, and Imports, 1980–1985.

Year	Value of Shipments	Exports	Imports	Ratio of Imports to New Supply	Ratio of Exports to Shipments
1980	$ 857,669	$23,939	$ 54,341	6.0	2.8
1981	1,039,903	26,813	142,136	12.1	2.6
1982	1,054,894	24,259	148,576	12.2	2.3
1983	831,153	27,714	453,706	35.3	3.3
1984	808,630	36,996	539,190	40.0	4.6
1985	1,220,289	37,322	483,901	28.4	3.1

Source: Compiled from official statistics of the U.S. Department of Commerce.

Department Study showed a phenomenal 586 percent increase in imports of telephone handsets for just the first nine months of that year (U.S. International Trade Commission 1984). Much of this growth could be accounted for by the boom in cordless telephones, *none* of which were manufactured in the United States. From 1982 to the end of 1983, the quantity of cordless phones imported into the United States more than quadrupled, from 1.9 million to 8.4 million. The import boom for all types of telephone instruments eased a bit in 1985, probably due to an oversaturation of the market with cheap, low-quality phones, though imports still accounted for about one-third of the U.S. market. And, although Taiwan and Hong Kong lost U.S. market share in 1984 and 1985, U.S. imports from South Korea and Singapore nearly doubled due to the number of firms opening production facilities in those two countries.

By contrast, the U.S. trade position looks fairly strong when one focuses on high-end customer premises equipment, such as PBXs, and other technologically sophisticated product categories, such as central office switching equipment. This is also true of some categories of transmission equipment where domestic economies of scale tend to mitigate the U.S. labor cost disadvantage. For example, AT&T's Atlanta fiber optics manufacturing facility was set to produce about 1.5 billion fiber optic circuit miles in 1985, double the 1984 production, but with only 10 percent additional labor. Total manufacturing costs were gauged at about 75 percent of the 1984 costs (*Communications Week* 1985: 6).

In general, exports have increased steadily, relative to shipments for central office switching equipment, reaching 14.9 percent in 1983, while imports, although rising, remained at less than 1 percent of domestic consumption (U.S. International Trade Commission 1984: Table 5). The trade picture darkens somewhat with the addition of data on private branch exchanges; the export/shipment ratio for all telephone switching and switchboard apparatus has declined from a high of 9.3 percent in 1983 to 4.5 percent in 1985. The ratio of imports to a new supply reached 10 percent in 1984, before falling back to 6.5 percent in 1985. Still, that 10 percent compares favorably with the 40 percent import ratio for telephone instruments in 1984 and the 12.8 percent for telephone and telegraph apparatus overall (see Table 6–4).

Japan accounted for roughly half of all U.S. imports of central office switches in the early 1980s. Canada is also an important source of imported switching equipment, mostly due to one firm, Northern Telecom. Canada supplied 15.9 percent of total U.S. imports of telephone and

Table 6–4.   Telephone Switching and Switchboard
Apparatus:[a] Producers' Shipments, Exports, and
Imports, 1980–1985.

Year	Value of Shipments	Exports	Imports	Ratio of Imports to New Supply[b]	Ratio of Exports to Shipments
1980	$4,254,301	$185,117	$191,110	4.3	4.4
1981	4,362,883	255,663	191,110	3.7	5.9
1982	4,447,803	370,795	183,821	4.0	8.3
1983	4,650,697	430,492	305,659	6.2	9.3
1984	5,533,142	390,690	612,833	10.0	7.1
1985	7,593,531	342,399	525,572	6.5	4.5

[a]Private branch exchanges and central office switches.

[b]New supply = producers' shipments plus imports.

Source: Compiled from official statistics of the U.S. Department of Commerce.

telegraph apparatus in 1985, of which switching equipment accounted for 65 percent (U.S. Department of Commerce 1986: 30–34).

A similar situation existed with respect to transmission equipment. Import penetration of the U.S. market for transmission equipment increased from 3.3 percent in 1979 to 6.4 percent in 1983, with Japan alone accounting for 34 percent (U.S. International Trade Commission 1984: Table 5). A smaller but potentially significant source of U.S. imports of cable, wire, and lightguide is Mexico, which accounted for 44 percent of such imports between 1979 and 1983. However, Mexico's import share of the U.S. market, which grew from 0.8 percent in 1979 to 2.7 percent in 1983, resulted primarily because U.S. firms took advantage of TSUS Items 806.30 and 807 (U.S. International Trade Commission 1984: 35). Domestic manufacturers have retained the dominant share in U.S. markets for cable and wire because few foreign suppliers produce these mature products to U.S. specifications. On the other hand, industry analysts expected the Japanese market share to rise rapidly for the newer lightguide, or fiber optic cable, technology, in large part due to the aggressive pricing strategy of Japanese suppliers.

In contrast to the CPE subsector, which is dominated by products that tend to be labor-intensive and require no substantial customization for the user and little significant after-sales service, switching equipment tends to be research and design-skill intensive in production and customized in use. Thus a number of foreign firms have established U.S. operations that specialize in final assembly of higher end products or in customizing imported equipment to meet the functional requirements of U.S. customers. Many foreign-owned firms have even established manufacturing facilities in the United States, with potentially important positive effects on domestic employment (see Table 6–5). Even as early as 1980, a U.S. Commerce Department study (1984) estimated that direct foreign investment accounted for 26,297 jobs in the U.S. communications equipment sector.

In general, then, the deterioration of the U.S. trade position in telecommunications equipment has been both dramatic and uneven. While the value of U.S. exports barely changed between 1982 and 1986 (in constant 1982 dollars, from $829 million to $809 million), the value of imports more than tripled (from about $816 million to over $2.6 billion). Clearly, the deteriorating performance was due more to the rapid rise in imports than to the slow growth of exports. And that performance was clearly consistent with a static comparative advantage perspective applied within the sector, as the imports were heavily concentrated in labor-intensive, low-end customer premises equipment.

EMPLOYMENT TRENDS IN THE U.S. TELECOMMUNICATIONS EQUIPMENT SECTOR

Despite sustained growth in demand and output, overall employment levels in the U.S. telecommunications equipment industry have tended to stagnate or decline since the early 1970s—an OECD study (1983) estimated a net decline of 17,600 jobs.[18] This pattern precedes the recent import challenge to employment levels in the more labor-intensive segments of the industry and can be explained almost entirely by rapid technological innovation in the production process. The shift from electromechanical to primarily electronic equipment has led to increased automation and improved production techniques. Testing and installation can now be accomplished quickly with the use of easily replaceable modular units, computer-controlled manufacturing systems and inventory control reduce labor requirements for moving and tracking parts and products, and robots are utilized to carry out the most unskilled and monotonous tasks. In short, far fewer people are needed to manufacture the industry's growing list of products.

Table 6-5. Foreign-Owned U.S. Manufacturing Facilities.[a]

Firm	Location	Equipment Manufactured
Canadian		
Northern Telecom	Santa Clara, CA	Digital PBX
	Richardson, TX	Digital PBX
	North Carolina (4 locations)	Digital CO switch telephone
	West Palm Beach, FL;	sets, terminals, computers, test
	Atlanta, GA;	equipment, transmission equip-
	Concord, NH;	ment (others include
	Moorestown, NJ;	components)
	Morton Grove, IL;	
	Nashville, TN;	
	San Diego, CA;	
	Minnetonka, MN	
Mitel	Vermont	Custom ICs for PBX
	Florida	PBX assembly
	Puerto Rico	PCB assembly
Japanese		
Alcoa-NEC Communications Corporation	Sidney, OH	Satellite television receiving systems
ASTRONET Corporation	Lake Mary, FL	Cellular mobile communications equipment
Fujitsu-America, Inc.	Richardson, TX	Cellular mobile and fiber optic, multiplex, and microwave equipment

IMC Magnetics	Westbury, NY	Fans/blowers for communications equipment
Iwatsu-America	Carlstadt, NJ	Key telephone systems
Matsushita Communications	Franklin Park, IL	Cellular mobile communications equipment
NEC-America	Hawthorne, CA	Cellular mobile and mobile paging equipment
NEC-America	Hillsboro, OR	Fiber optic equipment
NEC-America	Dallas, TX	PBX
NEC Information Systems	Boxborough, MA	Computers, peripherals
Oki-America	Norcross, GA	PBX, cellular mobile equipment
Sumitomo Electric	Research Triangle, NC	Fiber-optic cable

[a]Alcoa-NEC Communications is a joint venture of NEC (49 percent) and Alcoa (51 percent); ASTRONET is a joint venture of Mitsubishi Electric (49 percent) and the United Kingdom's Plessey Corporation (51 percent); IMC Magnetics is owned by Minebea Company; PBX = Private Branch Exchange; CO = Central Office; PCB = Printed Circuit Board.

Sources: Northern Telecom, Northern Business Information; most Japanese data are from the Japan Economic Institute.

Microelectronics is the transcendent force that drives these changes. The penetration of semiconductor technology, especially the large-scale and very large-scale integration that is associated with digital processing, has been propelled by a continuous decrease in price per circuit function, the result of a continuous increase in the number of electronic functions that can be implemented on a single computer chip. The employment implications of chips that are able to do more for less are staggering when measured in terms of their effect on direct labor requirements (see Table 6–6).

In attempting to assess the effects of trade on employment, then, it is crucial to bear in mind the fact that overall employment trends have been and will continue to be dominated by technological innovation in the production process, innovation that is driven at the high end of each product segment by the desired performance characteristics of the products themselves rather than by a desire to save on labor costs. That desire will become increasingly relevant in the low-end, labor-intensive product segments as import competition intensifies for commodity customer premises equipment.

It is important to bear in mind, also, that production of the family of products based on the previous electromechanical technological generation does not disappear all at once; such production continues to demand the participation of skilled manual labor and continues

Table 6–6. Estimated Work Forces for Production of Central Office Switches.[a]

Manufacturing Function	Total Number of Employees		
	Crossbar[b]	SPC-Analog	Digital
Material (PCB, components, metal FAB)	1,000	150	20
Assembly, wiring	2,000	900	50
Testing	250	200	50

[a]By production technique.

[b]Crossbar is an electromechanical process that uses a set of small metal switches that snap on and off to physically form the set of crosspoints required to make a telephone communication pathway; stored program control (SPC) analog and digital switches use solid-state (semiconductor) components to form the necessary connections. Analog switches convert sound waves to electronic current; digital switches convert sound waves to computer-readable numerical code.

Source: Arthur D. Little International (1983: 54).

to occur wherever centers of such labor are traditionally located. In the United States, for example, AT&T continues to manufacture a range of products and components at its older plants in the Northeast and Midwest. Nevertheless, the most clearly identifiable characteristic of such production is that it is declining. During the past several years, AT&T has been phasing out its four oldest plants—located in Baltimore, Indianapolis, and Hawthorne and Kearny, New Jersey—all of which produced products for which demand is now lagging or components that are now becoming obsolete.

This declining demand for skilled manual labor in the areas where it has been traditionally employed by the telecommunications equipment industry coexists with the industry's growing demand for a different type of skilled labor, which is more likely to be located near more recently developed agglomerations of high-tech R&D. The simultaneous increase in demand for unskilled and semiskilled assemblers leads telecommunications equipment producers to partake of the now-classic dual spatial structure of most electronics-based sectors, including the employment (sometimes offshore) of a less organized, lower paid, and mostly female production work force to complement its high-tech coterie of mostly white, male scientists and engineers.

These trends are insufficiently represented by existing aggregate employment statistics. Indeed, data on employment trends in the U.S. telecommunications equipment industry can best be characterized as scattered, inconsistent, unreliable, or merely unavailable. First, the level of disaggregation is frustratingly inadequate. Either occupational breakdowns are cross-tabulated with a too-highly aggregated breakdown by industry (SIC 36—electrical and electronic equipment) or relevant industry categories (SIC 3661—telephone and telegraph apparatus—and a portion of SIC 3662—radio and television communications equipment) are cross-tabulated with too-highly aggregated occupational categories (for example, "total employment" and "production workers").

Next is the problem of inconsistency. Figures from various sources—the General Accounting Office (GAO), input-output tables, censuses of manufactures and population, the BLS, and the U.S. Department of Commerce—sometimes differed by as much as 15 percent. Thus, unless otherwise noted, employment numbers in this section are taken from what appeared to be the single most complete and internally consistent source—the U.S. Commerce Department's *U.S. Industrial Outlook*. Finally, as previously noted, the telecommunications infrastructure does not reconfigure all at once. Thus available employment statistics probably reflect the shift from crossbar to analog technologies better than they reflect the currently accelerating shift to digital technologies. Nevertheless, given all these caveats, published data on aggregate employment are sufficient to suggest the magnitude, and indicate the true direction, of the overall trends.

Although no productivity measure for the telephone and telegraph apparatus industry (SIC 3661) is published by the BLS, new manufacturing technologies have clearly reduced unit labor requirements, causing employment growth to lag significantly behind the growth of output. Annual output growth averaged 4.7 percent between 1972 and 1983, while the average annual rate of change in employment amounted to 0.09 percent for the same period. Output grew an average of 4.2 percent annually between 1972 and 1978; it grew 5.3 percent between 1978 and 1983. Employment grew at an annual rate of 0.4 percent between 1972 and 1978, but declined at an annual rate of −1.1 percent between 1978 and 1983.

Despite a resurgence in output after 1982 due to divestiture, deregulation, and expanding demand for a growing list of new microelectronics-based products, the negative employment trends have continued. Although output grew at an average yearly rate of 11 percent between 1983 and 1986, total employment inched upward just 0.5 percent on average. In absolute numbers, total employment in industry SIC 3661 declined nearly 12 percent between 1981 and 1986, from the 147,000 employed in 1981 to approximately 130,000 in 1986 (see Table 6–7). Industry employment peaked in 1981 after five years of fairly steady increases following the mid-1970s recession. That recession apparently accounts for a sharp drop in total employment between 1974 and 1976 (down almost 28 percent, from 145,000 to 105,000). The employment downturn during 1982–83 reflects both recession and industry reorganization in anticipation of the Bell System breakup. Nevertheless, despite a brief period of growth in 1984, employment has not recovered (as in the late 1970s) to its pre-recession level. Indeed, employment declines are expected to continue through the end of the decade, even though the value of overall industry shipments is forecast to grow at a healthy inflation-adjusted rate of 9 percent annually.

Much of this projected employment decline can be traced to plans that were announced by AT&T Information Systems on August 24, 1985 to proceed with one of the largest corporate cutbacks in history, the eventual elimination of 24,000 jobs. These cuts can be explained by AT&T's increasingly difficult competition with lower-cost producers,

Table 6–7.   Employment in the U.S. Telephone and Telegraph Equipment Industry, 1971–1986.

Year	Total	Production	Ratio
1971	140,000	98,000	.70
1972	135,000	95,000	.70
1973	138,000	97,000	.70
1974	145,000	102,000	.70
1975	119,000	81,000	.68
1976	105,000	74,000	.70
1977	124,000	87,000	.70
1978	131,000	89,000	.68
1979	145,000	100,000	.69
1980	144,000	98,000	.68
1981	147,000	96,000	.65
1982	137,000	86,000	.63
1983	128,000	81,000	.63
1984	133,000	86,000	.65
1985[a]	132,000	84,000	.64
1986[b]	130,000	83,000	.64

[a]Estimated.
[b]Forecast.
Sources: *U.S. Industrial Outlook* (1984, 1985, 1986).

both foreign and domestic. Eighteen thousand of these jobs were to be cut in 1985 through attrition, reassignment, and layoffs, with an additional 6,000 to be eliminated outright in 1986. Although 30 percent of the cuts were to come from the ranks of middle management, the cutback also included the abolition of 1,877 hourly factory jobs at the company's telephone handset manufacturing plant in Shreveport, Louisiana. About 1,000 workers were expected to be hired at the new plant that AT&T planned to open in Singapore in 1986.

Aside from competition with lower wage labor in Korea, Singapore, and Taiwan (where electronics workers average no more than $1.75 per hour), well-paid, unionized telecommunications production workers in the United States are now in direct competition for jobs—and wages—with unorganized, lower paid American production workers from the electronic components industry. Although production workers' hourly earnings in SIC 3661 remained higher in absolute terms, their wages declined relative to the average manufacturing wage after 1983. Increased competition is apparently leading to a decline in the relative wage position of production workers in this industry (see Table 6–8).

Still relatively labor-intensive compared to other high-tech sectors, the ratio of production workers to all employees in industry SIC 3661 has hovered around 65 percent since 1981, as compared to an average of around 70 percent throughout the 1970s (see Table 6–7). Recession, reorganization, and robotization hit production workers particularly hard between 1981 and 1984, resulting in the employment of approximately 10,000 fewer people in production and related jobs in this industry despite the general economic recovery.

The employment picture brightens considerably when data are added from SIC 3662—radio and television communications equipment—but these figures must be viewed with extreme caution since the data are not adequately disaggregated for our purposes. We wish only to examine the category of products that are grouped as "communications systems and equipment" (except broadcast), which includes many of the more technologically advanced telecommunications products, such as fiber optics systems and equipment, mobile radio equipment, facsimile equipment, and space satellite communications systems. Products in this category accounted for about 23 percent of total product shipments in 1985, up 11 percent from their share in 1984. It must also be kept in mind that the radio and television communications

Table 6–8.   Average Hourly Earnings of Production Workers in Selected Electronics-Based Industries.

	Year				
Industry	1981	1982	1983	1984	1985
All manufacturing	7.99	8.49	8.83	9.19	9.53
Telephone and telegraph apparatus	9.52	10.25	11.04	11.28	11.29
Radio and television communications equipment	8.76	9.64	10.35	10.91	11.58
Semiconductors and related devices	8.15	8.51	9.06	9.16	9.25
Electronic components	6.39	7.42	7.81	not available	not available

Sources: *U.S. Industrial Outlook* (1984, 1985, 1986).

equipment sector is heavily dependent on the U.S. Department of Defense and thus is substantially insulated from the commercial vagaries of international trade. Forty-five percent of this sector's output went directly or indirectly into Pentagon products in 1979; by 1987 the military's share is expected to approach 63 percent (Markusen 1986: 499–501).

Despite our inability to separate out employment data for the telecommunications portion of SIC 3662, trends as a whole seem quite consistent with what we would expect to find in such an advanced technological sector (see Table 6–9). Both total employment and employment of production workers have increased steadily throughout the 1970s and through the mid-1980s, but the rate of increase in the production work force has slowed to about half the rate of increase in the nonproduction work force since 1981. Indeed, although total industry employment increased by 10 percent between 1984 and 1985, more than half—nearly 30,000—of the 53,000 new jobs that were created were for nonproduction workers, reflecting a continuing high demand for engineers and technicians. The ratio of production workers to the

Table 6–9. Employment in the U.S. Radio and Television Communications Equipment Industry, 1971–1985.

Year	Total	Production	Ratio
1971	325,000	154,000	.47
1972	319,000	162,000	.51
1973	323,000	163,000	.50
1974	318,000	160,000	.50
1975	316,000	160,000	.51
1976	316,000	159,000	.50
1977	334,000	172,000	.51
1978	376,000	192,000	.51
1979	386,000	199,000	.52
1980	413,000	212,000	.51
1981	427,000	218,000	.51
1982	464,000	228,000	.49
1983	478,000	225,000	.47
1984	520,000	246,000	.47
1985[a]	573,000[a]	269,000	.47

[a]Estimated.

Sources: *U.S. Industrial Outlook* (1984, 1985, 1986).

total has slipped decidedly below the 50 percent or more that reigned throughout the 1970s.

Just as estimating overall employment trends is difficult because data are inconsistent, inaccurate, or incomplete, coming up with a numerical estimate of the employment effects of trade is made difficult by the configuration of existing data bases. Several input-output-based studies of trade-related employment have been undertaken in recent years, but data for IO Sector 56 include not only figures for SIC industries 3661 and 3662, but also for SIC 3561 (radio- and television-receiving sets), one of the most trade-impacted industries in the United States, with an import penetration ratio topping 60 percent in 1985. Even so, the trade impact on employment in this industry, and for the industry with which we are most concerned (SIC 3661), has clearly been swamped by employment creation in high-tech, military-driven SIC industry 3662. A U.S. Commerce Department study released in 1983 reported, for example, that total U.S. exports of telecommunications equipment (SIC 366) generated 65,000 American jobs in 1980 alone (U.S. Department of Commerce 1983).

Thus, although the USITC's study of trade-related employment found that trade had cost 95,970 jobs in IO Sector 56 between 1980 and 1984 (representing 13.57 percent of the industry's total 1984 employment), actual employment still *increased* between 1980 and 1984. The increase was equivalent to nearly 8 percent of the industry's total 1984 employment, or about 57,000 jobs (U.S. International Trade Commission 1986: Table 4). Moreover, looking at the data we have for SIC 3661 alone, one thing is abundantly clear: declining employment trends *preceded* the beginning of serious import competition in 1983 and have not accelerated since, despite tremendous surges in both imports and domestic output during the same period.

As the production processes of telecommunications equipment and other electronics products converge, so too do the employment structures and the geography of production characteristic of each sector. Large telecommunications producers increasingly exhibit the classic electronics spatial structure, consisting fundamentally of the locational separation of management, research, and development from parts of the production process that require a skilled manual labor force and from the increasing proportion of production work that requires unskilled and semiskilled labor, mostly for assembly operations. Until recently, telecommunications equipment producers were less likely than electronics component producers to set up offshore assembly facilities, in part because assembly operations accounted for such a small share of total production costs. However, this cost calculation has begun to change due to intense competitive pressure from overseas suppliers as well as a growing desire to create a presence in, and thus gain access to, overseas markets. Thus, for example, AT&T moved its residential phone plant from Shreveport, Louisiana, to Singapore.

The great exception to this pattern stems from the necessity of continuing to manufacture a range of products and components that serve many of the same functions as do the latest microelectronics-based gadgets but are themselves at a prior stage of technological development. Doreen Massey (1984: 145–49) has identified the manufacture of telecommunications equipment as the classic case of such "staged development," proceeding simultaneously from the production of electromechanical, through semielectronic, to fully electronic products.

As Massey notes, investment in the new technologies no longer requires the locations that are traditionally favored for the production of electromechanical instruments. Indeed, the decline in market demand for products that are based on older technologies, combined with intense competitive pressure on firms in the industry to update their manufacturing techniques, means that "new investment in the new techniques in the new areas now has to be compensated for by closures of the old techniques in the old areas" (Massey 1984: 146). Thus the closures of AT&T's component plants in New Jersey free capital for the construction of its new semiconductor facility in Orlando, Florida; the opening of its new handset production facility in Singapore follows the removal of its residential handset line in Shreveport.

But the changing spatial structure of telecommunications equipment manufacture within the United States does not merely replicate the international division of labor in electronics. The national spatial structure is embedded in the international one and reflects the place of the United States in the international hierarchy. Thus all stages of production are present in the United States. The existence of "Silicon Valleys" — the coexistence of production facilities and advanced research and development centers—distinguishes the organization and employment structure of industrial production in the United States from telecommunications equipment manufacture in other countries, where only production facilities are located. So, too, does the continued manufacture of older products and components.

Thus we must be careful when trying to isolate the employment effects of increased international trade in this sector. Indeed, within the

United States it is perhaps not the skilled and highly organized manual labor force that is most uniquely vulnerable to the changing geography of telecommunications equipment production. These workers are vulnerable, all right, but they are vulnerable because the products that they make, along with the skills that are required to make them, are being entirely phased out. Less skilled wafer fabrication technicians and assembly workers that are employed in the manufacture of more labor-intensive microelectronics-based customer premises equipment are more vulnerable to a deteriorating trade position; unlike some of their Third World counterparts, United States assembly workers earn more than twenty cents an hour.

In general, the intraindustry employment structure of regions in the United States that currently provide sites for different stages of the telecommunications equipment production processes reflects their relative "generational" position in the technological cycle as well as in the national and international division of labor. Thus what Massey (1984: 149) says about the sector in the United Kingdom applies as well to the industry in the United States: While other parts of the country—Route 128, Research Triangle, Colorado Springs—try to gain good-paying technical and engineering jobs by competing with Silicon Valley, "the regions with only assembly jobs may lose even them to a Third World Free Production Zone, or win production back only when there has been sufficient automation to reduce substantially the critical importance of labor costs, and therefore the number of jobs."

THE DOMESTIC EMPLOYMENT EFFECTS OF TRADE IN TELECOMMUNICATIONS EQUIPMENT

Competition and technological innovation have accelerated electronics-based product lives, forcing substantial cost-cutting in manufacture and assembly, necessitating real differentiation of products in the market, and often requiring that firms produce a family of related products in order to realize higher gains from their initial investments. As the competition has intensified, state-of-the-art production techniques have come to constitute the core of global manufacturing strategies that are geared to win competitive advantage.

Manufacturing location decisions have likewise been driven by the desire to penetrate new markets, tempting domestic producers offshore when the axis around which competition revolves is price and keeping them in the United States when success in the market requires sophisticated custom-finishing and long-term after-sales service on the customer's premises. As Andrew Sayer has noted, the spatial implications of the new manufacturing technologies are characteristically double edged. Microelectronics-based innovations influence location strategies by "simultaneously facilitating the coordination of spatially-separated activities and hence allowing dispersion, but also allowing localised location factors such as labour markets with top technical skills to become relatively more important" (Sayer, 1985).

A brief examination of the manufacturing strategies of major telecommunications equipment producers in two important product submarkets suggests a particular pattern to these choices. It can be argued, in fact, that the organizing principle in telecommunications equipment production is product differentiation: choices about manufacturing techniques, the use of labor, and the location of production are driven by the needs of final users, as expressed in the performance characteristics of the products themselves.

Telephone Handsets

The market for consumer telephones is at the low end of the submarket for CPE. Because these are standard commodity products, very much like other consumer electronics products, there is no requirement to customize each handset for any particular user during the production process, nor is there any need for considerable after-sales service—if it breaks, the customer can simply throw it away or trade it in for one that works. Handsets are not software-intensive or circuit design-intensive; the manufacturing process begins and ends with standard circuit pack and final assembly operations.

It is precisely these standard manufacturing operations, however, that can be made more or less labor-intensive, depending primarily on a firm's evaluation of the cost of labor relative to the cost of automating. There is considerable incentive to automate when manual assembly of circuit packs costs twenty-five cents per component and when custom software is a major characteristic of the product. When the need for user-specific functionality disappears, it becomes possible to rely on more labor-intensive assembly, which remains cheaper overall than automated assembly, even in the United States. It is cheaper still, of course, in Hong Kong, Korea, and Taiwan.

Industry analysts agree that the U.S. market is probably oversaturated with cheap, low-quality phones that are manufactured in the Far East. Imports of telephone handsets amounted to 34.2 million units in 1983, yet total sales to dealers, including domestic production, came to only 19.7 million. This oversupply led to price reductions in some cases to as low as $4 per phone. Given these realities, production in offshore export platforms in the Far East has become an increasingly attractive strategy for small, independent American handset companies, such as Teleconcepts, which specializes in sales of small business systems to the small-to-middle-sized retail market, and Dynascan, which specializes in the production of cordless phones and answering devices. Indeed, imports of low-cost cordless phones from the Far East have caused U.S. firms to completely discontinue their production in the United States. As we have seen, by mid-1985 even AT&T was unable to resist the attraction of a production site in Singapore for the manufacture of its standard telephone handsets.

Fortunately for domestic employment and for the long-range competitive position of American firms, some U.S. producers have identified a manufacturing strategy that is compatible with high-wage American labor and that enables them to remain internationally competitive in the market for telephone handsets while simultaneously developing the market and technological resources that are necessary for success in the telephone equipment markets of the future.

Understanding that they cannot match the extraordinarily low costs that are achieved in foreign export platforms in the Far East, these firms are positioning themselves to dominate the high-quality, high-value-added, custom-specialty segments of the telephone handset market. AT&T, for example, has chosen to meet its continuing price disadvantage head-on by stressing the high quality of its product—"you get what you pay for" —and by incorporating useful features, such as number memory and automatic redialing, into its phones.

Another domestic manufacturer, Comdial, has traded on its semiconductor expertise to enter the market for high-quality feature telephones; significantly, Comdial has maintained its U.S. manufacturing facilities in Virginia.[4] Like AT&T, however, Comdial has turned to state-of-the-art automation to reduce its manufacturing costs. Between 1982 and 1984 the size of Comdial's engineering staff increased fivefold; during the same period, the company cut its production work force by approximately 40 percent.

Parts of Comdial's production process have remained relatively labor-intensive, even as other production operations—plastics molding, computer-aided design of printed circuit boards, circuit pack assembly, and testing of finished circuit packs—have become completely automated. In 1983 Comdial opened a new manufacturing plant in Shenandoah, forty miles away from its Charlottesville operation. Labor rates are lower in Shenandoah than in Charlottesville, thus enabling the company to cut costs for labor-intensive subassembly work—the insertion of components that are too sensitive, too expensive, or too limited in number to warrant automatic handling. At the same time, the new plant's proximity to Comdial's Charlottesville R&D facility assures a quick response on the production line to new product or process innovations, requests from customers for service, repairs, or systems upgrades, or shifts in market demand that require alteration of Comdial's product mix.

While Comdial's move to the highly automated production of high-quality or high value-added telephone handsets has enabled the firm to maintain its manufacturing operations in the United States, it purchases raw materials and standard electronic components from offshore producers, both domestic and foreign owned. As is the case with low-end commodity handsets, the axis around which competition revolves for standard components and raw materials is *price*; it is cheaper for Comdial to buy and transport integrated circuits, capacitors, resistors, and the like from low-cost offshore producers than it is to purchase or manufacture them for itself in the United States.

The locational and employment consequences of the two major manufacturing strategies are thus clear; they vary with the performance characteristics of the product. Low-end components and commodity handsets are extremely price-sensitive and thus vulnerable to offshoring; when competition is based on quality, custom functionality, and systems upgradeability, manufacturing is very likely to remain near the U.S. market, utilizing a much smaller labor force that is split between high-tech glamour jobs and relatively monotonous fabrication and assembly work.

Private Branch Exchanges

Due to the growing demand from business users of automated office equipment for a product that can control the voice and data flows between various pieces of workplace equipment while serving as the major internal link to external public and private communications networks, the PBX is being positioned as an indispensable digital network integration device.

But, unlike the producers of standard telephone handsets, PBX producers seem to have little choice about where to locate the production of their product, at least during the final stages of manufacture. Although the PBX market is itself fragmented into niches, differentiated in terms of the number of internal connections (lines) from the PBX to terminals, all PBXs utilize very complex and highly customized systems/subsystems software. Foreign producers have thus set up U.S. domestic manufacturing operations in order to adapt their hardware in final assembly to meet the particular requirements of American customers, as well as to make sure that they have incorporated the latest technological advances into their increasingly software-driven products. These characteristics of the product and its use explain the near absence of imports of finished PBXs into the United States.

Price competition has been intense in the U.S. market—competitors have accused each other of predatory pricing in order to gain market share and thus position themselves for more lucrative future sales of add-on equipment and services—but production costs are a less important determinant of competitive success in the PBX market than are system features, reliability, and configurational flexibility. Indeed, aggressively low-priced Japanese PBXs actually lost market share between 1979 and 1982.

Although the vast majority of PBX equipment is manufactured to customer specification and finished domestically, the organization of production varies considerably between firms, with varying implications for the use of labor. PBX manufacturing by AT&T and Northern Telecom, for example, is highly vertically integrated. Both firms have attempted to lead the high end of the PBX market. AT&T's PBX production line in Denver is highly automated, though final assembly remains, for the moment, relatively labor-intensive. Like AT&T, Northern achieves economies of scale in components production through the use of a distributed manufacturing setup. Northern combines components that come from six different plants in the United States and Canada, and its PBX production is split between its plant in Belleville, Ontario, and its plant in Santa Clara, California.

Flexible manufacturing systems, such as those used by AT&T and Northern Telecom, respond directly to the particular product characteristics on which competition in this market is based. Rolm, which has been most successful at dominating the middle-sized segment of the PBX market, achieves manufacturing flexibility by purchasing components—integrated circuits, printed circuit boards, metal parts and castings, and commodity peripheral equipment—from outside vendors. Although this strategy leaves Rolm vulnerable to supply fluctuations, it also permits the rapid incorporation of technological innovations that are generated by electronic component suppliers. It may also add to the stability of Rolm's production employment because Rolm can respond to market downturns by cutting back its orders from outside vendors instead of cutting back on its own work force. Rolm's domestic PBX production takes place in three plants—in Santa Clara, Colorado Springs, and Austin, Texas. Similar to AT&T, the basic manufacturing process—in the case of PBXs, the initial one-fourth of the process—is identical for all systems; once the basics are set, each system is customized for the user. It bears repeating that the increasingly custom and software-driven nature of PBXs—as well as other digitally based switching and transmission equipment—*requires* manufacturing near the point of sale because customization occurs during the process of production.

Mitel of Canada currently dominates the low-end (under 100 lines) segment of the PBX market, but it has had some trouble managing the transition to a digitally based product. Significantly, Mitel's current troubles stem in part from its previous strategy of pursuing a low-cost manufacturing position for its analog-based PBX product. Mitel relies heavily on labor-intensive assembly. Its own custom-integrated circuits are manufactured in Vermont and Canada, its printed circuit boards are assembled in Puerto Rico (for tax and low labor-cost advantages), and final assembly is done in Florida for the U.S. market. Although Mitel has been quite successful at incorporating analog systems design into the design of its custom integrated circuits, its analog-installed base is inappropriate for digital network integration and it has not gained extensive experience in the design of complex, user-functional software.

Japan's NEC seems to be in a good position to take advantage of Mitel's dilemma, though the competitive pricing strategies of Japanese producers have not been successful so far in overcoming their technological disadvantages in the U.S. market. Like other foreign firms, NEC has sought to overcome its technological disadvantages by establishing a manufacturing presence in the United States; about half of NEC's PBX production takes place in its Dallas, Texas, plant. A domestic presence also helps to inspire confidence in customers who depend on the continued availability of after-sales service and systems upgrades. Furthermore, domestic production enables the Japanese to finesse possible trade disputes, an important consideration given the relative closedness of the Japanese telecommunications equipment markets to American producers. There is some evidence, however (mostly anecdotal at this point), that the Japanese prefer to import Japanese design engineers to work in their U.S. plants, a practice that would tend to further limit the range of new domestic employment opportunities for Americans, despite the growing demand for foreign telecommunications products that are manufactured in the United States.

Underlying the convergence of product markets, spatial patterns, and employment structures among the producers of telecommunications and data processing equipment is, again, the increasing microelectronics content of telecommunications products. At the simplest level, the production process for every type of modern telecommunications product is virtually identical—semiconductor chips are inserted onto boards, and the boards are stuffed into boxes or cabinets. The chips will differ in complexity, and the boxes and cabinets are of different sizes, shapes, and colors, but these differences are irrelevant to the organization of production lines.

As we have seen, however, it is useful to divide telecom equipment into two broad segments for the purpose of analyzing firms' strategic choices about how to reorganize production in response to new technologies and new trade pressures, choices about what to automate and where to produce. We can distinguish between low-end, low value-added products, such as commodity telephone handsets, and high-end, high value-added products, such as PBXs, that are more software driven and tend to be more customized for the user.

For low-end telecom equipment, it makes little competitive sense for U.S. firms to choose domestic automation over offshore platform production. Only when it is possible, as in the case of business handsets, to sell the equipment as part of a higher value-added system (such as a PBX with many extensions) does domestic production remain a viable strategy. In contrast, high-end products often must be functionally customized for each user, a process that must generally begin during the manufacturing process. Initial sales depend on the customer's evaluation of the potential availability of such after-sales services as maintenance, worker training on the equipment, and upgrading. Most important, in terms of long-term competitive position, initial sales create an installed base that lends itself to continuous upgrades and future sales of enhanced software. The combination of these characteristics both permits and requires onshore production in the major markets of Asia, Europe, and the United States. Here, automation appears to be the only viable strategy for domestic producers because of the high custom software content of the products and the need to move rapidly to meet, and to anticipate, the changing needs of the customers of successive product generations.

In looking at the various manufacturing strategies of major telecommunications producers in a low-end CPE market—the market for telephone handsets—and a high-end one—the PBX segment—we have seen how the very different labor and merchandising requirements of each product submarket drive production organization and location decisions that are mandated by the twin challenges of trade and technology. In both submarkets, the production of telecommunications equipment can be seen taking on the classic spatial attributes of most modern electronics production—R&D, fabrication, and assembly operations are increasingly separated geographically, due in part to their dependence on very different categories of labor. This new microelectronics-based spatial division of labor is being superimposed on an older spatial division, one that persists with the continuing production of replacements and upgrades for telecommunications equipment of a *prior* electromechanical technological generation. In a very real sense, the new geography of production feeds off of the scraps of the old; a new employment structure, bifurcated between highly paid scientific and engineering jobs and low-paid assembly work, is growing at the expense of thousands of skilled manual production jobs that are rapidly disappearing in other sections of the country.

CONCLUSIONS

As noted earlier, continued deterioration in the trade position of U.S. producers of telecommunications equipment would portend a worsening employment situation, either in terms of fewer jobs that are created through trade or a greater number of jobs that are destroyed. But the direct impact of increased trade in this sector is clearly marginal relative to the pervasive effects of technological innovation in both products and production techniques. Declining employment trends in this industry *preceded* the beginning of serious import competition in 1983 and have not accelerated since, despite tremendous surges in both imports and domestic output over the same period. Regardless of the trade situation and despite projected continued rapid growth in demand for and output of a growing list of microelectronics-based telecommunications equipment, domestic employment in the telephone and telegraph sector will most likely continue to decline.

An increased demand for highly trained software and circuit designers, electrical engineers, and technicians will accompany the gradual automation and elimination of skilled and semiskilled production and craft work. The retention and expansion at home of high value-added equipment production (switching and transmission equipment, network integration products, such as PBXs and electronic key telephone sets) will accompany the offshoring of labor-intensive standard components and such commodity terminal equipment as one-piece telephone handsets. Although automation is a feasible response to foreign competition in these standard product segments, it becomes economically attractive only insofar as such products can be manufactured and sold as part of a higher value-added package.

In general, increased international trade is pressuring U.S. firms to seek their strategic advantage in the markets for high-end telecommunications equipment. In this sense, trade in this sector is generating domestic employment. The highly custom, software-intensive nature of such products probably requires that production for the U.S. market be located in the United States. Thus even foreign producers will be forced to locate production in the United States in order to compete successfully with their domestic competitors.

These trade-generated jobs cannot be expected to compensate, however, for the trade-related loss of employment in the production of more labor-intensive commodity products or for the pervasive effects of increased automation in the manufacture of more customized and service-intensive products and components. New employment opportunities, whether with U.S. or foreign firms located in the American market, will be for a rapidly growing but relatively small contingent of software designers, technicians, and engineers.

The policy implications of all of this are twofold. On the one hand, industry representatives have expressed concern that the United States lags behind some of its chief economic competitors in the number of students that graduate with advanced degrees in engineering, the physical sciences, and mathematics. Corporate leaders are acutely aware that a shortage of appropriately skilled labor could impose limitations on high-technology development that are no less serious than financial or production constraints are, especially if the United States must compete on the basis of high-end product innovation. Aside from continued corporate assistance to universities in recognition of this problem, the relationship of the nation's educational system to the broader competitive position of U.S. firms in the world's high-tech markets would seem to warrant increased government attention at the federal level.

At the other end of the skill spectrum, displacement of production and craft workers could become a serious problem in the telecommunications industry if the quickening pace of technological advance in the entire range of electronics-based industries further reduces employment opportunities or constrains the degree of labor mobility between the various equipment-producing sectors. These workers tend to possess skills—not to mention homes and community ties—that are better suited to the manufacture of an earlier, electromechanical generation of telecommunications gear. More industry-specific retraining and placement programs may be required to ease the adjustment of workers who are downgraded or displaced from the telecommunications equipment sector due to the combined effects of technological change and increasingly successful competition from abroad.

NOTES

1. Unless specifically noted in the text, the term "telecommunications equipment" refers to the products of the telephone and telegraph equipment industry corresponding to SIC 3661. These products include switching and switchboard equipment, telephone instruments, teleprinting and telex equipment, and other telephone and telegraph apparatus and parts. Certain other telecommunications equipment, such as microwave systems, mobile radio systems, fiber optics and cellular radio equipment (except network switches), and data and satellite communications equipment, are classified in SIC 3662—the radio and television communications equipment industry. The manufacture of products that are included in SIC 3661 is, in general, more labor-intensive and trade-impacted than is the manufacture of the relevant products of SIC 3662, whose production is increasingly oriented toward the defense market and is thus characterized by a very different competitive dynamic.
2. For a detailed analysis of the role played by technological breakthroughs in undermining AT&T's domestic monopoly, see Borrus et al. (1984).
3. Imports are valued on a customs basis. Data have been adjusted to ensure comparability between 1972 and 1984.

4. Information on Comdial is based primarily on personal interview with the company's manager of offshore operations.

REFERENCES

Arthur D. Little International. 1983. *Trends in Telecommunications Technology.* Final Report to the Commission of the European Communities. CEC Contract No. AH-83-365-I/II, November.

Borrus, Michael, François Bar, and Ibraham Warde, with James Millstein and Patrick Cogez. 1984. "The Impacts of Divestiture and Deregulation: Infrastructural Changes, Manufacturing Transition, and Competition in the United States Telecommunications Industry." Berkeley Roundtable on the International Economy Working Paper No. 12, University of California, Berkeley, September.

Communications Week. 1985. July 8, p. 6.

Markusen, Ann. 1986. "The Militarized Economy." *World Policy Journal* 3, no. 3 (Summer): 495–516.

Massey, Doreen. 1984. *Spatial Divisions of Labor: Social Structures and the Geography of Production.* Methuen, N.Y.: MacMillan.

Sayer, Andrew. 1985. "New Developments in Manufacturing and Their Spatial Implications." Working Paper 49, Urban and Regional Studies, The University of Sussex, October.

U.S. Department of Commerce. 1986. *U.S. Industrial Outlook, 1986.* Washington, D.C.: U.S. Government Printing Office.

U.S. Department of Commerce. Bureau of the Census. 1984. *Selected Characteristics of Foreign-Owned U.S. Firms.* Series FOF #6. Washington, D.C.: U.S. Government Printing Office, April.

U.S. Department of Commerce. International Trade Administration. 1983. *Domestic Employment Generated by U.S. Exports.* Prepared by Lester A. Davis, Office of Trade and Investment Analysis. Washington, D.C.: U.S. Government Printing Office, May.

U.S. International Trade Commission. 1984. *Changes in the U.S. Telecommunications Industry and the Impact on U.S. Telecommunications Trade.* Publication 1542. Washington, D.C.: U.S. Government Printing Office, June.

——— . 1986. *U.S. Trade-Related Employment: 1978–84.* Publication 1855, Washington, D.C., May.

7 THE CHANGING SHAPE OF DOMESTIC EMPLOYMENT IN A HIGH-TECH INDUSTRY
The Case of International Trade in Semiconductors

Carol A. Parsons

Once an economic bright spot and an industry on which many were pinning the nation's economic hopes, the semiconductor industry is now hard hit by international competition and, like its brethren in America's older manufacturing core, it is crying foul play against its foreign rivals and asking for government aid and protection. Indeed, the industry's recent history shows troubling parallels with smokestack manufacturing—intense foreign competition, mounting trade deficits, loss of domestic employment, declining market share in critical product segments, and layoffs and plant closures. These discomforting similarities cast doubt on the usefulness of economic development strategies that are based on easy divisions between sunrise and sunset industries. They also imply that high-technology industry may not be a solution to the employment problems of traditional manufacturing.

TWO PERIODS OF FOREIGN TRADE IN SEMICONDUCTORS

This chapter examines the effect of international trade on domestic employment in the semiconductor industry. As a starting point it is useful to recognize that there have been two periods of foreign trade in the semiconductor industry's development. In the first period—dating from the industry's genesis until the mid-1970s—direct foreign investment was the central strategic principle driving production organization, which includes the level and composition of labor demand. In the second period—from the mid-1970s to the present—foreign competition, mainly from Japanese producers, drove the domestic industry's production strategy and has shaped the domestic industry's demand for labor.

During the first period, U.S. merchant firms dominated the world industry.[1] Foreign trade during this period was the result of domestically headquartered companies that shipped partially completed circuits outside of the United States for final assembly. The impetus behind this movement of low-wage production jobs overseas was intense price competition among U.S.-owned firms. Dating from about the 1978 recession, when Japanese firms seized a large share of the U.S. market—Japanese imports rose from 7.7 percent of total U.S. imports in 1977 to 16.5 percent in 1978—trade in semiconductors literally became foreign trade. While the reimportation of domestic firms' output continued to be an important part of U.S. semiconductor imports, the composition of those imports shifted as the output of Japanese firms manufacturing in Japan claimed an expanding share of total imports.

Just a brief look at the import figures for the last fifteen years supports the validity of this characterization. From 1969 to 1978 approximately 80 percent of the value of semiconductor imports resulted from the reimportation of the output of domestically headquartered companies. These product flows are itemized under TSUS Items 806.30 and 807.00. Enacted in 1963, the Item 806/807 provisions allowed U.S. firms to export semifinished goods for final production and then reimport the goods and pay duty only on the value that was added offshore. In 1969 Item 806/807 imports accounted for 95 percent of the value of all semiconductor imports (see Table 7–1). And while this percentage declined rather bumpily, falling to 70 percent or so during recession years, these duty-free imports still constituted 85 percent of the value of all imports in 1978. Beginning that year, however, and continuing steadily ever since, the share of imports taken by Item 806/807 declined. Even during the industry boom in 1984, imports exempt from tariffs fell to 58 percent, reaching an all-time low of 49 percent during the 1985 bust.

The decline of Item 806/807 marks the transition to the second stage of international trade. Over the same period that the Item 806/807 share of imports fell by 27 percent, Japanese imports grew from 7.7 percent

Table 7-1.   806.30 and 807.00 Imports as a Percentage of Total U.S. Imports and Total Shipments, 1969–1984.

Year	806/807 Imports ($ millions)	Total U.S. Imports ($ millions)	806/807 as Percentage of Value of Total U.S. Imports	806/807 as Percentage of Value of U.S. Shipments
1969	127	134	95	8.1
1970	160	168	95	10.7
1971	178	187	95	11.1
1972	254	329	77	9.4
1973	413	611	68	11.3
1974	684	953	72	15.9
1975	617	802	77	18.8
1976	879	1098	80	19.6
1977	1120	1358	82	21.0
1978	1478	1775	83	23.0
1979	1916	2427	79	23.2
1980	2506	3326	75	23.9
1981	2825	3553	80	24.1
1982	3131	4128	76	27.7
1983	3383	4881	69	25.2
1984	5000	7800	64	28.2

Source: 806/807 data from Flamm (1984: 74); value of shipments from Census (various years); approximate 1984 figures from U.S. Department of Commerce, Bureau of the U.S. Department of Commerce (1985).

of the total value of imports to 24.4 percent, an increase of 16.7 percent. This increase in Japanese imports reflects the loss of the commodity memory chip market by U.S. firms. While U.S. companies held 73 percent of the metal oxide semiconductors (MOS) memory chip market in 1980, they only held a 44 percent share by 1984. Over the same period, Japanese companies' share of the MOS segment had grown from 26 percent to 51 percent (Integrated Circuit Engineering Corporation 1986).

These data suggest that the task of determining how trade in semiconductors has affected the level and composition of domestic employment can actually be divided into two separate questions: What effect has the offshoring of employment by domestic producers had on domestic employment? And how has domestic employment been affected by Japanese competition? The discussion that follows will indicate that during the first period, on balance, trade in semiconductors created more jobs in the United States than it destroyed. During the second period, international trade showed up as real job loss, not just lost "job opportunities," as U.S. firms lost domestic market share to the Japanese. In both periods international trade tilted the domestic occupational structure toward technical and managerial jobs while reducing domestic production employment. This increased job opportunities for educated, white male employees while reducing job slots for less educated female and minority workers.

At the same time, some Japanese semiconductor producers chose to build production facilities in the United States, with consequent employment opportunities for American workers. Thus the urgent need that Japanese manufacturers feel to maintain access to the U.S. market may provide a measure of insurance for a very small number of U.S. workers whose jobs might otherwise be threatened by continued Japanese successes (and American failures) in semiconductor trade. Quite recently, in fact, the dollar's depreciation and the growing lobby favoring protectionist legislation have begun to make the United States a desirable location for Japanese producers. Yet it is also clear that the continuing automation of semiconductor production, especially of the formerly labor-intensive assembly stage of production, will mean an increasingly weak tie between direct foreign investment and employment (Parsons 1987).

When examining trade and its domestic employment outcomes during these two periods, one should keep two caveats in mind. First, technological innovation is constantly and quickly pushing the industry into more advanced products and manufacturing processes. Quite aside from trade's affect on labor demand, these technical advances by themselves have had and continue to have a decisive impact on labor demand. As the industry shifts from one generation of product technology to another—from the earlier generation of large-scale integration (LSI) to the most advanced product technology of very large scale integration (VLSI)—companies are introducing new products and new, or vastly improved, manufacturing processes. With VLSI, which is a shorthand for changes in the manufacturing process that make it possible to place more electronic circuits on each semiconductor chip, firms are choosing among a wide range of strategic options. Firms are investigating automating previously labor-intensive segments of the production process, a step that could ultimately require the geographical reintegration of production steps—wafer fabrication, assembly, and testing—that have traditionally been kept geographically separate. Constant incremental (and sometimes radical) innovations in products and their manufacturing processes have had, in short, an enormous effect on the industry's pattern of labor demand. For the purposes of this chapter, technology will be treated as an exogenous variable. But it would be misleading to overlook the central role of technical innovation in the changing occupational structure and geographical distribution of employment.

The other warning flag is the role and importance of state industrial policies. Because of the strategic importance of the semiconductor industry, and the constant technical innovation that is a requirement for market success, the role of government-led industrial development policy has played a crucial role in shaping the industry's growth and production strategy (Borrus, Millstein, and Zysman 1980). Industrial policies link together, for purposes of this analysis, technical change on the one hand and the structure of production on the other.

Profile of International Trade in Semiconductors

Trade in semiconductors has accelerated rapidly over the last fifteen years. In the decade between 1972 and 1982, total imports grew at an annual average rate of 23.9 percent. Exports during the same period increased each year by only 13.4 percent on average (U.S. Department of Commerce 1986). Throughout the 1970s the U.S. trade balance in semiconductors remained comfortably in surplus. Beginning in 1981, however, the trade balance in semiconductors slipped into deficit and in six years slid from a $156 million surplus in 1980 to a $1.2 billion deficit in 1986 (see Table 7–2).

To a large extent, trade levels reflect variations in the demand for final products for which semiconductors are used. This variation in end-users leads to an uneven demand for semiconductors. The 1984 boom market in semiconductors, which was driven by the growth in computer sales and orders by computer producers to replenish their flagging inventories, exemplifies the underlying cause of volatile demand conditions in the industry. During the 1984 boom, imports soared by 55 percent. In 1985, when computer sales slumped, semiconductor sales took a nose dive and imports plummeted by 30.5 percent. With a slight lag, then, the

Table 7–2. U.S. Imports and Exports of Semiconductors (in $ thousands).[a]

Year	Imports	Exports	Balance
1972	$ 330,000	$ 470,000	$ 140,000
1973	619,000	849,000	224,000
1974	961,000	1,248,000	287,000
1975	803,000	1,054,000	251,000
1976	1,107,000	1,400,000	293,000
1977	1,352,000	1,503,000	151,000
1978	1,765,000	1,933,000	168,000
1979	2,447,000	2,609,000	162,000
1980	3,291,000	3,447,000	156,000
1981	3,665,000	3,579,000	− 86,000
1982	4,215,000	3,787,000	− 428,000
1983	5,038,000	4,352,000	− 687,000
1984	7,754,000	5,313,000	− 1,568,000
1985	5,788,000	4,219,000	− 1,568,000
1986	6,079,000	4,847,000	− 1,232,000

[a]SIC 3674.

Sources: U.S. Department of Commerce (1986); unpublished U.S. Department of Commerce data.

demand for semiconductors mirrors the demand for the final products for which semiconductors are used.

The reason the 1985 slump was felt so keenly in the U.S. market was due, in large part, to the differences in the relative specialization of the end-users in different national markets. Overall, the world market fell by 16 percent between 1984 and 1985; in the United States, demand tumbled twice as far, down by 30 percent. In Japan and Europe, demand declined quite moderately, by 2 percent and 4 percent, respectively. This difference in performance hinges on the differences in the end-user markets: the U.S. industry sells almost one-third of its semiconductor output to the computer sector, compared to 10.4 percent for Japanese producers and a 20 percent share for Western European producers (United Nations Centre on Transnational Corporations 1986).

Variations in the structure of demand are a central determinant of the changing pattern of trade. A fuller explanation, however, hinges on an exposition of the two distinct stages of international trade in semiconductors and the competitive conditions each period represents.

Domestically Created Foreign Trade— Stage One

The internationalization of trade in semiconductors initially resulted from direct foreign investment by U.S. companies, which shifted labor-intensive assembly operations to low-wage countries in Latin America and the Far East. The batch manufacturing process made it practical to keep chip design, requiring skilled engineers, and wafer fabrication, requiring expensive equipment and controlled handling, in the United States while taking chip assembly offshore. This international division of labor was at the heart of foreign trade in semiconductors. Between 1964 and 1972 chips assembled offshore by U.S. companies accounted for 95 percent of semiconductor imports.

During the first decade of the industry's development, the technical characteristics of production and the cost advantage of offshore assembly created a self-reinforcing logic. By moving labor-intensive assembly work to low-wage countries, U.S.-headquartered companies reduced total production costs and simultaneously brought competitive pressure to bear on their competitors to offshore their own assembly operations in order to keep their costs competitive. The cost advantage of cheap labor seems indisputable. Industry analyst William Finan (1975) estimated that the lower wages in assembly plants in the Far East and Latin America could reduce *total* manufacturing costs by 50 percent. "For example," he wrote, "the total manufacturing cost of an MOS integrated circuit in 1973 was approximately $1.45 per device with assembly done in Singapore. If the *same device* was assembled in the U.S., the total manufacturing cost would be about $3.00" (Finan 1975: 23). This cost advantage produced a wave of direct foreign investment. Beginning when Fairchild opened a semiconductor plant in Hong Kong in 1964 (no doubt partially in response to the Item 806/807 tariff provisions that were enacted in 1963), U.S. semiconductor firms quickly constructed plants and hired workers. There were twenty-three plants in 1971; there were eighty-two in 1979 (see Table 7–3). And while the industry employed 50,000 workers outside the United States in 1971, this number had reached 89,000 by 1978 (see Table 7–4). While offshore employment continued to be significant throughout the late 1970s and on into the 1980s, up-to-date and reliable estimates of world employment outside the United States are scarce. Recent estimates tend to overlook employment by subcontractors and therefore tend to understate the level of offshore employment. And as multinational companies

Table 7-3.   The Development of Offshore Investment in Various Third World Locations by Major U.S., Japanese, and Western European Semiconductor Firms, 1971–1979.

Country	Number of Firms Present[a]				
	1971	1974	1976	1979	1982
Korea	6	8	8	8	8
Hong Kong	1	6	6	7	6
Indonesia	0	3	3	3	3
Malaysia	0–2	11–13	13–14	14	14
Philippines	0	0	1	6	10
Singapore	9	10	12	13	11
Taiwan	3	3	6	1	7
Thailand	—	—	1	1	1
Brazil	0–2	2	5	5	b
Mexico	—	—	12	13	b
Barbados	0	0	0	1	1
Puerto Rico	—	—	2	3	b
El Salvador	—	1	1	2	1
Morocco	—	—	1	1	1
Malta	—	—	1	1	2
Portugal	—	—	2–3	3	2

[a]The sample included twenty-four U.S. firms, six European firms, and seven Japanese firms. Each firm was counted once, even if it had more than one plant in each country. The U.S. companies were AMD, Burroughs, Fairchild, General Electric, General Instrument, Harris, Hewlett Packard, Intel, International Rectifier, Intersil, ITT, Litonix, Mauman, Monsanto, Mostek, Motorola, National Semiconductor, Pulse Engineering, Raytheon, RCA, Rockwell, Texas Instruments, and Zilog.

[b]Figures for 1982 are from the update in the United Nations Centre for Transnational Corporations (1986).

Source: United Nations Industrial Development Organization (1981: 240).

from Japan and Europe adopted offshore assembly as part of their production strategy it became more difficult to establish the ownership of foreign plants—an increasingly difficult problem as transnational joint ventures and other strategic alliances proliferate. After wrestling with problems of this type, the United Nations Centre on Transnational Corporations (1986) estimated that in 1980, employment outside of the United States in U.S.-owned semiconductor firms was between 115,000 and 130,000, with one estimate going as high as 200,000.

Estimating the Effect of Offshore Employment on the Domestic Work Force. What effect, if any, did this wave of DFI have on the level and

Table 7–4. World Employment in the U.S. Semiconductor Industry, 1966–1978.

Year	United States	Abroad[a]	Total
1966	82,000	4,000	86,000
1967	85,000	10,000	95,000
1968	87,000	20,000	107,000
1969	99,000	40,000	139,000
1970	88,000	45,000	133,000
1971	75,000	50,000	125,000
1972	98,000	60,000	158,000
1973	120,000	80,000	200,000
1974	133,000	85,000	218,000
1978	131,000	89,000	220,000

[a]Until 1974, the majority of foreign employees were located in Third World locations. In 1974, for example, only 5,000 of 85,000 foreign workers were employed in Western Europe or Japan.

Sources: For 1966–1974, U.S. Department of Commerce (1979); for 1978, U.S. International Trade Commission (1980: 6).

composition of U.S. employment in the semiconductor industry? Counterfactual analysis, that is, asking what domestic employment would have been if there had been no offshore production, is one way of gauging the employment effect of DFI. When applied to the 1964–1978 period, counterfactual analysis has one notable strength and one weakness. On the positive side, counterfactual analysis conforms to the fact that until approximately 1977, employment by U.S.-owned firms and worldwide employment in the semiconductor industry were virtually one and the same thing. This means that during the period when U.S. firms dominated the industry, it is reasonable to identify total employment outside of the United States as the maximum estimate of forgone domestic employment due to offshore production. When U.S. firms were effectively responsible for all DFI in semiconductors, counterfactual analysis offers a credible estimate of the maximum number of domestic jobs forgone. If the labor content of offshore assembly were the same as domestic assembly, a largely accurate assumption, especially from the early 1960s through the mid-1970s, then the maximum forgone employment amounted to between 150,000 (U.S. Congress, Office of Technology Assessment 1983) to 185,000 jobs (Flamm 1985). This estimate is reasonable on its surface because assembly was very labor-intensive, whether it was done in the United States or overseas.

The problem with this estimate, and the weakness of counterfactual analysis, lies in its implicit assumption that domestic production at higher wage rates would not have reduced the demand for semiconductors and, therefore, the demand for labor. Of course, the degree to which employment would decline with a rise in production costs and price is an empirical question, with the magnitude of the effect depending on how sensitive buyers are to price changes.[2]

Estimating Price Elasticity. Kenneth Flamm (1985) of the Brookings Institution estimated the employment effect of offshore assembly on U.S. employment, based on an analysis of changes in employment over a range of price elasticities (see Table 7–5). Flamm separated jobs lost and jobs gained into assembly jobs and nonassembly jobs, an imperfect indicator of low-wage and high-wage jobs, and then asked how the composition as well as the level of employment would have changed with different price elasticities.[3] According to his estimates, if demand were relatively price elastic, then a maximum of 4,000 jobs would have been lost in 1977. If, on the other hand, demand were fairly insensitive to price changes, there would have been a net gain of 32,000 jobs.

Table 7–5.   Elasticity Estimates and Their Employment Effects in the Semiconductor Industry, 1977 (in thousands of jobs).

Estimated Demand Elasticity	Cost Advantage Assembly Offshore	Net Gain, Assembly Jobs	Net Loss, Nonassembly Jobs	Net Gain, All Jobs
−1.5	0.07	57	9	48
	0.10	53	13	40
	0.13	˙48	17	32
−2.3	0.07	52	14	38
	0.10	45	20	25
	0.13	38	26	13
−3.0	0.07	47	18	29
	0.10	38	26	13
	0.13	30	33	−4

Note: Flamm assumes that 70 percent of assembly is done abroad and that labor, given U.S. factor prices, is used in fixed proportion to output. Figures are rounded.

Source: Flamm (1985: Table 3–23).

The range of effects that Flamm identifies covers a lot of ground—from 30,000 to 57,000 assembly jobs gained and from 9,000 to 33,000 nonassembly jobs lost. When confronted with this range, one may ask which of these estimates is the most likely? To answer that question, we need to know what the likely price elasticity of demand is.

Finan and Amundsen (1986), in a study done for the U.S. Trade Representative, estimated the demand elasticity for the U.S. semiconductor market at −1.8. Baldwin and Krugman (1986) found this estimate convincing when they compared it with the change in price and quantity from 1978 to 1981—the period when 16K dRAMs were the commodity memory. "It is apparent," they argue, "that the elasticity of demand for semiconductor memories must be more than one but not much more, given that the price per bit has fallen 99 percent in real terms over the past decade. If demand were inelastic, the industry would have shrunk away; if it were very elastic, we would be having chips with everything by now."

Combining this elasticity and Finan's high-side estimate of the cost advantage of offshore assembly, we would argue that Flamm's −1.5 price elasticity estimate and the estimated .13 percent cost advantage from offshore assembly is the most likely estimate of the range that he calculated. If we are correct, then domestic assembly would have yielded a net gain of 32,000 jobs: 48,000 assembly jobs gained and 17,000 nonassembly jobs lost.

With a price elasticity of −1.5, 2.8 assembly jobs would be gained for every nonassembly job lost. But what does this job trade-off imply concretely for the quality of the industry's domestic jobs? The jobs gained through domestic assembly most likely would have been, on balance, less skilled and lower paid than the jobs lost. It is not possible to say that every job lost would be a $20 an hour engineer and every job gained would be a minimum wage assembly job. The industry's total domestic wage bill only would decline if the average wage of a job lost were 2.8 times higher than the average wage of a job gained. The average hourly wage in semiconductors was $8.61 in 1983 (U.S. Department of Labor 1985), while assembly wages were quite a bit lower, ranging from $5.22 to $8.82 per hour (see Table 7–6). Unfortunately, these data are not sufficient to answer the question. We need to know the distribution of industry employment by wage level—from data that are not available.

Job Opportunity Studies. Aggregate studies of job opportunities—measured as the direct labor content per dollar of industry output—are

Table 7-6.   Hourly Wages for Electronics Production Workers in California's Silicon Valley, July 1984.[a]

Category	Average	Minimum	Maximum	12-month Change
Assembler 1	$5.22	$4.80	$ 6.72	+1.0%
Assembler 2	6.58	5.55	7.85	−1.0
Assembler 3	7.65	6.38	9.12	+3.5
Assembler 4	8.82	7.25	10.46	+4.6%

[a]Sample based on 100+ companies.
Source: Hauser (1984: 10).

another way of estimating the effect of trade on domestic employment. Aggregate studies of foreign trade in semiconductors during the 1960s and 1970s demonstrate that the employment effects of trade were positive; trade was a net job generator for the United States. Since most input-output models do not estimate job opportunity effects at the four-digit SIC level, the estimates of job opportunities cover a sector that is broader than semiconductors, but the findings are congruent with the U.S. industry's competitive success in a growing world market. The job opportunity studies that cover the period indicate that demand swamped the job-destroying characteristics of semiconductor production. Not only did trade create employment, but trade generated domestic employment at a quickening pace as commercial markets for semiconductor devices expanded. In electronic components and accessories, a broader industrial category that includes semiconductors, trade created 6,987 job opportunities between 1964 and 1972; by 1972 the industry was growing so quickly that by 1974 trade had created an additional 5,388 job slots (National Commission for Manpower Policy 1978: 275). Over this early period, export growth and the growth of the world market, and the dominant position of U.S. firms within it, produced employment growth.

Aho and Orr (1981), also relied on a job opportunities model and estimated net trade-related job opportunities between 1964 and 1975. Defining job opportunities as the number of jobs required to produce a dollar value of output in the U.S. industry, they identified semiconductors as one of the twenty industries that were most favorably affected by trade between 1964 and 1975. While there were 5,000 net trade-related job opportunities in 1964, by 1975 job opportunities had more than doubled: net trade-related job opportunities grew by 6,200 between 1964 and 1975. This pattern mirrors the growth in exports and sales that grew from $4 million in 1962 to $1.2 billion in 1974 (Borrus, Millstein and Zysman 1980).

Foreign Trade and Domestic Demand. During this early period of the industry's development, trade played a relatively minor role. While DFI was a crucial element of the organization of production, sales and therefore domestic employment, were driven by domestic demand. Using an accounting framework, Lawrence (1984) estimated the role of manufacturing trade flows in aggregate U.S. manufacturing employment between 1970 and 1980 and 1973 to 1980. Based on the fifty-two-category input-output model, he found that between 1970 and 1980, value added in electrical components and accessories increased by 212.5 percent. Of that change, -6.2 percent was due to foreign trade (including both the direct and indirect effects), a change that was more than counterbalanced by the 218.6 percent increase in value added due to domestic use. Between 1973 and 1980 the trends were the same: Value added grew by 109.7 percent; the -3.4 percent from foreign trade was swamped by the 113.1 percent growth in domestic use.

According to Lawrence, the effects of trade on employment followed predictably from these conclusions. Between 1973 and 1980 total sectoral employment increased by 35 percent, with trade pulling 4 percent to the bad and the domestic effect pulling 39 percent to the good. Between 1970 and 1980 employment in electronic components increased by 51 percent: -7.8 percent due to trade and 59 percent due to domestic demand. Over the longer haul the trends held steady. Lawrence summarizes three conditions that propelled domestic job growth during the first phase of the industry's growth. The industry was, first of all, comprised of U.S.-owned firms, the U.S. market was at the same time the world's fastest growing market, and the end-users were largely government buyers (primarily the U.S. Defense Depatment and NASA). The total effect of these three factors was a fast-growing domestic market that was, even with DFI, a net job creator.

Direct Foreign Investment and Occupational Restructuring. While the burgeoning market for semiconductor devices kept the demand for labor bouyant, DFI was changing the composition of domestic employment. Shifts from direct to indirect labor apparently mirror industry reorganization in response to recession, which is characterized by domestic producers cutting back higher cost U.S. assembly operations. In early 1981, for example, manufacturers who cut back on production reported little or no effect on their foreign assembly operations (Flamm 1985: n. 126; Russell 1981; "Layoff Set by Texas Instruments" 1981). And to round out this pattern of cyclical rationalization, when demand rebounded, reduced U.S. assembly capacity was typically replaced by new or expanded assembly plants that were located offshore. Existing information on foreign employment, though sketchy, supports the view that offshore employment expanded most rapidly just after each major recession in the United States. There was a sharp increase in the proportion of semiconductor devices that were manufactured offshore following the mid-1970s recession and the attendent Japanese drive into the commodity chip market in the United States. In relation to DFI, U.S. firms pursued a double-edged strategy: rationalization in the United States during the downswing followed by expansion offshore during the upswing.

The commitment of the domestic industry to a global division of labor directly influenced the occupational composition of semiconductor employment in the United States. It is clear that production employment has been harder hit than nonproduction employment during each recession. Production employment registered a 36 percent drop between 1974 and 1975, from 81,600 to 52,400 (see Table 7–7). And while production employment has rebounded in absolute terms after each recession, the ratio of production to nonproduction employees has shifted markedly after each downturn. The ratio of production workers to all employees dropped from 64 percent to 54 percent between 1974 and 1975 and again from 54 percent to 48 percent between 1980 and 1982.

To some extent, of course, the declining ratio of semiconductor production workers is in tune with the broader occupational shift from direct to indirect labor that has been occurring in most of manufacturing since the end of World War II. Technical change and rationalization, changes that are on the whole unrelated to trade, are the principle cause of this shift in the structure of jobs. In the semiconductor industry firms' decision to move production work offshore has most likely accelerated the pace of the occupational shift but has not been its only cause. In fact, both rationalization and offshore production stem from the same cause—the desire to reduce direct labor costs.

Interpreting the Occupational Shift. The meaning of the occupational shift can be read in two different ways. Read one way, the export of low-level production work was a clear swap of jobs for wages. In dollars

Table 7-7. Domestic Employment in the U.S. Semiconductor Industry, 1971–1985 (in thousands of workers).

Year	Total	Production
1971	74.7	45.5
1972	97.6	58.4
1973	120.0	74.7
1974	133.1	81.6
1975	96.7	52.4
1976	102.5	57.9
1977	114.0	63.5
1978	130.8	73.6
1979	142.9	81.1
1980	160.7	87.3
1981	169.5	84.9
1982	167.0	81.3
1983	169.0	84.1
1984	195.0	96.0
1985	188.0	90.0
1986	184.0	75.7

Sources: U.S. Department of Commerce (1982, 1985, 1986).

and cents the international division of labor meant that while industry employment was fairly evenly divided, with about half in the United States and half outside of the United States, overwhelmingly the industry's wages and salaries were paid to U.S. workers. In 1983, for instance, 47 percent of the U.S. merchant semiconductor manufacturers' work force of 270,000 was employed in the United States. Yet because two-thirds of production or assembly employment was located offshore, 82 percent of the industry's wages and salaries were paid to the domestic work force (Finan and Amundsen 1986). Earlier data on the international distribution of wages are not available, but it seems prudent to assume that the relative magnitudes were similar. The domestic industry engaged in the classical price/quantity trade-off: employing fewer domestic workers but employing them at a higher wage.

The alternative way to read the same fact is to note that trade has had the ironic effect of pitting the jobs of female workers in the United States against the jobs of female workers in the Second and Third worlds. While women made up one-third of total U.S. employment in manufacturing in 1983, they accounted for almost half of employment in semiconductors.[4] While nationally the total electronic component work force was 51 percent male and 49 percent female, operatives—mostly assemblers and wafer fabrication assistants—were only 26 percent male and 74 percent female. Put the other way around, the Equal Employment Opportunity Commission reported that in California's Silicon Valley, the home base of the semiconductor industry, men made up 55 percent of the total work force that was engaged in component production but only 27 percent of the operatives. In the only detailed study of its occupational structure, done in 1977 by the Bureau of Labor Statistics, women held 90 percent of assembly jobs, 88 percent of inspector and tester slots, and 73 percent of processing operative jobs. So while it is true that net job opportunities and total employment grew during this first period of the semiconductor industry's development, it is also clear that offshore production that was accompanied by technical change and rationalization reshuffled job opportunities—away from women, many of them minority women, and toward white men.

Foreign Production Locations—Stage Two

As we have seen, the first stage of competition—competition among U.S. producers—generated an international division of labor that continues as the dominant production model for U.S. merchant producers. In the second stage of competition, however, there was a decided shift in the terms and character of international competition. Instead of competing against one another, as had been true for over a decade, U.S. firms found themselves competing against Japanese firms that had established themselves as the low-cost world producers. This period of the industry's development dates from 1974 to 1978, when Japanese firms' share of the world market for semiconductors increased substantially, making inroads into markets that were previously held by U.S. producers. According to the USITC, "Much of the increase in Japanese market share was gained at the expense of U.S. producers." Whether the competitive success of Japanese manufacturers was the result of low wages, low-cost manufacturing processes, or dumping, the initial effect of their success was to accelerate the prevailing trend among U.S. producers toward offshore assembly and testing.[5]

Reflecting the sunk costs of existing overseas production facilities and a commitment to low-wage labor as an effective and efficient way to organize production, U.S. firms indicated an enduring attachment to

offshore production. In fact, U.S. firms became even more commit-
ted to offshore production and an international division of labor in
the period of Japanese competition than they had been earlier. In 1981,
for example, between 70 percent and 80 percent of all U.S.-based
semiconductor shipments were finished in assembly plants located
overseas, primarily in Mexico and Southeast Asia (Flamm 1985:
81–85). Since IBM and AT&T, which assemble their domestic output in the United States, accounted for about 28 percent of all U.S.
shipments of integrated circuits in 1981 (U.S. International Trade Commission 1982: 2), between 85 percent and 95 percent of all semiconductor devices that were shipped by merchant firms (that is, firms that
produce integrated circuits for sale rather than for internal consumption, such as AT&T and IBM) were assembled offshore (Flamm 1985;
Linebade 1985; U.S. International Trade Commission 1982). U.S.
firms' first response to the Japanese cost advantage was to continue
to economize on labor costs. Yet with this competitive strategy firm-
ly in place, Japanese imports still soared. The Japanese share of total
U.S. imports of semiconductors grew from 6 percent in 1977 to 11
percent in 1981 to over 25 percent in 1985.

The Domestic Employment Consequences of Trade with Japan.   The
effect of Japanese firms' competitive success on U.S. employment is considerably less bright than the aggregate studies reported earlier. There
have been several input-output studies of the employment effects of trade
in the semiconductor industry since the late 1970s, the period that we
have designated the second stage in international trade in semiconductors. Following on Leontief's work, the International Trade Commission's (1986b) study of the effects of trade on employment between 1978
and 1984 is based on an estimate of the labor content of U.S. merchandise trade. The ITC study's assessment of the labor content of imports
and exports of electronic components and accessories (input-output sector 57) is measured in thousands of work-years. While the sector's net
labor content has been in deficit since 1978, when it posted a modest
deficit of 19,000 work-years, the deficit doubled to minus 40,000 work-
years in 1983, and then more than doubled again in 1984 to minus
97,000 work-years. Overall, then, between 1980 and 1984 the labor
content of exports minus the labor content of imports moved the sector toward deficit by 890,000 work-years, 13 percent of the industry's
1984 employment. During this period trade reduced gross industry
employment opportunities by 89,000 jobs.

The biggest problem with this approach is that the value of imports is assumed to have the same labor content as an equal value of domestic output. This assumption is problematic, especially when applied to sectors in which technical advance is central to the organization of the production process, as is the case in semiconductor production. First of all, some imports do not have a close domestic substitute. Many industry analysts argue in this vein that semiconductors that are produced by Japanese firms are a higher quality product than are U.S. firms' chips. If this is so, then the validity of the substitutability assumption is questionable. But much more importantly for the semiconductor industry, the equivalence that is assumed between the price and quantity of labor that is needed to produce some value in different production locations seems farfetched. The method obviously does not capture differences between U.S. and offshore production in the unit price of labor inputs. In assessing the employment effects of trade, therefore, this method indicates the quantity of trade-related employment generated or forgone, assuming, however, that labor that is paid, say, $20 an hour, is exactly equivalent to labor that is paid $4 an hour or fifty cents an hour.

The 480 INFORM input-output model that was developed by Interindustry Economic Research (Davis 1986) at the University of Maryland describes the total domestic input-output requirements for domestic merchandise for each year included in the model. The employment estimates are only for export-related job opportunities, which are measured as full-time equivalent employment. This measure is defined as export-related output multiplied by a labor productivity measure, which is in turn defined as the ratio of full-time equivalent jobs per unit of output. For electronics components, a category that is broader (and includes lower productivity sectors) than the semiconductor industry alone, there were 8,800 job opportunities created for each $1 billion of direct exports in 1984.[6] For solid-state semiconducting devices, total export-related employment measured as full-time equivalents fluctuated from a low of 64,000 in 1980 to a high of 75,000 in 1983, before dropping back to 70,000 in 1984 (Davis 1986).

The loss of job opportunities in the industry's domestic labor market coincides with the erosion of U.S. firms' share of the market in high-volume commodity chips. These new competitive conditions meant that the industry's continuing reliance on offshore assembly and testing affected the domestic work force differently in this period of slow market growth and slipping market shares than it had in the earlier high-growth period. First, total employment began to decline (see Table 7–7). And second, the industry abandoned its commitment to a no-layoff policy.

According to Aho and Orr (1981), industries that were net job opportunity losers during the 1960s and early 1970s were import sectors with work forces that were disproportionately female, minority, very low income, and decidedly less educated than workers in sectors that gained from trade. And although the microchip business was clearly a net export sector and job generator during that early period, these characteristics, absent the low-income characterization since the average production wage in semiconductors was essentially the average manufacturing wage, are also good descriptors of the semiconductor industry's production work force. And as the sector moved deeply into the red in the early 1980s, the jobs of these workers were clearly at risk.

Japanese Competitive Success and Domestic Employment

Nonetheless, simply the fact that Japanese imports grew, even as dramatically as they did, is not enough, in and of itself, to demonstrate that foreign trade reduced domestic job opportunties. Fieleke (1985) notes that between 1980 and 1984, across a range of industries, overall changes in sectoral employment have not been correlated with the degree of net import competition. Instead, job decline is, he argues, the result of either industrywide overcapacity or the loss of market share. It is possible for a firm to increase output and employment and lose market share in a growing market. During the second wave of internationalization, these two factors, summarized by a growing trade deficit in semiconductors, strongly point to job destruction resulting from trade.

Japanese Competition in Standard Products.   To a large extent the story of job loss in this industry begins with takeoff of Japanese imports, particularly the Japanese domination of the market for memory chips. Most of the U.S. trade deficit has occurred in memory chips, where Japanese shipments to the United States nearly doubled in 1983 to more than $400 million. And even though total imports dropped by 30.5 percent in 1985, the U.S. industry continued to lose its market in commodity memory chips, the MOS memory segment of the market. The segment of the memory market that was held by U.S. companies fell from 73 percent in 1980 to 44 percent in 1984. Over the same period Japanese companies' share of the MOS memory segment grew from 26 percent in 1980 to 51 percent in 1984 (Integrated Circuit Engineering Corporation 1986). The share of the total U.S. chip market that was held by

Japanese imports increased from 7.7 percent in 1978 to 24.4 percent in 1985. Beginning with the 16K generation of dynamic random access memories (dRAMs) in 1976, and moving, by 1980, into the 64K generation, the Japanese have captured ever increasing shares of the dRAM market, holding 40 percent of the U.S. and world market for 16K chips in 1980 and 65 percent of the world market for 64K memories in 1983. Moreover, even during the 1985 slump, Japanese companies cut back their production less severely than did other foreign producers and cut their prices considerably less.

Japanese Imports and the Overvalued Dollar.   The argument has been advanced that the surge in Japanese semiconductor imports and the loss of market share—especially in commodity memory chips—was primarily a consequence of the overvalued dollar. In order to test how important exchange rate changes were, one would need to do an econometric test of the exchange rate effect on the real volume and price of imports. Such a test would permit us to disentangle the effects of exchange rate changes, the alleged dumping by Japanese manufacturers of chips in the U.S. market, and technical change. Unhappily, the data to perform this test are not available. Data on the real volume of imports, firm level production costs data, and data on costs by product type are not available. Moreover, because one would expect changes in import levels to vary substantially as exchange rates vary for such price-sensitive products as commodity memories, one also would need data that were disaggregated by product type. Again, no such data series exists.

Because an econometric test was not possible, the best way of gauging the direction and magnitude of the domestic employment effect of foreign trade in semiconductors—determinining how the appreciation of the dollar affected import levels—was out of reach. As a second-best approximation, there are indirect indicators of the effect of exchange rates on semiconductor imports. These admittedly imprecise tools suggest that the exchange rate effect was relatively minor. According to the International Monetary Fund average exchange rate index (1980 = 100), the yen depreciated by 11.6 percent against the dollar in 1982, while semiconductor imports increased at triple that pace, shooting up by 35.4 percent, a rate that is much faster than the price elasticity of −1.5 implies.[7]

Over the next three years, even as the yen appreciated modestly against the dollar, imports remained stubbornly unresponsive. In 1982 and 1983 imports continued to increase. In 1982 imports of semiconductors from

Japan increased by 35.4 percent, though the average exchange rate index fell by 13.4 points, from 100.6 in the fourth quarter of 1981 to 87.2 in the fourth quarter of 1982. Imports were up by 37.1 percent in 1983 as the index climbed to 96.4 points; when imports surged by 52.7 percent in 1984, the index fell to 91.8. Over this period, the pace of growth of imports from Japan outstripped the dollar's rise by four-and-one-half times in 1982 and by twenty-two times in 1984. Even more telling is the fact that while the index records that the yen appreciated by 50.3 percent against the dollar between July 1985 and July 1986, the value of Japanese imports will, if the rate of growth of imports in the first half of 1986 holds, only fall at one-fifth that rate, declining by a modest 10.8 percent. The pattern of currency values, when juxtaposed to the growth in imports from Japan, implies that Japanese semiconductor imports are relatively insensitive to fluctuations in the value of the dollar.

Economic theory predicts that there is a lag between a currency depreciation and changes in the level of imports. Figure 7–1 suggests, however, that, even allowing for substantial lags, there has been very little correlation in the behavior of the yen/dollar exchange rate and the rate of change in imports.

Accusations of Dumping.   Over the last several years, American merchant firms have filed a series of complaints with the USITC alleging that Japanese firms have dumped chips on the U.S. market. It is difficult to substantiate this claim with the price series information that is publicly available from the USITC (June 1985a, b; 1986a, c). The publicly available USITC price series, which are the weighted average of company level production cost data, do not document a clear and convincing series of underselling. But according to analysts with the USITC and the U.S. Trade Representative's office, confidential company-level cost data supported the dumping charge.

While not disputing the finding of dumping, we would also point out that the export price, in yen, of Japanese semiconductors was falling rapidly in third markets and in Japan. Between 1980 and the first quarter of 1986, the export price of Japanese semiconductors fell more rapidly than the yen/dollar exchange rate over the same period. Using indices of the average yen/dollar exchange rate and an index of Japanese and U.S. export prices for semiconductors and integrated circuits, the semiconductor price index declined more than the IMF index in every quarter between 1981 and 1986. With 1980 as the baseline case for both

Figure 7-1. Yen per Dollar Exchange Rate and Semiconductor Imports from Japan, 1978–1985.

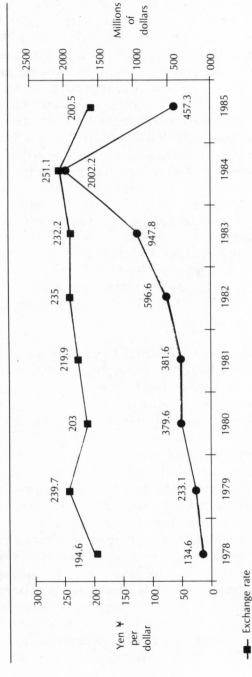

Sources: International Monetary Fund (various issues); unpublished Department of Commerce data.

indices, the gap between the average exchange rate and the commodity exchange rate widened. This implies that the yen price of semiconductors—the price that has exchange rate effects stripped out—was falling. To some extent (which we cannot precisely quantify), the decline in the export price of Japanese chips was unrelated to the depreciation of the yen. It is quite likely, we think, that the fall in the yen price of exports, and the growth in market share for Japanese producers, reflects technical advances in the Japanese semiconductor manufacturing process.

In sum, then, there are two distinct periods in international trade in semiconductors. In the first period, trade was domestically generated by U.S.-headquartered firms that engaged in DFI, principally in a few countries in the Far East. In the latter period, trade became more truly international. The central fact of this period was the increasing market dominance of Japanese-headquartered semiconductor producers.

ALTERNATIVE FUTURES FOR THE INDUSTRY

One possible scenario for the industry's development is that Japanese domination of the commodity memory chip market and the potential for government trade sanctions will accelerate the move toward DFI in the United States. Yet because automated production processes appear to be central to manufacturing successfully VSLI chips, Japanese state-of-the-art production facilities, even those that are located in the United States for the manufacture of random-access memories, should not be expected to create significant employment opportunities for semiconductor fabrication and assembly workers. The NEC plant in Roseville, California, for example, one of the most automated semiconductor plants in the world, is equipped with the latest generation of semiconductor production equipment—for wafer fabrication, assembly, and test—and will have a throughput of 75,000 to 80,000 wafers per month when it is fully operational (Parsons 1987). The combination of high levels of automation and the manufacture of the latest generation of semiconductor products makes the NEC plant an excellent exemplar of the potential employment effects that are associated with the decision to automate in the United States. Projected employment figures for the plant in 1981 estimated that 600 employees would work three shifts when the plant is at full capacity. Typical employment figures for a plant with similar throughput would have been closer to *1,500* (United Nations Industrial Development Organization 1981). Along with reduced labor requirements comes a reduction in skill requirements and assembly automation. With automated bonding equipment, for example, it only takes two weeks worth of training compared to three months for a worker to become competent at manual bonding (United Nations Industrial Development Organization 1981: 91).

More likely, slots will be available for well-trained manufacturing process engineers. At the same time, U.S. firms maintain their greatest strengths in new product design and are concentrating more than ever on the markets for custom, semicustom, and programmable application-specific chips. These chips are essentially different from the dRAM chips that are used in personal computers and video games and whose production has been dominated by Japanese firms. Advances in custom chips, for example, rely on innovations in the design of the advanced central processing units—microprocessors—that form a computer's "brain." Thus future employment growth in U.S. firms can be expected to favor highly skilled software designers as well as specialists for automating both chip design and manufacture.

A second possible future is that there will be substantial government protection. The industry and the U.S. government have recently concluded that some Japanese manufacturers have been selling chips in the U.S. market below the cost of production, the classic definition of dumping. While the publicly available price series do not suggest a pattern of dumping, experts at the USITC and the U.S. Trade Representative have stated that a clear pattern of underselling was evident among many Japanese firms. As we suggested above, some of the cost difference also appears in the yen price, implying that technical advances in manufacturing by Japanese firms may be at least partially responsible for a lower selling price.

Whatever the truth of the dumping complaint, the two governments agreed to set a floor under the price of 256K dRAMS and erasable programmable read only memories (EPROMs). The agreement, which was intended to protect domestic markets from cutthroat competition by Japanese producers, promises several unintended consequences that may boomerang on the domestic industry and its employees.

The agreement may have the perverse effect of speeding up the pace of offshore production by systems makers. Deep discounting in third markets was reported within weeks of the final agreement. The immediate response by systems producers was to publicly note the incentive this provided to relocate to be close to low-cost suppliers. The agreement also has the ironic effect of guaranteeing Japanese producers high profit levels. It thus becomes a guarantor of crucial R&D capital. As the industry's capital requirements have escalated rapidly over the last decade, the ability to sustain investment in advanced processes today largely determines market share and profits tomorrow. It is becoming clear that with a high and sustained level of investment, firms hold and increase their success in international markets.

A third strategy U.S. firms could pursue is to build fully integrated production facilities at the market. To a large extent, the advantage of integrating production comes from firms' desire to penetrate new markets. Using industrial location as a tool for generating competitive advantage in final markets is not new to semiconductor producers. The desire to gain market position in new markets has driven the location decisions of European and Japanese firms in locating their production facilities in foreign markets (Finan 1985). The new wrinkle in this strategy is the interest in locating fully integrated production facilities at the market. The spatial reintegration of production at the market is an attractive way to realize the dual advantages of integrated production: fast turnaround time and close contact with the customer during applications engineering and after-sales service, and the ability to take up domestic resources and adjust transfer costs. To a large degree, the shifting contours of the market itself dictate a new location strategy. The market for semiconductors outside the United States, Japan, and Western Europe—particularly the market in the Far East—is projected to be as large as the 1984 consumption in Western Europe, which is the United States's largest export market (Semiconductor Industry Association 1984: 49–50; Scott 1985: 26).[8] The appeal of locating production at the market, in combination with the declining importance of direct labor costs at the plant level, means that in the future the location of offshore manufacturing facilities may result from an attempt to penetrate new markets rather than mirroring, as it largely has in the past, the search for cheap labor.

There are two countervailing tendencies, although they are rather small quantitatively, to the continuing erosion of the domestic employment base in semiconductors. One of these is a shift in the structure of the semiconductor industry, the convergence of circuit design and system design. The ability to directly design systems in silicon is narrowing the differences between chips and systems.[9] The technical capabilities of computer-aided design systems permit design and systems engineers (which, because of the convergence of circuits and systems, will be increasingly difficult to separate as distinct engineering disciplines) to become the technical core of a new segment of the semiconductor industry—the design and prototyping of custom VLSI chips. This is one part of the strategic response of the industry to the high design costs of VLSI—the "unbundling [of] the overall process of making semiconductors from design through production" (Borrus 1983). As the boundary between systems and chips blurs, there is a critical and yet to be resolved set of incentives that operates on both sides, the motivation to vertically integrate—for semiconductor firms to move into systems and, conversely, for systems houses to move strongly into captive design and, perhaps, production. One piece of the unbundling is the emergence of design centers, essentially engineering service businesses, which will specialize in design and perform limited prototype production. These firms will service systems producers and farm out production to merchant firms or silicon foundries (Bourbon 1984: 120). These "design centers" may also act as brokers between systems houses and silicon foundries. The design services may recommend alternative production facilities to their clients, the systems houses, in much the same way that stockbrokers recommend investments to their clients. Another permutation of unbundling is the shifting of design from integrated circuit manufacturers to systems producers per se. In the next five years, it is likely that the design of custom chips will be almost completely broken off from the merchant firms (see Table 7–8).

If design centers (or in-house design) become as significant as these figures indicate, there will be an incentive to locate silicon foundries close to systems producers.[10] The separation of design and manufacture, at least for custom chips, has several advantages for both manufacturers and systems producers. On the manufacturer's side is the incentive to share the heavy design costs with systems houses. This logic is even more compelling given the cost of new facilities, which are expected to rise at a 25 percent compound annual rate (Integrated Circuit Engineeering Corporation 1986: 94). The systems producers would tend to favor silicon foundries that are not tied to the existing or potential systems producers that they compete against. By using Japanese silicon foundries, U.S. producers would be put at a competitive disadvantage since semiconductor and systems producers are typically part of vertically integrated electronic companies (Borrus, Millstein, and Zysman 1980). Thus both domestic production *and* ownership seem likely.

Table 7-8. Responsibility for the Design of Custom and Commodity Semiconductors.

	1984		1990	
	Silicon Manufacturing	Customer	Silicon Manufacturing	Customer
Custom	73%	21%	11%	89%
Commodity	100	0	100	0

Sources: Bourbon (1984: 120); Borrus (1984).

CONCLUSIONS

Foreign trade in the semiconductor industry, while first driven by the logic of competition among U.S.-owned firms and then by the growing success of Japanese producers, has produced a clear and consistent set of domestic employment effects. In both periods, the effect of trade alone has reduced job opportunities, particularly for low-level assembly jobs that are most often filled by women. In the first period, however, the fast-paced growth of domestic demand propelled domestic employment creation and swamped the job-destroying effects of trade. In the second period, the story about trade is the same—trade substantially reduced domestic job opportunities for the low-wage workers in the industry. And because of the success of Japanese producers and the slump in the market for computers, those lost opportunities translated into layoffs when the weak domestic market did not counterbalance the loss.

NOTES

1. Semiconductor firms that produce for sale on commercial markets—companies known as merchant firms—are the focus of this analysis. Captive producers—companies like IBM and AT&T that produce chips for internal consumption—do not trade on the world market.
2. The price elasticity of demand is defined as the percentage change in quantity resulting from a 1 percent change in price.
3. Flamm (1985: Table 3–21) used the U.S. Department of Commerce, Bureau of Census (various years) to separate out assembly workers from all other production workers. According to the census definition, non-assembly jobs include managerial, technical, professional, clerical and nonassembly production workers.

4. Women accounted for 32.33 percent of total manufacturing employment in 1983 and 46.38 percent of semiconductor industry employment. (U.S. Department of Labor, Bureau of Labor Statistics 1986).

5. In March 1985 the United States and Japan concluded a bilateral agreement that eliminated tariffs on semiconductors and integrated circuits. From a research standpoint, this means that after 1985 it is impossible to track reimportation of devices that domestic firms ship offshore for partial assembly and processing. This will become an especially significant lacuna as countries that have been and continue to be important sites for offshore production by American firms also develop domestic semiconductor capacities of their own. The reduction of bilateral tariffs on semiconductors and integrated circuits is another mark of the transition to the second stage of international trade. For, even as offshore assembly and testing continued to be important sources of imports—even after the abolition of tariffs—this international division of labor did not prove to be a successful response to international competition coming primarily from Japanese producers.

6. One should keep in mind that the value of semiconductor (SIC 3674) shipments represents about 35 to 40 percent of the value of shipments of the broader category of electronic components (SIC 367).

7. A fall in the index means an appreciation of the yen.

8. Scott points out that the market for semiconductors in Southeast Asia has grown quickly over the last decade and that 16 percent to 18 percent of semiconductor shipments from U.S.-owned branch plants in Southeast Asia are made within the region.

9. The relationship between a circuit and a system changes as technology changes. As the number and sophistication of functions increases, "components are technically able to implement basic features of what previously had been regarded as an electronic system" (Borrus, Millstein, and Zysman 1980: 22).

10. Design centers are the companies that provide circuit design and prototype construction but do not manufacture circuits themselves. Silicon foundries are companies that manufacture semiconductors that are designed by outside sources (in this argument, they are either design centers or circuits that are designed by the systems producers themselves). It is presently standard practice for merchant firms to use one or more of their production lines for contract work, essentially a silicon foundry type of arrangement. However, this is typically only done during periods of excess capacity.

REFERENCES

Aho, C. Michael, and James A. Orr. 1981. "Trade-Sensitive Employment: Who Are the Affected Workers?" *Monthly Labor Review* 104, no. 2 (February): 29–35.

Baldwin, Richard, and Paul R. Krugman. 1986. "Market Access and International Competition: A Simulation Study of 16K Random Access Memories." National Bureau of Economic Research Working Paper Series #1936, Cambridge, Mass., June.

Borrus, Michael. 1984. Discussion with author.

———. 1983. "Responses to the Japanese Challenge in High Technology." Working Paper, Berkeley Roundtable on the International Economy. University of California, Berkeley.

Borrus, Michael, James Millstein, and John Zysman. 1980. "U.S.–Japanese Competition in the Semiconductor Industry." Policy Paper in International Affairs No. 17. Institute of international Studies, University of California, Berkeley.

Bourbon, Bruce R. 1984. "ICs Tailored to Applications Gain Ground." *Electronics Week*, September 3.

Davis. International Trade Administration. 1986. "Contributions of Exports to U.S. Employment." Staff Report, Office of Trade and Investment Analysis, March.

Fieleke, Norman S. 1985. "The Foreign Trade Deficit and American Industry." *New England Economic Review* (July/August): 43–52.

Finan, William. 1985. Interview with author, May.

———. 1975. *The International Transfer of Semiconductor Technology Through U.S.-Based Firms.* Washington, D.C.: National Science Foundation.

Finan, William F., and Chris B. Amundsen. 1986. "An Analysis of the Effects of Targeting on the Competitiveness of the U.S. Semiconductor Industry." Prepared for the Office of the U.S. Special Trade Representative, the Department of Commerce, and the U.S. Department of Labor.

Flamm, Kenneth. 1985. "Internationalization in the Semiconductor Industry." In *The Global Factory: Foreign Assembly in International Trade*, edited by Joseph Grunwald and Kenneth Flamm. Washington, D.C.: Brookings Institution.

Hauser, Dedra. 1984. "Surviving at the Bottom of the Ladder." *San Jose Mercury News*, November 5, p. 10.

Integrated Circuit Engineering Corporation. 1986. *Status 1986: A Report on the Integrated Circuit Industry.* Scottsdale, Ariz.: Integrated Circuit Engineering Corporation.

———. 1985. *Status 1985: A Report on the Integrated Circuit Industry.* Scottsdale, Ariz.: ICE.

International Monetary Fund. Various issues. *International Financial Statistics*.

Lawrence, Robert Z. 1984. *Can America Compete?* Washington, D.C.: The Brookings Institution.

"Layoff Set by Texas Instruments." 1981. The *New York Times*, May 30, pp. 29 & 32.

Linebade, J. Robert. 1985. "Automation May Ease Offshore Edge." *Electronics*, April 21, pp. 92, 95.

National Commission for Manpower Policy. 1978. *Trade and Employment: A Conference Report*. Special Report No. 30 November.

Parsons, Carol A. 1987. "Flexible Production Technology and Industrial Restructuring: Case Studies of the Metalworking, Apparel and Semiconductor Industries." Unpublished Ph.D. dissertation. University of California, Berkeley.

Russell, Sabin. 1981. "Semiconductor Firms Wriggle Work Schedules." *Electronic News*, March 30, p. 42.

Scott, Allen J. 1985. "The Semiconductor Industry in South-East Asia: Organization, Location and the International Division of Labor." Working Paper Series #101, Department of Geography, UCLA, December.

Semiconductor Industry Association. 1984. "The International Competitive Environment for the U.S. Semiconductor Industry, 1985–1990." Unpublished paper, September.

Sparth, Anthony and John Marcom, Jr. 1981. "Asia Defies a U.S. Microchip Slump." *The Wall Street Journal*, September 18, p. 35.

United Nations Centre on Transnational Corporations. 1986. *Transnational Corporations in the International Semiconductor Industry*. New York: United Nations.

United Nations Industrial Development Organization. 1981. *Restructuring World Industry in a Period of Crisis—The Role of Innovation: An Analysis of Recent Developments in the Semiconductor Industry*. New York: United Nations, December 17.

U.S. Congress. Office of Technology Assessment. 1983. *International Competition in Electronics*. Washington, D.C.: U.S. Government Printing Office.

U.S. Department of Commerce. 1986. *U.S. Industrial Outlook, 1986*. Washington, D.C.: U.S. Government Printing Office.

———. 1985. *U.S. Industrial Outlook, 1985*. Washington, D.C.: U.S. Government Printing Office.

———. 1979. *Report on the Semiconductor Industry*. Washington, D.C.: U.S. Government Printing Office, September.

———. Bureau of the Census. Various years. *Census of Manufacturers, Selected Metalworking Operations*. Washington, D.C.: U.S. Government Printing Office.

———. 1982 *Census of Manufacturers*. Washington, D.C.: U.S. Government Printing Office.

U.S. Department of Labor. Bureau of Labor Statistics. Various issues. *Employment and Earnings.*

———. 1979. *Industry Wage Survey: Semiconductors—Survey of 1977* Bulletin 2021. Washington, D.C.: U.S. Government Printing Office, April.

U.S. International Trade Commission (ITC). 1986a. *Dynamic Random Access Memory Semiconductors of 256 Kilobits and Above from Japan.* Determination of the Commission in Investigation No. 731-TA-300 (Preliminary) Under the Tariff Act of 1930. Publication 1803. Washington, D.C.: ITC, January.

———. 1986b. *U.S. Trade-Related Employment: 1978–84.* Publication 1855. Washington, D.C.: ITC May.

———. 1986c. *64K Dynamic Random Access Memory Components from Japan.* Determination of the Commission in Investigation No. 731-TA-270 (Final) Under the Tariff Act of 1930. Publication 1862. Washington, D.C.: ITC, June.

———. 1985a. *64K Dynamic Random Access Memory Components from Japan.* Determination of the Commission in Investigation No. 731-TA-270 (Preliminary) Under the Tariff Act of 1930. Publication 1735. Washington, D.C.: ITC, August.

———. 1985b. *Erasable Programmable Read-Only Memories from Japan.* Determination of the Commission in Investigation No. 731-TA-288 (Preliminary) Under the Tariff Act of 1930. Publication 1778. Washington, D.C.: ITC, November.

———. 1982. *Summary of Tariff and Trade Information—Semiconductors.* Publication 841. Washington, D.C.: ITC.

INDEX

269

ABOUT THE EDITORS

Laura D'Andrea Tyson is a principal faculty member of the Berkeley Roundtable on the International Economy (BRIE) and an associate professor of economics, both at the University of California at Berkeley. She is a summa cum laude graduate of Smith College and has a Ph.D. in economics from the Massachusetts Institute of Technology. She has served as a consultant to the World Bank, the Office of Technology Assessment, the Rand Corporation, the President's Commission on Industrial Competitiveness, and the Council on Competitiveness. Her major publications include *American Industry in International Competition* (with John Zysman), "Creating Advantage in High Technology Industries" (with Michael Borrus and John Zysman), and "The U.S. Trade Deficit: A Black Hole in the World Economy" (with Lester Thurow). She has also published a number of books and articles on the Eastern bloc economies.

William T. Dickens is an associate professor of economics at the University of California, Berkeley, and a research associate of the National Bureau of Economic Research. He has also taught industrial relations at the Massachusetts Institute of Technology, where he received his Ph.D. in economics in 1981. He has had several grants from the National Science Foundation to study the structure of labor markets and was a member of a team of researchers from BRIE that conducted a study of the employment effects of trade for the Congressional Office of Technology Assessment.

John Zysman is director of the Berkeley Roundtable on the International Economy and professor of political science, both at the University of California, Berkeley. He is a graduate of Harvard College and the Massachusetts Institute of Technology (Ph.D.). He has served as an OECD examiner of French innovation policies; a panel member on international competition in biotechnology and on technology, innovation, and U.S. trade for the Congressional Office of Technology Assessment; and a consultant to the U.S.-Japan Advisory Commission and recent President's Commission on Industrial Competitiveness. Professor Zysman's major publications include *Manufacturing Matters: The Myth of the Post-Industrial Economy* (with Stephen S. Cohen), *Government, Markets and Growth: Finance and the Politics of Industrial Change, American Industry in International Competition* (with Laura Tyson), *The Mercantilist Challenge to the Liberal International Trade Order* (with Stephen S. Cohen), *Political Strategies for Industrial Order: State, Market and Industry in France,* and *U.S.-Japanese Competition in the Semiconductor Industry* (with Michael Borrus and James Millstein).

ABOUT THE CONTRIBUTORS

Kevin Lang received his M.A. in philosophy, politics, and economics (PPE) from the University of Oxford; his M.Sc. in economics from the Université de Montréal; and his Ph.D. in economics from the Massachusetts Institute of Technology. He is an associate professor of economics at Boston University and a faculty research fellow of the National Bureau of Economic Research. He presently holds an Alfred P. Sloan Foundation Faculty Research Fellowship and has been an Olin Fellow at the National Bureau of Economic Research. He has received three grants from the National Science Foundation for work on labor market segmentation and on hours constraints. He has published extensively in economics journals and is co-editor, with Jonathan Leonard, of *Unemployment and the Structure of Labor Markets*.

Carol A. Parsons is an assistant professor of urban and regional planning at the University of Iowa. She is a graduate of the University of California, Irvine and holds a master's degree in urban and regional planning from the University of Southern California. She has a Ph.D. in city and regional planning from the University of California, Berkeley, where she was also a research associate at the Berkeley Roundtable on the International Economy. She has served as a consultant to the Office of Technology Assessment; the states of California, Utah, and Nevada; and the cities of Los Angeles and Oakland, California. She is the author of several studies detailing the relationship between technological innovation in manufacturing, changing patterns of industrial location, and labor market restructuring.

Robert E. Scott is an assistant professor of business and public policy in the College of Business and Management at the University of Maryland at College Park. He is a doctoral candidate in the Department of Economics at the University of California, where he was also a research fellow for three years with the Berkeley Roundtable on the International Economy. He holds a B.S. degree in technology and human affairs from Washington University in St. Louis. Scott was a recipient of the Herman Kahn Fellowship at the Hudson Institute, where he contributed to a study on economic development for the state of Oklahoma. He is a co-author (with Carol Parsons and Bruce Guile) of a BRIE study on the diffusion of new production technologies in metal machining industries in the United States. He is currently working on several studies on the effects of trade and industrial policies on economic development in the United States. He has also published several articles on energy and environmental issues.

Jay S. Stowsky is a research fellow at the Berkeley Roundtable on the International Economy, University of California, Berkeley, where he is also a doctoral candidate in the Department of City and Regional Planning. He holds a master's degree in public policy from the John F. Kennedy School of Government, Harvard University, and received his A.B. from the University of California, Berkeley, in the political economy of industrial societies. Mr. Stowsky has served as a consultant on economic development issues for the U.S. Congress, the states of California and Massachusetts, and the government of Spain. He is the author of several studies detailing the relationship between high-technology sectors and economic development in advanced industrial societies, including "Beating Our Plowshares into Double-Edged Swords: The Impact of Pentagon Policies on the Commercialization of Advanced Technologies."